HUMBLED

HUMBLED

THE JOURNEY TO UNDERSTANDING LIFE AND CHRONIC LYME DISEASE

DAVID BUGENHAGEN

LIVE HUMBLED

PUBLISHING

ISBN: 979-8-218-36246-1

Library of Congress Control Number: 2024902415

LIVE HUMBLED
PUBLISHING

Live Humbled Publishing
Mauston, Wisconsin

Typeset by Michelle Cline

CONTENTS

Dedicated to all the lives affected and lost due to the complications of tick-borne illnesses such as Lyme disease. My story is just one of many and is a sampling of the devastation that has and can happen.

To those who understand the plight.

To anyone struggling.

I pray you find healing, comfort, and support.

"For He shall give his angels charge over thee, to keep thee in all thy ways."

Psalm 91:11 KJV

PREFACE

Where does one start? I have never written a book before. I don't think I ever considered writing one in my thirty-plus years. Years ago, I kept a journal of sorts; it was a notebook where I wrote down some thoughts. But I threw that notebook out long ago because of the embarrassment I felt reading back through it. I'm sure we've all been there: something happened in your past that you wish you could forget about. It's happened to me, and I'm sure it's happened to you as well.

It is amazing the ordeals people go through and live to talk about to others. I often wonder how in the world people made it through daily life even as little as one hundred years ago.

I've read quite a few books in my life, and it is fascinating the trials and tribulations that certain individuals have endured. For example, it's difficult to fathom being a prisoner of war (POW). How anyone could endure being tortured and deprived of the basic necessities of life for years on end, wondering if their situation would ever get better, is difficult to process.

I can't imagine being in the shoes (or maybe *no* shoes) of people who had to leave everything behind—their home country, family, friends—to get on a ship and embark on a voyage across endless miles of ocean. How do you handle that? How do you assimilate to a place with no money, no connections, and no place to live? All you have is your faith and determination to make a better life for yourself. People are still fleeing their homelands today in search of new beginnings, and they will one day have a story to tell as well. Most everyone has a journey or an account they could chronicle that would captivate an audience. I have read and heard many stories of people who have been down on their luck and then turned their lives around to make something of themselves. It's been done in the past, it's happening now, and it will continue to happen. As long as there is a dream or goal to strive for, there will always be someone running after it at full speed to see if they can catch it.

I've had goals, and I've had dreams. However, I'm at the age now where a lot of those are never going to happen. As a kid, I thought I was going to play Major League Baseball when I got older. Baseball was my favorite sport. I tried to emulate my favorite player, Ken Griffey Jr., on the field, and if I could have copied those skills successfully, I may have had a shot. Unfortunately, I couldn't hit very well after I reached the age of ten. My vision became worse, and I had a hard time seeing what I was trying to hit. If the pitcher threw slow enough, I could track it in and put a good swing on the ball. But as I got older, the pitcher threw harder, and I couldn't catch up. I was good at a lot of sports but never great, and good doesn't cut it in professional sports. In general, good gets you a normal life. Good gets you by. Good is what some people dream about. Good is food on the table every day, clothes on your back, and a clean and warm place to live. Good is great for a lot of people. I had always wanted to be better than good, though.

I learned at a young age that life isn't fair. The sooner you learn that lesson, the better off you'll be. There is no sugarcoating it. We are not all destined for fame and fortune. Some are, though, and that is fantastic because it gives people something to strive for to make a better life for themselves. If we were all the same, life would be quite mundane, and society would fall apart. If everyone were rich and famous, who would pick up your trash at the end of the driveway? Who would provide service at restaurants? Who would take care of the elderly in nursing homes? Who would do the tough and dangerous jobs? Who would get their hands dirty? Systems would crumble. Therefore, we all must do our part, big or small, because we all have a hand in making the world go round.

I've been up, and I've been down, and so have a multitude of other people throughout history. I've felt on top of the world where no one could touch me, and boy is that a great feeling. I can't imagine how it would feel to be on cloud nine all the time, but I imagine it would be something spectacular.

On the flip side, I've also been in a deep, dark pit that I didn't think I could ever get out of. It's lonely at the bottom. To be honest, it's terrifying. Nearly everyone has felt a similar way at some point in their lives—hopelessness, despair, depression, and isolation. It's only natural to feel sad when life doesn't go as planned.

I believe all of us are a copy of a copy of a copy of the initial perfect genetic code that God made. However, through the years, our genes have become a little mixed up, and our wires have gotten a bit crossed. We've got our mental issues that need to be addressed from time to time. Sometimes, though, we are our own worst enemies. Some of us love it when others feel bad about our situation and empathize with our feelings. It sure feels nice to have someone share in the pain, so as to not feel so alone in the struggle. However, if five, ten, or twenty years go by and you're still feeling bad about everything, that's not a healthy way to live. You must find a way out of your despair, or it will slowly destroy you. Why be down in the dumps and not try to have a better attitude? Living in a constant depressed state is a big waste of time for the one life you've been given. I don't know about you, but being happy is way better than feeling like a sack of trash and sad about everything all the time. I know because I've been there. Dealing with mental health is not easy, but with a little help and practice, you can improve it greatly.

That's why I wanted to write this book. Everyone struggles and deals with their own issues. Some people are rich and famous. But guess what? They still experience times of despair, get depressed, have friends and family die, and have bad things happen to them, just like the guy working at the local gas station at ten o'clock on a Wednesday night to support his family. Bad things can happen to anybody at any time.

Money can make things better, but it will never solve all your problems or the problems of the world. How much money have governments thrown at poverty and hunger? Quite a lot, I'd imagine, and yet there are still people struggling for food and money. The Bible talks of people who were beggars, invalids, hungry, deaf, and blind. And I would take a bet that in the future, people will still be down on their luck and in the same types of situations.

A fascinating thing I have seen and read about is that people who may be down and out or live in poverty can be the most gracious and thankful people you'll ever meet. A small gift like a pair of socks or shoes will bring a huge smile to a person who really needs that item. How about someone who gets a new house or car gifted to them after a tragedy? You can't wipe the grin off that person's face for a long time. Being appreciative of what you do have, no matter how small, can sometimes be a difficult lesson to learn.

What the opening of this book is trying to convey is this: appreciate what you have and stay humble with the gifts and abilities you possess because, like Job in the Old Testament of the Bible, it can all be taken away if you're not careful.

If you've ever read the book of Job, you'll know that Job had it all: money, friends, family, land, possessions, and health. Everyone liked him, but he was proud and self-righteous of all that *he* had done. God had to remind Job that all good things come from above. God also allowed bad things to happen to Job. He allowed the devil to bring death, despair, and destruction into Job's life. Sound familiar? It does to me.

After all these bad things happened, Job's friends came over to console him. Job's kids had recently all died, his possessions went away, and his health was in poor shape. His friends couldn't figure out what sin or evil Job could have done to warrant all these horrendous things that were happening. Job's wife wanted him to curse God and die because of all the turmoil, but Job wouldn't do that. Instead, he remained adamant that he had to accept the good along with the bad. Job was impressed with his righteousness and how well he'd handled adversity, remaining convinced that he had done everything right and nothing wrong. However, after he couldn't find any obvious reason for his hardships, Job began to question why God was being unfair to him. He could not see why

God had even allowed him to be born to endure all that he had, especially after he had it so good.

God then stepped in and asked Job multiple, hard-hitting questions. God showed Job the power of the things He had created and basically asked, "Can you do this? Can you do that?" Job couldn't answer because he knew he didn't have the power to do *anything* on his own. In that moment, Job realized God was in charge and repented his sin of pride and self-righteousness. As a result, God restored unto Job twice as much as he had before.

Once you figure out that you're not God and that you are completely powerless if left butt naked out in the frozen wilderness or dumped into an ocean with no tools, no supplies, no help, and no life raft, you quickly realize you need God's help.

We are renters of this planet. We didn't create the earth; God did. Therefore, He owns everything. This book you're reading is printed from the trees that God created and planted. Everything good and bad that people have made is possible because of what God provides. Humans, as hard as we may try, can't create anything out of nothing. It's not possible. But with God, anything is possible. We might not always get what we want, but it might be what we need.

Not all of us go through horrendous times when we feel like we are helpless. Thank God for that! However, if you do find yourself going through a rough time in life, remember that God is in control. I know that you might not feel that way right away, but He is. You may not understand the reasoning for your troubles. It could take a lifetime to understand. If you're not right with God, He might be trying to get your attention. Sometimes we must endure a lot of hard times and troubles until we turn our hearts to the Lord.

I recommend reading *Unbroken*, the story of Louis Zamperini, an American prisoner of war in World War II. You'll see just how stubborn and hardheaded some of us can be until we realize God is trying to get us to trust in Him. It took me some time to do that as well, but I'm glad I listened. I don't know where I would be right now if I didn't. Even knowing that lesson, I still need to be reminded of it from time to time. Sometimes I forget that God is in charge. Sometimes I think that I'm the big man on campus. Sometimes ego and pride can get in the way. And sometimes all it takes is being served a healthy dose of humble pie to correct my heart and mind on where they should be. When that happens, I turn to God for help and guidance.

Why did I write this book? I know there are people out there struggling with all sorts of things. My hope is that I can help at least one person with what I've gone through. But, and it is a big *but*, I wouldn't be writing this if God wasn't part of my existence. I might have been that major leaguer living large, but if my life was full of shallow vanity, it would have all been in vain. You see, you can have everything on this earth, but if you don't have a place in heaven prepared for you, all the possessions and fame of this world will not save you. We all need saving from our sins, the consequent death, and the fiery hell we deserve because of our sins. I'll let you in on a secret that's not really a secret: we all die. Think about it. We all get old, fall apart, have failing health, and die.

Want to feel helpless? Live your whole life without knowing where you're going when you die. Then get to the point where you're lying in a hospital bed, you're unable to help yourself, you can't use the bathroom on your own, you can't eat without assistance, and you can't do anything except lay there to die. Who's going to help you now? You're going to be dead for a *long* time. I mean, a really long time. Do you think that this is it? That this life was all there was? So, you had fun, fame, glory, and did whatever you wanted for seventy or eighty years, then you shrivel up and die. What? How is that fair? All that living and all that fun for what? To end up like everybody else?

Life isn't fair, and death doesn't discriminate. We all will eventually die. And if you don't know where you're going after you eventually pass away, you might want to think about it for a few minutes. Go ahead, take a little time.

Did you think?

I hope and pray that you do, and that the rest of the book will help you along your way.

Buckle up! It's going to be a journey. I never would have expected how complicated and messed up a mysterious illness like Lyme disease would totally change the trajectory of my life. I'm not sure how I feel letting the world into my own small space between my ears, as I relive the chaos that was. However, I believe God has given me the talents and ability to use them the best I can to get into your mind and, more importantly, into your soul so that you, too, can become *humbled*.

CHAPTER 1

BACKGROUND AND EARLY LIFE

In order to get where we are going in this book, it is important to know where I've been. I can't get to the meat and potatoes of the book before we have an appetizer and a salad, so to speak.

Wisconsin, Brookfield, to be exact, about twenty minutes west of the heart of downtown Milwaukee, is where all the fun and games started for me. I don't have the slightest clue if there have been any popular or best-selling books written by anyone in my part of town. Maybe this will be the first one. God willing, that would be fantastic.

My dad wasn't drunk, abusive, or missing in action. I suppose that would make for a more interesting and sadder story, but that's simply not the case here. My dad was always busy and hardworking, performing well in different sales positions over the years. He brought home many awards and trophies for always being one of the top producers. More importantly, he was able to provide a nice home and food on the table to feed everybody. He was the one to lay down the law if I or any of my five brothers were out of line. My dad has a bit of a rougher voice, and when he hollered, we sure listened, or we started to cry because we didn't like being yelled at. Honestly, though, I'll take that over getting whacked with a belt any day. What always stuck with me the most is that Dad would always say, "If you're in trouble or need a ride, I don't care if it's two in the morning, I'll come get you." Dad was always willing to lend a hand when any of us needed it, and that's what a good dad does.

Mom got to stay at home and raise my brothers and me. It was a hard job, but she was always more than up to the task. Mom was the gentle one, and knowing what I know now, she should easily qualify for sainthood. She not only raised five kids successfully but also was the primary caregiver to many of my elderly relatives over the years. That was Mom's job. She was always there to help. Without her, who knows where any of us would have ended up. I am very fortunate to have the mom I do.

Having both parents around while growing up was very helpful, and they were both very instrumental in helping us boys get to where we were trying to get in life. We didn't always see eye to eye, but at the end of the day, they were always there for me and everyone in the family.

I was fortunate to have both a mom and dad raise me, and I know that not everyone is as blessed as I was. If you're a single parent raising kids, that must be over-the-top difficult, especially if you have a mob like us five boys, who were constantly wrestling with each other, to deal with. Surprisingly, when we did wrestle in the living room, we were never seriously injured. There was a hearth extension from the fireplace about ten inches off the ground that stood out about another twenty and was made of stone and cement. It was a miracle that none of us cracked our heads open and bled to death by hitting that thing.

Talking about brothers, where do we all fit in? Somehow, I got stuck being the youngest, so yep, I was picked on and beat up by all four of my brothers at one time or another. Mike is the oldest. He's got me beat by about fifteen years. Next is Matt, who has twelve years on me. Mark is next, and he came along eight years before me. And Paul Jr. (PJ) is six years older than I am. I find it weird that my oldest brothers helped change my diapers once or twice. That's crazy to think about. They probably got stuck with some of the nasty ones at times, so a little bit of beating by them was probably warranted.

The family dog, Tahoe, was a black Labrador Retriever and a professionally trained hunting dog. However, due to possible hip dysplasia, the trainer didn't feel right selling her to someone knowing her hips might be bad. We took her in knowing the situation and got her for a lot less than would have been a normal price for that time. I was just a baby when we got her, but she quickly turned into my best buddy. With Tahoe, my lifelong attachment to black Labs started.

Now that the pleasantries and introductions are out of the way, we can start to dive into a little more of how I got from where I was to where I am now.

I was a quiet kid, and, for the most part, I'm still on the reserved side of things. I was never one to ask too many questions or talk loudly. I'm not quite sure why that is, but one guess would be what my dad always said: "Little kids should be seen and not heard." I believe that was meant to keep us quiet at the dinner table when we were all goofing off. Dad wanted some peace and quiet during his dinner, and I don't blame him. I don't always like the sound of kids being all snotty and goofy when I'm eating, either. Another reason I can think of is that being the youngest of five siblings, I was always the clueless, dumb, gullible little brother. I didn't know much more than them. After all, they had been around a lot longer, so it wasn't a fair fight at that time in my life. Thirdly, I think it's just my natural tendency. I kept to myself. I had my little plans of what I wanted to do, and I didn't want others to know for fear of looking foolish or someone saying, "Well, that's just a stupid idea." I didn't like revealing much then, and I still don't now, but I'm getting better at it.

Being born in 1986, I don't recall much, if anything, from the eighties, so my claim to fame is that I'm a product of the nineties. To some, I may sound like a young person. To others, I may sound like an old-timer.

I grew up in a unique time just before the internet, cable, or smartphones. Sometimes I wish I could go back to those days. It was a simpler era, and time didn't go so fast. Life was just better and easier, and we were allowed to be kids. I had to call my friends on an actual landline telephone with a cord attached or walk down the street to see if they were outside so we could get together and play. Video game systems were still in their early days, so there wasn't much time spent in front of a TV gaming. However, if it was raining out or you were sick with something, you got stuck watching soap operas that were downright terrible. On the bright side, if you had the TV on at the right time, hearing, "Come on down, you're the next contestant on *The Price Is Right!*" was always something worth watching. I loved seeing the prizes and trying to figure out the games. My favorite was Plinko. I'm not sure why, but it was fun to watch. Oh, and I believe Bob Barker had a pretty good gig. He got to work with a bunch of "lovely" ladies, as he would call them. Even at six years old, I didn't mind the sight of a pretty woman. Though it probably would have been better if I thought all girls had cooties going through my young years versus being enamored with them and wanting them to all like me. But what can you do?

In the suburban neighborhood where I lived, there were quite a few families that had kids my age, so there was always fun to be had. We had a nice town park down the biggest hill I had ever seen at that point in my life. Man, if you want to live on the edge, take your bike and fly down that thing. Even better, take your roller blades without a helmet or pads. You'll be dodging cars, cracks, and rocks as you zoom toward the bottom. When you realize you can't stop, you just hit the curb and see how far you can fly until you land awkwardly on the grass. How I didn't die, I don't know. I'm glad I didn't tell Mom about that one, until she reads it here. I'm sure she'll be shaking her head but will laugh, thankful I was coordinated enough to stay upright and not need a panicked ride to the ER with blood gushing from my head.

At the park, there was a baseball field made up of mostly weeds and rocky sand. If you slid into home plate, or anywhere on the infield, you would no doubt get up with skin missing somewhere. It's where I got my first taste of baseball, and I loved it.

My friends and brothers would often go down there to hit and shag balls until we all got tired and had to get home for dinner. I recall pitching to one of my friend's older brothers. At the time, he was in his late teens and was much stronger and faster than I was. Well, I fired one right down the plate, and he swung and tagged the ball right on the barrel. In a split second, the ball rocketed back at me. I did some sort of kung fu-like martial arts move to avoid being hit, and luckily, I was able to. Boy, was I fortunate not to get taken out by that screaming liner; otherwise, I'm sure I would have needed a ride to the hospital.

It wouldn't have been a bad idea for me to live in a bubble for most of my young years. As we go along, you'll find out my guardian angel has had to work overtime on me.

I don't know if parents or kids could go back to those days like I had. On weekends or when school was out for the summer, we'd be gone all day. We would leave in the morning, have lunch at a friend's house, and then be out again doing whatever until it got dark. You knew it was time to go home when you could smell supper cooking, or if the phone rang, you knew it would be Mom looking for you. I'm sure our parents worried or wondered what we were doing. I often thought that perhaps they had a secret phone line we didn't know about so they could keep tabs on all of us. For the most part, we didn't really get into any big trouble. They knew we couldn't travel too far on our bikes, so as long as we kept showing back up and letting them know where we were going to be, it was never much of a problem.

I hated thunderstorms as a kid. They freaked me out like crazy. I feel a bit embarrassed that I was so scared of them, especially at night. I would go into my parents' bedroom and lay on the floor with my pillow on Mom's side of the bed whenever the thunder started to roll. I survived every storm we had, so I'm not sure what my problem was, but once that bright lightning and loud thunder hit, I was like a scared puppy and wanted to hide somewhere. Wisconsin isn't exactly in Tornado Alley like the states a bit to the south of us, but we still can get them. I remember seeing the destruction a tornado can cause on TV and how people panicked when sirens would go off. I didn't understand the weather and why or how it happened. I simply did not like storms. I'm sure the unknown portion of it was the worst. I worried that our house might be wiped out by a massive wind. I was terrified that I'd be flying on my mattress and land somewhere in the woods where it was dark and cold, and something would try to eat me. My imagination and envisioning of these bad things happening did not help the matter one bit.

I do want to insert here a little story about one storm in particular, probably when I was the age of six or so. It started out like storms always do. The wind picked up and blew eerily through the screen, sounding like a train blowing its horn as it barreled toward me. The windows in my room started to shake violently, as if someone was trying to get inside and steal me away. The rain started out light and eventually started to pick up. It was only a matter of time before lightning struck, and not even a second later, a thunderous boom followed.

That was my cue to haul out of bed and get into my parents' room, which I'm sure they got accustomed to as soon as the weather got rough. I hunkered down next to the bed and tried to close my eyes, which sometimes was a major battle if it was God's Fourth of July fireworks happening outside. If it wasn't too bad, I would eventually fall asleep, and by the morning, everything would be sunshine and roses.

This experience only happened one time. I have no clue what it really was, but it reminded me of the story of Samuel in the Bible. Samuel kept hearing his name being called and kept going to Eli, because he thought he was calling him. Eli would say, "I did not call you. Go lay back down." This happened a second time and then a third. The third time, Eli realized God was calling Samuel, so Eli said to Samuel, "If he call thee, that thou shalt say, 'Speak, LORD; for thy servant heareth'" (1 Sam. 3:9).

Listening to the Lord is sound advice. With the experience I had, I don't know if I was being called or if I was dreaming. There's no way to tell for sure, but it has always stuck with me.

I was lying on the floor, half asleep, in my parents' bedroom during a storm when I heard the most deep, clear, God-like voice you could imagine say, "David."

I immediately shot up, and my heart was racing because I didn't know who said my name. My dad was fast asleep. I could hear him sawing logs—or gently snoring, you might call it—so I knew it wasn't my dad's voice. It only happened one time, and it never happened since, but maybe it was God saying my name to let me know He was there and in charge, and I would be okay through the storm.

I wanted to throw that little experience into the book because I think it will tie in well with some other things shared later. I don't know who or what said my name or if I was simply dreaming it happened. That moment has stuck with me ever since. When I later heard of the story of Samuel, it took me back to this experience. What it truly meant, I'll never know, but I like to think God was watching over me.

As you can probably tell by now, I'm a Christian. I've read the Bible cover to cover and have used it many times to help give me guidance. I attended a private Lutheran school, though I didn't have much say in the matter. I didn't know there was such a thing called a public school until I was a bit older.

My mom was raised Catholic, and my dad was raised Lutheran. I don't know the details of how it was decided that I would go to a Lutheran school rather than a Catholic school, but that's what happened. On Sundays, Mom would get up earlier than everyone else and attend Catholic Mass. After that, she would come home and make sure everyone else was ready for church at the Lutheran services. My mom got a double dose of church on Sundays. I didn't really think there was much of a difference in the two church services at the time. But what did I know? I was just a kid. I did like the Lutheran church more at that age. I attribute that to the fact that I would see my school classmates there, and as a bonus, there would be free doughnuts after the service. I was always up for some nice, sugary goodness. The Long John doughnut with chocolate frosting and sprinkles was my favorite and still is today.

I'm glad I was raised to learn about God and the Bible and all that goes with it. Granted, I was too young to fully understand it, but building that faith and having a firm foundation turned out to be extremely important down the line.

In school, we had some sort of Bible class every day. During my early years, I memorized lots of scriptures and songs. Later, Scripture became more involved in the teachings that we believed in and how they can be applied to everyday life. I wasn't the greatest at remembering all the words. It was a bit nerve-racking to have to go up to the teacher and recall multiple verses. It was especially difficult when the whole class could hear you stumble and mumble while you tried to come up with the correct wording.

One passage I remember well, which also turned out to be my confirmation verse, is from Psalm 91:11, which states, "For He shall give his angels charge over thee, to keep thee in all thy ways."

I picked out that verse as one I liked in second grade, well before I knew I had to choose a verse for confirmation in eighth grade. While a lot of kids were scrambling to find a verse that suited them, I had mine picked out years in advance. I always felt like it's been my special verse because of that.

I'll be getting back to faith, God, and the Bible as we go deeper into this book. I wanted everyone to know that from an early age, I was taught Christian values. I realized that we are all sinners in need of forgiveness. I know I have that forgiveness because of what Jesus did for me. Hey, if someone can offer to pay for my multitude of sins, shortcomings, bad thoughts, and failures so that I don't have to go to hell and be punished eternally for them, I think I'll take that offer. I'd much rather be saved from the bad things that I've done than be condemned for them. That's like a "get out of jail free" card in Monopoly. If you don't have that card, you can get one. It's not that hard. Maybe by the end of this book, you'll be convinced that you need one.

The early years of my life aren't filled with a ton of excitement, drama, or trauma, but there are certain areas I want to poke around. I believe doing so will give you a better picture as to what shaped me and maybe give a few reasons for why I am the way I am.

My brothers and I were all quite active in sports and athletics. In many ways, I envied my brothers for their athletic accomplishments, and I wanted very much to be as good as, or better than, they were.

My oldest brother, Mike, was big into baseball and basketball. The Chicago Bulls were the star team in the nineties, and one of my fonder memories I had was when Mike and I would play against Mark and PJ at my parents' house. We had a decent hoop and driveway to play in, and we wore that hoop out over the years. Mike would pretend to be Michael Jordan, and I would always be Scottie Pippen. I thought that was awesome. Of course, I was roughly five or six years old and couldn't make a basket to save my life, but I tried. It was thrilling playing with my brothers. Mike and I always won, at least that's how I remember it.

Mike had moved out and gotten married by the time I was eight years old. He was off living his own married life well before mine even started, but those early days were some that I like to think about from time to time.

I do want to inject a little humor here before we get down to all the serious business at hand. All my brothers, except Mark (so far), have inadvertently tried to kill me at one point or another. I'll start with Mike, since we are on him now, and go down the list from there.

My mom's sister Frances, who I call Aunt Frances, and her husband, Bud (Uncle Bud to me), have a house in the farm region just west of the Wisconsin Dells. Behind their house is a field with a very large bluff. A bluff in Wisconsin is like a mountain in Colorado. A bluff isn't that big, though, maybe a few hundred feet tall but quite steep. In the wintertime, it turns into an awesome sledding hill. Any of my relatives that ends up reading this will know what I'm talking about. There have been toboggan races, sledding with jumps, and loads of fun happening on that hill for many years. The fun part was flying down that snowy hill. The not-so-fun part was carrying our sleds all the way back to the top. When you're a little guy like I was with short legs, it felt like an impossible task. Luckily, my brothers were nice and would carry it up for me, sometimes. So, we have me, a tiny six-year-old on a sledding hill with snow and ice, with brothers and cousins ten times the size of me speeding down the hill. What could possibly go wrong? Well, I set off on my tiny sled and got a bit stuck in the snow halfway down the hill. The snow was abnormally deep that day, so I couldn't get out of the way very fast. Mike started off down the hill and quickly picked up speed and barreled straight toward little old me. I was still in my sled and didn't see him coming. In no time at all, I got run over and squished into the snow by Mike and his sled. I didn't know what hit me or what happened next. I may have had a bloody nose or a good bruise, but I do remember Mom coming to check on me and take me inside to get fixed up. Could I have died getting run over by a sled? I don't know, but I don't really want to try it again. I could see the flip side of it now if I ran over one of my nieces or nephews in the same fashion. I'm sure some significant damage could ensue if I hit someone the wrong way. Luckily, I survived the first attempt at cutting the share of the will from everyone getting a fifth to everyone getting a fourth.

All my brothers and I wrestled to some degree in our lifetimes. Matt could more than hold his own on the mat, and even though I have very little memory of him wrestling, one time sticks out.

With me being the youngest, I looked up to all my brothers at some point in time. I thought they were the coolest dudes to do what they got to do. They had friends, played sports, and had girlfriends, the whole nine yards. Matt loved wrestling (and still does). The guy can talk about it all day, every day. In high school, there was a dual match where one team would face off against another team. Matt had a match against one of the better wrestlers at the time. I was super young, so I may not have the details correct, but everyone was screaming and yelling. The cheerleaders were by the edge of the mat, cheering him on. Mom was next to me, tense and nervous and hanging on every move and every point in the match. Suddenly, eruption and elation came from the crowd as he had won his match. It was pandemonium. His teammates mobbed him on the mat and picked him up and carried him off on their shoulders. If you've ever seen the movie *Rudy*, just picture the scene where his teammates are carrying him off the field; that's how cool it was to me. If that's exactly how it happened, no one can remember, but that's the story I'll go with.

I wanted a piece of that when I got older.

While that was an awesome moment, the next one wasn't as great, but it's a funny story to tell now.

This was attempt number two at trying to take me out and get the inheritance from a fifth to a fourth. The event took place a bit later in my life. I think I was twenty years old. We were playing a round of golf in the Northwoods of Crivitz, Wisconsin. The golf course doesn't exist anymore, but it was the course I played at the most growing up. It was a challenging but shorter course. The fairways were lined with thick forests, so if you had an errant shot, you would be in some deep woods and likely never find your ball again. I always thought it would be awesome to see how the pros would handle a course like that.

Back to the near-death experience: we were on the front nine playing on hole number seven. PJ was there, and Matt's wife, Jenny, was there as witnesses to the event. I'm able to one-up my brothers in golf, as it's the one sport I could usually beat them at, even from a young age on. It was no surprise that I was sitting about 250 yards down the middle of the fairway while everyone else was hacking up the golf course behind me. Matt could hit it a country mile when he connected, but many times you didn't know which direction the ball was going. I do blame myself a bit for this incident, as I should have known better than to walk ahead of my brothers before they hit. I now know to either stay behind them or to the side for safety's sake.

So, there I was, taking a stroll to my first tee shot, and Matt was behind, taking a swing or two, or maybe three at this point. It was a sunny day, and we were all having a good time until I heard Matt's voice yell, "David!" Of course, my natural reaction was to turn to him and say, "What?" At that moment, I was eye to eye with a screaming golf ball heading right for my face. I could see the hard curve it had, and I knew the impending path. I was going to get hit. It's amazing how your body can slow time down when something bad is going to happen. I could literally see the words "Top Flite" on the ball before it hit me. I turned my head to the right at the last possible second to avoid a direct blow to my eyes or temple, which could have proven to be quite painful. I estimate the ball was coming at least one hundred miles per hour, but who knows for sure. The ball whacked me on the left side of my face, just above my jawbone. I immediately saw stars and spun around, then fell like a sack of potatoes. I was lying there, trying to process what happened, and I heard my brother PJ come over and yell, "David, say something! David, say something!" I groaned a bit, but I don't think I lost consciousness. All I could say was, "Ouch!" My face started to swell up, but I wasn't bleeding—no teeth missing or any major issues. PJ called the clubhouse to see if they could bring me an ice pack to help with the swelling, and we played the rest of the holes. I still did par that hole even after taking a hit. We laugh about it now, but that could have been quite serious, and I'm glad I survived that attempt to have my life cut short. Today, I tell Matt that if he's golfing with me to, next time, yell "Fore!" so that I don't look in his direction and get another golf ball to the face.

All my brothers had a hand in raising me, but the two who were closest to me in age were around a lot more when I was growing up. Mike and Matt were both out of the house by the time I was six years old.

Mark was a decent athlete as well. He was good at wrestling, and he and PJ would always test their skills against one another in the living room. The carpet in there sure got its abuse over the years. Eventually, the flooring got replaced with hardwood. So, the days of wrestling in the house are pretty much over. That's probably a good thing now since we're all older. After all, one of us might break a hip.

Mark really liked baseball about as much as I did. I always had a good time when he'd hit me some grounders and pop flies in the front yard. It was even more fun when he would take me down to the park and throw me balls for batting practice.

Around the time I was ten or eleven, Mark became my Little League baseball coach. It was a fun time, and I felt mighty important, as we were always the ones to bring the gear we needed for the team. Mark coached the team for two years until he went to college in Iowa. I was more skilled than most of the players on the team, and Mark usually had me batting in the leadoff position or in the second or third spot. I liked it at the top of the order. It meant I got more at bats during a game. I was excellent at getting on base, and when I did, I would always steal bases. I don't think I ever got thrown out because I was Speedy Gonzalez out there.

When I took the field, I was quite often the shortstop or second basemen, as that's where most of the balls were hit. I was put there because not very many of our guys could catch the ball and throw it accurately to first base, so I was constantly in the action.

One position I was always a bit scared to be was the pitcher. That meant all eyes on me, and I wasn't sure I was ready for that. I have to give Mark credit for pushing me and making feel like I could be effective out there on the mound. I very much doubt that if I had any other coach, I would have been the one throwing balls and strikes because I know I never would have volunteered. I was nervous as I could be before I took my first trip to the mound. There was no bullpen, so a teammate and I warmed up in the parking lot until Mark called me into the game. I was shaking, sweating, and having a hard time keeping my heart rate down, as I settled in for my first-ever pitch in a real, live game. I had thrown many times with my brothers, and I wasn't half-bad. I had much better control than a lot of other guys on the team, so I couldn't be much worse. I tried to mimic the big-leaguers I saw on TV. I put my face in my Rawlings glove and pretended I was reading the signs from the catcher, even though there were no signs. At that age, it was all about throwing the ball and seeing what happened, so I did. I believe the first one I threw was a ball, and probably the second one too, but then I started to relax. I was extremely relieved when I heard the umpire yell out that first "Strike!" I have no clue if we ended up winning or losing the game, but that's not really the point of the story. The point was to show that doing something I've never done, while nerve-racking, got easier the more I did it. At my age now, I know when a new opportunity comes up that it is better to act quickly versus letting it eat at you. Otherwise, you sit there and think about it, which isn't always bad when it's a big decision. However, once you have your mind made up that you're going to do something, you might as well just do it because you're going to anyway, so there's no sense in worrying about it too much. That one moment that I took the pitcher's mound was scary, but I got through it, and I ended up really liking being the pitcher and having more control over the game. I was never great at it, but I was a lot better than most of the other kids because I could consistently throw strikes. Everyone else was airmailing balls all over the place. You never knew where one would end up.

As of the writing of this book, Mark is the only brother who hasn't tried to take the inheritance down to a fourth, either purposely or otherwise. I do bet there were a few times when I got on his nerves being that annoying little brother. Thankfully, other than a few times of getting my butt kicked in wrestling and getting held down until I said I was a baby, nothing sticks out. We should have quite a few years left in us, so there is still time for something crazy to happen, but I'd rather bypass that possibility.

PJ, on the other hand, was probably the closest to taking me out. Don't worry; it wasn't on purpose. I was roughly six years old at the time, which probably helped me to not die or get seriously injured. Also, being young, I was still very flexible, which helped my body bend and bounce instead of break.

We took a family trip out to Colorado. Mark, PJ, my parents, and I were all along for the long road trip out there. I don't know exactly why we went out that way, but we stayed at a family's house that my parents knew of. In the backyard was a giant trampoline, you know, the one where pretty much everyone gets hurt on at some point in their life. Yep, it was one of those. It was just PJ and I bouncing around on it. Where everyone else was, I can't recall. We were having a good time, and then PJ got an idea. I, being the dumb younger brother, always went along with whatever my brother said, especially if he said it would be *"fun."* It started out sounding like a blast. PJ lay on his back on the trampoline, loaded his legs back into his chest, and said, "Come on. Sit down on my feet, and I'll launch you into the air." My job was to sit there and try and do a somersault and land back on my feet. At least, that was the plan. When you're six, hardly anything goes according to plan. We gave it a try anyway without any practice. We gave it the old one-two and awaited what was to happen. I remember thinking, *Man, this is going to be awesome.* As PJ took a deep breath in and used all his teenage strength to launch his legs up as high and as fast as they could, I went flying into the air. When I got lifted up, my head and neck tilted back instead of to the front, which made it really hard to try and somersault, end over end, in time to land on my feet. I tried to spin and rotate forward, but it was obvious I wasn't going to get all the way around in time. It wasn't looking too good for me, and as I was starting to come down, I tried to tuck as much as I could, but it was no use. My head landed first. My chin probably touched my chest, and the back of my neck was stretched farther than it ever had before. I remained conscious, but I felt a terrible pain in my neck and upper back. I started to cry, but PJ was quick to my side and said, "Don't cry! Don't cry!" I think he knew he was in big trouble if I went crying back to Mom and told her what had happened. I wasn't the type of kid who tattled. So, you know what I did? I sucked it up and only cried a little, even though I was hurting pretty bad. I toughed it out, yes. I was in pain, yes. I wanted to cry to Mom, but for the most part, I was okay. Granted, I probably should have gone to the hospital at that point, but I wanted to show I wasn't a wimp. Being the youngest sibling, I was often told to not complain and to be tough. It was mind over matter. It was great advice, but I wasn't old enough to realize when to use that advice or when there was a moment to ask for help. This could have been one of them, but thankfully, I'm still here. The next day, we had breakfast at a restaurant, and I was rubbing my neck a lot. Mom could tell I was in discomfort. She thought I slept on my neck wrong and gave me an aspirin for the pain. I started to feel better. That trip could have been a lot worse. Fast forward a bit, to save money, Mom has always cut our hair. When she gets to my neck area, she often points out that one side of my neck sticks out and looks a bit goofy, and she never knew why. I have a feeling that my poorly executed somersault flip in Colorado had something to do with it, but there's no way to know for sure.

With PJ having six years on me, it was only natural that he became the brother I was around the most and, therefore, did the most things with growing up. I was eight years old when he was in his freshman year of high school and twelve during his senior year. PJ was active and excelled in all kinds of sports: cross-country, wrestling, and track. Because of that, he had a lot of friends. The high school teams would often come over to our house at the end of their respective seasons for a party. Our house had an indoor pool that was heated to a nice and toasty eighty-eight degrees, even in the wintertime. It was no surprise that all the other high schoolers loved to come to our house and have a good time. You would expect that PJ would tell me to get lost whenever there was a party going on (they were supervised, so not too many shenanigans went on). On the contrary, I was always there. I, oftentimes, felt like a "big-timer" when teenage girls were over and I got to show them around the house. They would think I was "so cute" or something along those lines. I even remember a time where I didn't feel the greatest, and one of the girls read me a bedtime story. She was quite attractive too. Even when the guys were there, I was allowed to take them on in ping-pong or video games. I remember a lot of fun times playing on the Sega Genesis, and then things really got fun when the N64 and Golden Eye tournaments would happen. I was the younger brother hanging out with the older crowd. It felt great to be included and interact with people I looked up to.

PJ's friends became my friends, and still to this day, we get together on occasion for poker night, birthdays, or some other weekend getaway. Having that exposure to older guys and girls when I was younger and having a good time really got me excited about the high school experience and what it could entail. I was already well-liked in grade school and very athletic, so it was only natural to want to meet and even exceed what my brothers were able to accomplish when they were there. I couldn't wait until it was my turn.

Having four older brothers was sometimes a pain in the butt. They all had a hand in raising me, teaching me stuff, and taking turns in beating me up. All that comes with being the last one in line. Of course, with me being the youngest, they'll say that I was spoiled and had it easy. I'm sure there is some truth in that.

Considering my parents had four kids and then adding me as the fifth, they knew what to expect and maybe softened a bit once they got to me.

Moving on to some other highlights (or lowlights) from the early years. My family is into hunting, especially when it comes to deer season. I was always left at home because I was too young to be out in the woods. I wasn't to be trusted to sit still for hours on end while freezing my fingers and toes off. We all stayed at my aunt and uncle's house, about a two-hour drive from our home.

The "hunters" would always get up while it was dark outside, have breakfast, use the facilities, and then bundle up to get to the stand before the sun got too high in the sky. I didn't know what to think about all that, but I'd be at the house waiting until around noon for the convoy of trucks and vans to pull back into the yard for lunch to see if anyone got anything. I would run outside if I saw a deer on the top of a vehicle or in the back of a pickup, especially if someone got a nice buck. Everyone would hoot and holler (okay, maybe not that), but they would be excited, and everyone would want to know who got it and how they did it. Harvesting a deer was a big thing for our family because it meant food on the table. When you have five kids to feed, a nice deer or two helped with that.

Around the age of nine, after sitting and waiting in the house my whole life, I finally got my chance to go out into the woods. I was eagerly awaiting the opportunity to see what all the fuss was about. Dad took me out for my first time. He wasn't always an early riser, so we were always the last ones out the door. I was all bundled up in my blaze-orange hunting gear as we made our way to the stand. I remember the walk to get to our stand took a while, but once we got there and set up, it became a waiting game. The sun was already lighting up the sky and started to warm things up a bit. There is a huge difference in how comfortable you can be out in the woods if you have a little bit of sun on you and no wind. If you sit out there long enough, you start to get sleepy and can fall asleep quickly. I think that's what my dad was experiencing because, all of a sudden, I heard what sounded like a boulder rolling down the hill behind my right shoulder. It was so loud! We were set up in a berm, which is a strip of trees and brush in the middle of a cornfield that had been picked. The ground was frozen, so any sound hitting the dirt was amplified. If you can imagine the sound of a stampede, that's what I can most compare it to. Then the noise stopped. I turned to my right, and all I saw were huge, creepy-looking eyes staring at me about twenty yards away. It was a decent-sized buck! I had never witnessed anything like this, and I think that buck was thinking the same thing. I bet he was wondering, *What in the heck is in my bedding area?* I couldn't believe what I was seeing, and I also couldn't believe Dad didn't seem to even notice. I whispered, "Dad, behind you!" But there was no response. I spoke louder. "Dad, behind you!" I think I woke him up because he seemed startled. I whispered again, "Dad, *behind* you," and this time, he turned and saw what I was looking at. Dad reached for his gun in front of me, so I ducked down a bit to get out of the way. Then I heard a tremendously loud bang! I think I almost fell out of my chair. My ears were ringing uncontrollably after Dad shot off a round from his .30-06 that I started to freak out and cry because of the shock. I was afraid, but I wasn't sure of what. I couldn't process why it was so loud and why my ears would not stop ringing. Before I knew it, Dad was leading me in the direction of where he shot, and a few minutes later, we heard another shot that came from where the buck dashed off to. We found some blood and began tracking, heading toward my brother Matt. We were surprised to see he had shot it as well and had it down on the ground. I still had terrible ringing in my ears as Matt was field-dressing the deer. All I wanted to do was go back home. I didn't like being out in the woods after that experience, especially alone. Not to mention the sight of the dead deer gave me the creeps. It took a long time for me to start liking the outdoors and feeling comfortable by myself out there. I'm still not a fan of being in the woods when it's dark outside, but I'm getting better at it.

If I wasn't traumatized enough from that experience, two years later, I was back out in the same spot with my dad. We must have been getting cold, so we got up to walk over to where PJ was. We slowly walked through the cut cornfield and made our way into the woods, down through the marshy area. Dad was leading, and I was right behind him. There was no way I was letting someone leave me alone out there. I was a few feet behind and to the left of my dad when a streak of blue whizzed by us at what seemed like one thousand miles per hour! Then a shot rang out. Dad was quick thinking and knew what was happening. He got us both behind a large tree nearby. Not even two seconds after I moved, another blue streak screamed by the exact spot where I had just been standing a few seconds prior, followed by another loud bang! I really had no idea what had happened at that moment, but after a minute to process, it was clear that we were being shot at! I don't know who was shooting and whether it was on purpose or by accident. All I know was that it could have been bad news for both of us. If we hadn't taken shelter behind the tree, I believe one or both of us would have gotten shot. It all happened so quickly, and nothing bad ultimately occurred. Still, escaping death or serious injury was starting to become commonplace.

That same area wasn't done with me yet. Only a few years later, my life would completely change. All I was doing was minding my business, being helpful, and enjoying nature. We'll come back to this place I call "the swamp" because that's what it was, a swamp.

CHAPTER 2

THE HIGH BEFORE THE LOW

The years before I turned fourteen years old were some of the best years of my life. Grade school was unique because I got to know and grow with kids from the time we were four years old until we graduated eighth grade. I can still remember the names and faces of basically all the kids in my class, as well as the ones above and below me. I haven't seen or been around some of them for over twenty years.

I would say I was more on the popular side during that time but never had any great friendships where we would get together outside of school or sports. The time spent with friends during those activities must have been more than enough. I remember going to a few birthday parties, even hosting one myself, but other than that, I wasn't getting together with anyone on a regular basis.

During summer break or on the weekends throughout the school year, there were a couple of neighborhood friends I would hang out with. We would play video games, race our Hot Wheels, build fun stuff out of LEGOs, or simply just watch a movie and eat snacks. With Mark and PJ being around for a lot of those years, I ended up doing more things with them than anyone else. I always enjoyed throwing the football or baseball around in the yard, and the basketball hoop in our driveway got worn out by how many times we would play HORSE. I didn't win many games, but I was also a lot shorter and younger than them. When I did magically win once or twice, though, I felt on top of the world.

Growing up and going to school in the nineties was a far different time compared to now. I can remember using a computer for the first time when I was six. My parents had one for their business that required you to input code through the command prompt to get the computer to do what you wanted. The GUI (graphical user interface) was new for home computers and quickly made computer games the newest trend. One of the most popular games was *Wolfenstein*. Man, did my brothers and I play that game like crazy. It was addicting! I'm not sure how I was allowed to play it at that age, as it's more suited for older kids, but I did, and I turned out all right.

In school, we started using computers roughly in the third grade, when I was nine years old. They were ancient and slow compared to what I'm using right now, but they served a good purpose. The screens were green with white lettering, and I recall some programs were developed with education in mind. There was a math game where you had to input the correct answer as fast as you could, then you were ranked with how quickly you accomplished a section. I must have been quick with my answers because I was the only one who could get a better score than the teacher! I felt good about myself and proud that I was able to accomplish that feat. I'm sure my records were never broken since that game probably became obsolete by the next year. Technology always seems to move fast.

Learning about computers and how to utilize them was probably one of the greatest things I was taught in grade school, and by far, the most useful program was *Mavis Beacon*! You may not be a nineties kid if you don't know how much of an impact that program or tool had. In simple terms, *Mavis Beacon* was a teaching tool to help someone learn how to type on a keyboard. You had to accurately type words or phrases in order to advance, and the faster you went, the higher words per minute you earned. I believe I was somewhere around sixty to seventy words per minute back in my day, which was definitely better than most but not quite the best in the class. My dad could have used that program, as he is one of those one-finger s-l-o-w typists. That skill is now allowing me to type this a lot faster than I would have if I had to use one finger at a time. I can't imagine using a typewriter, either, with no spellcheck. It would be even worse if I had to use paper and pencil. Yikes!

Along with typing, another great skill school taught was Microsoft Word and Excel (circa 1995). It's amazing how much I used Word and Excel at that time and how much I still use it now. With Excel, we used to go bowling for a physical education class. We then had to come back and input the numbers and make formulas that would add up and average all the scores to see who was doing the best and the worst. I didn't realize at the time what Excel and Word would mean to the coming generations, but I'm sure millions of papers and millions of spreadsheets have been made to make things easier for countless people. I'm glad I learned those skills when I had the chance, unlike algebra, which so far has been useless. Not once have I ever used the quadratic formula in real life, and I probably never will. Microsoft Word, however, is how I've written this whole book. It's been such a useful tool.

The internet was in its infancy, and I wasn't exposed to it until I was thirteen. Cable was starting to become popular, and nobody knew what a cellphone was. Car phones were a luxury. I only saw them on TV. I have no clue how anyone communicated and got things done. If our current technology gets knocked out for a while, I'm sure mass hysteria will ensue. One of my earliest encounters with a TV was an old black-and-white model where you had to get up to change the channel as there was no remote. There were only five channels to choose from. The only way you could get them to come in clearly without static was by taking a little probe and moving some dials on the control panel to the right of the screen. To go from that to having a sixty-inch flat-panel 4K TV that I can use to stream wirelessly any content from anywhere is quite remarkable. I can only imagine what my hundred-year-old grandpa thinks about all this nonsense. I give him credit that he knows how to operate the remote!

I knew very little of the world outside of my little bubble in Wisconsin. I had scant knowledge about politics or global happenings. I knew some world history from school, but at the time, I wasn't very interested in it, though I am now. One of the first things I can recall being a newsworthy moment was the Oklahoma City bombing. The local stations were covering it on TV, and the image that stuck with me was the massive collapsed side of the building that had blown up. I didn't know what it was supposed to look like, but it looked bad. I know now how bad it was, but at the time, I couldn't comprehend exactly what happened. I don't think I knew if someone purposely tried to blow it up or if it happened by itself.

In 1996, the Summer Olympics were held in Atlanta, Georgia. Mom, Dad, Mark, PJ, and I drove down there. It took many hours of driving to get there with a few stops along the way. We stayed at a campsite where we could pitch a tent for the night. I'm sure it was a lot cheaper to do that than to find a hotel for all of us in Atlanta. A day or two before we arrived, the bombing of Centennial Park occurred. I was quite oblivious to what that meant. Being only eight years old, I'm sure my parents shielded me from knowing much of what went on for my own sake, but it is interesting now to go back and look at what was taking place at that time. The Olympic Games were fun to see in person. I know we took in a baseball game, track and field, handball, and wrestling. I'm glad we made it there and back safely, knowing what I know now.

One Thanksgiving, when I was in the fifth grade, the whole family was up in Mauston for deer hunting and family time. (I'm including this story, as it will tie in later on in the book.) It was a brisk turkey day, and the backyard football game was getting underway. Being only eleven years old and seventy-five pounds soaking wet, I didn't stand much of a chance of contributing a whole lot. How the next events unfolded is still a blur, but my cousin Danny had the football and was barreling toward me. Danny wasn't the biggest guy, either. But he was at least twice the size of me at the time. I was like a deer in headlights as he plowed me over, sending me flying through the air. My body hit the ground, and a split second later, my head snapped down onto the cold, hard ground. I was seeing stars for a few seconds. People came running over to check on me as I tried to get up. I thought I was okay and walked it off a bit. No one seemed too concerned. A little while later, I was complaining that my head was hurting, and I told Mom what had happened. I was given a couple of aspirin, which helped, but my problems had only just begun. The next few days, I was getting very bad headaches, and I couldn't stand bright lights or sounds. Mom took me to the hospital, and I was diagnosed with a stage two concussion that was borderline stage three. There wasn't a whole lot that could be done except to take it easy. At that time, school was still going on, so I had to try and get through my classes. For a few weeks, it was quite a struggle. The lights and noise in the classroom were giving me killer headaches, and more than a few times, I had to lie down in a dark room to get some relief. I know Danny still feels bad for "taking me out," but things happen. I recovered eventually, but it was difficult keeping up with schoolwork. I didn't like being behind and having to catch up, but that was going to be the story of my life more than I knew in the not-so-distant future.

On a lighter note, I'm going to share one of the most embarrassing moments of my life that I'd be willing to bet will at least make you smile. During my fifth- grade year, I was late for the school bus that stopped at the end of the street in front of our house. I grabbed my stuff and ran out the door with reckless abandon to get there before it left without me. I was fast enough to make it on time, and I made my way toward the back to take my usual seat. I settled in for the twenty-five-minute ride to school when all of a sudden, I caught a whiff of something foul. There was a water treatment facility not far from my parents' house that sometimes emitted a rather stinky odor, if you know what I mean, so I attributed the stench to that. The bus made it to school, and I headed on in for class. I was sitting in the front row, and that putrid aroma again filled up my olfactory nerves. I couldn't figure it out! Did someone crap their pants? The teacher started class with the unpleasant smell still lingering. I was trying to figure out who the culprit was but to no avail. As the teacher was speaking, he walked in front of me and stopped to pick up a piece of dirt in front of my desk. As he picked it up, his face scrunched up like it would if you caught a whiff of death. I then knew what it was, and so did the teacher. During my hasty dash of running to try and catch the bus, I did not realize that the family dog, Sheena, decided to do her morning duty in the front yard. I had zero clue I stepped in it until that moment the teacher picked it up and gave it a sniff. I was busted! The teacher looked at my shoes and then at me and said, "This isn't dirt. This is dog poop!" All over my left shoe was a colossal splattering of brown doggie doo-doo. I gingerly got up and walked out of the room on the sides of my feet, as to not track any more remnants through the classroom. I made my way to the bathroom to try and clean off my shoes, and after a good ten minutes, I returned. For quite some time, I was then known as

Mr. Poopy Shoes by my classmates. I am thankful the name didn't stick around for very long. How embarrassing!

Now that we've all had a good laugh at my expense, I want to continue on to what I consider some of my "highs." I've done a little bit of skipping around, and I'm almost getting to a point where timelines will fall one after another instead of going a little back and forth, so bear with me.

One sport I participated in during grade school was wrestling. I hated it for the most part. I think the reason I didn't like it was simply because I had to go to tournaments on Saturdays. I already went to my brother's wrestling matches on Saturdays, and I didn't like giving up play time with friends or having fun around the house. Also, it could have been the fact that to get to these tournaments, I had to be up at six o'clock in the morning to get there on time. However, once I got to a tournament and into the flow of the matches, I wanted to win, and I won *a lot*. I rarely lost, so I had quite a few first-place medals. When I won a tournament, I also got to keep the bracket poster that had my name as the champion on it. Most of my matches would be done in less than thirty seconds, sometimes in less than ten. I pinned most of my opponents, but sometimes if I knew a guy wasn't going to stand much of a chance, I would take him down and get two points and then let him up. I would continue to do that as a means of practice, and eventually, I'd have enough points that the ref would stop the match and declare me the winner in what was called a "technical fall."

I don't have any real memorable moments from wrestling at an early age, but I was better than most of the kids I faced. I do know I had two straight undefeated seasons. And if my memory is correct, I also never got pinned. It may have happened, but I honestly can't recall losing very often, so it's not too farfetched to believe that no one was ever able to pin me. I took a lot of pride, I guess you would say, that I would not give up and I would not give in. I didn't want to lose, I didn't want to let my team down, and I didn't want to give my opponent the satisfaction of beating me. That's the way I operated when I was on the mat. I didn't like going, but when I was there, I gave 100 percent.

I stopped participating in wrestling after sixth grade. The only reason I can think of was that I didn't want to do it, and I didn't want to put the time in for it. Either way, I do regret that decision because I was quite good at it. It's not my biggest regret of my youth, but it's in the top ten.

Another sport that I was very gifted at was soccer, but again, I hated practices, and I hated giving up Saturdays to go play a game. However, when I was playing, you could not stop me. I was fast, I had excellent coordination, I had strong legs, and I had a fierceness come out of me that really didn't show up anywhere else except on the soccer field.

I played mostly as a right winger or a center striker. My favorite thing to do was to get a breakaway along the right side of the field. I would pull away from the defenders and either make a centering shot to the middle so that my teammates could have a chance to score or take it all the way and launch the ball into the back of the net. I was fortunate to have those opportunities many times.

Matt B. was the only other guy who was as good as, or better than, me. Thankfully, he was always my teammate. He had a massively good left leg that rivaled my right leg, so it was natural for us to play across from each other.

During the games, it was always "The Boogie (my nickname) and Matt B. Show." People called me Boogie because of my last name. I believe every male in my family was called that at one point or another. Anyway, either I was scoring the goals, and he was assisting me, or he was scoring, and I would do the assisting to him. We made a great duo, and because of that, we hardly ever lost.

Matt B. and I played together in the town league and then also on the grade school soccer team. I know I didn't play in fifth grade, and that was something I regret a lot. I remember my school won the championship that year, and a couple of guys in my class were on the team. For some reason, I didn't think I would be good enough, and maybe that was correct because the sixth, seventh, and eighth graders were all on that team too. Who knows if I would have even played, but it would have been nice to find out.

I did get on the field in sixth grade, and I found myself in my usual striker or right-wing role, competing and holding my own against the seventh and eighth graders. I still hated practices, but as I got a little older and wiser, I knew they were important, so I didn't dread them as much. I lived for the games. We won our fair share of them my sixth-grade year, but we ultimately fell short of the championship.

The next two years, it was a different story. Matt B. and I were unstoppable. I consider this run of success to be the most fun I have had in any sport. We knew we always had a chance to win when we were both on the field, and we did just that. It also helped that we had a great goalkeeper named Ryan. He kept our opponents off the scoreboard, and our offense usually scored more than enough goals to win convincingly.

Matt B. and I would make the school newsletter after every game. It was fun seeing my name mentioned in a positive light. I was starting to imagine what it would be like being a professional soccer player and having stories written about me. It made me feel good, and I wanted to continue seeing things like that in the future. It made me want to work and play even harder. I wanted to score, win, and see my name in the news articles. It was a major motivating force for me.

One memory of a game was intense. The ball literally hadn't been touched yet by the other team after the ref blew his whistle to start the clock. The opposing players looked a tad confused on who was going to touch the ball off at midfield. I was standing there, noticing their confusion, and decided to bust off like a Kentucky Derby horse out of the gate and steal the ball before they knew what happened. I then stormed down the field and blew past all the defenders and rifled the ball into the back of the net for an early one-to-nothing lead. The fans in the stands were shocked but then erupted into celebration as I ran back to my side of the field with a big smile on my face. I surprised everyone with that play, and I still get a kick out of it.

Another fun highlight was when I was on the right wing at midfield when the ball got sent to me, lining up for me to throttle back my right leg and send it flying. It was very much like playing kickball, if you can imagine, where the pitcher rolls it in nice and easy, and you can get a running start. I squared that ball up perfectly, and boy did that thing fly. The goalie backpedaled in a panic toward the goal and jumped up, but he couldn't quite reach, as the ball went over his head and under the crossbar as the net caught the missile I sent. All I did was smile and give a nice fist pump. It was a very satisfying moment to know I had that much kick in my leg. The fans in the stands loved it. It was one of my most favorite goals ever.

We had an undefeated season going in seventh grade, rolling through teams all the way up to the championship game. For some reason, we struggled in the title match and were tied zero-zero and had to go to a shoot-out or penalty kicks, as they are also referred to. I didn't like shoot-outs. I would rather keep playing until someone legit scored a goal, but I didn't make the rules. There wasn't much drama. Matt B., another teammate, and I made our first three shots, and the other team was unsuccessful with their first three. We were the victors and brought home the trophy. It was one of my first real championships as a team, and it was exciting to share that moment with my fellow teammates. Then there was next year.

Eighth-grade year, we were top of the class. We knew we were the team to beat, and it was going to be disappointing if we didn't win the championship again. It was basically a carbon copy of the previous year, with Matt B. and I leading the way. I don't know how many goals and assists I had in those two years, but there were a lot. I also had a few hat tricks (three goal games) thrown in there and one where I scored four. Nothing major really jumps out during the season as a major highlight. We did what we were expected to do, and that was to win.

We did that all the way up to the championship game, and again, we were undefeated with one game to go. The final game was tough, just like the previous year. Matt B. and I didn't score a single goal in regulation or overtime. It was uncanny!

I had a great chance, and it still is a replay in my head I can't forget. I got the ball on the right side and just took off. I was surprised that I had a defender who stayed with me the whole time down the field, which normally never happened. I split between the last two defenders by faking them up to the right and skipping the ball past them on the left, and then coming down with a shot on goal with only the goalie in my way from outside the penalty box. With the one defender still bearing down on me, I reared back my right leg and crushed the ball as hard as I could. I could hear the ball sizzle through the air as the crowd gasped. I saw the trajectory of the ball. I hit it too high. I watched it fly just inches over the top cross bar. The ball soared over the back fence, landed in the parking lot, and bounced off some cars.

I had missed the best opportunity of the game. I felt like I let the team down at that point, but we were still tied at zero. And that's the way it stayed until the shoot-out, *again*! I can't believe that we never had a shoot-out in the regular season, but in the big game, we had to do it twice. It was very much like the previous year, but I was fourth this time and didn't even have to kick as we did the same as last year. We made our first three, and the other team missed their first three. The celebration was on. We were back-to-back champs and had back-to-back undefeated seasons. Life was good. I was ready for more.

Many times during that season, opposing coaches and parents would come up to me after the game and tell me how impressed they were with my play on the field. It made me feel like a little bit of a celebrity. I knew I was good at soccer, and I wish I would have stuck with it more. For some reason, it didn't click in my head to keep going with it. It probably wouldn't have mattered in the long run, considering all that was about to happen.

Basketball was a sport I knew about but never played on an actual team until I was in sixth grade. I was stupid again and didn't play my fifth-grade year when I had the chance, simply because I was intimidated by my classmates who had been playing with each other on teams for a few years prior. I didn't think I stood a chance at being good, and I didn't want to be laughed at for stinking up the court.

By the time I did get out on the court in sixth grade, I wasn't very good, but I wasn't as far behind everyone else as I had thought. I had been expecting everyone to be dunking and hitting all sorts of shots and being able to handle the ball with ease. That definitely wasn't the case. Our basketball team was nowhere near as good as our soccer team was. After a few practices and games, I wasn't nearly as intimidated by my fellow teammates who had been doing this a lot longer than me. They could dribble better and knew how the game worked more than I did, but it didn't matter. We usually lost more than we won.

I was in a tough position. I was a guard, and the other two starting guards on the team were also the two coaches' kids. They were a little more skilled than I was in the beginning, so I wasn't too concerned about it at the time because I was always the first guy off the bench. I was good at defending and not much else. I couldn't handle the ball very well, and my shot was quite ugly most of the time. I got lucky once in a while and made a few baskets, but they were few and far between. I liked basketball. I had never really watched it on TV or in person, so for the most part, I didn't know what I was doing, but it was fun. I'll be getting back to basketball a little later on, as it ties into some pretty important happenings, so continue reading on. There's a lot more craziness coming.

I felt that I was on my way and had a great future during my seventh- and eighth-grade years. I had good friends, good family, good grades, and performed well in sports. I felt the sky was the limit. Every day was a great day. It was easy to be optimistic and have big dreams.

It wasn't too long after my first soccer championship in seventh grade that another piece of the puzzle of what I thought was a magical run of high moments happened.

Somehow, one of the things I wanted most took place. I had a girlfriend.

Holy smokes and shut the front door. How did that happen? Well, I'm not entirely sure, but it did. I was thirteen and in seventh grade, and she was fourteen and in eighth grade. How in the world did I pull that off? Did I have handsome looks? Did she like my athletic ability? Who cares? It happened, and to me, it was what I thought were the beginnings of a fantastic relationship.

Brittany was her name. She had a younger brother in my class, so I knew her family quite well. Brittany's family had moved to Wisconsin from Nebraska because her dad got a job as the fifth-grade teacher at our school. Her brother and I were chatting one night on the now-extinct AOL Instant Messenger or AIM, as it was referred to, when he mentioned that Brittany wanted to chat with me. *Why would Brittany want to chat with me?* I thought. I was nervous and excited at the same time. I quietly had a small crush on her but didn't do too much about it, fearing rejection. It was just the two of us typing back and forth, going on about this and that. I always found it was so much easier to say what you want when you have time to type it out and not have to worry about stuttering and looking like a noob. What did we talk about? It's hard to know now, but somehow, we admitted that we both had an "interest" in each other, and we became an item the next day.

Stop the presses! Get on the horn! David and Brittany were born. The gossip quickly spread throughout the roughly two-hundred-kid school, and we were transported into another realm of popularity that neither of us knew existed. Even the teachers had some fun with it. I can remember one instance where a teacher said, "Anyone with a steady girlfriend gets to go to the front of the line." The fact that a teacher knew Brittany and I were a couple and teased us a bit about it only showed that it was a big deal throughout the whole school.

Brittany and I were very much, stupidly, into each other in a very short period of time before we really even knew much about each other. She was the daughter of one of the teachers in school (red flag, I know that *now*), but I didn't see it as an issue. I saw it as an opportunity to show her dad that I was a good enough guy for his daughter. I did wholeheartedly believe at the time I was, but I was thirteen. I didn't really know much at the time, but of course, I thought I did. Brittany was beautiful, athletic, and had a great smile with long blonde-brown hair. We weren't that far apart in age, either. I was old for my class, so with her being only eight months older, it didn't seem like a far stretch that she'd have her eyes set on a guy a grade below.

Our relationship came together quickly. Every day, we couldn't wait to see each other in the morning as we hung out outside of the eighth-grade classroom. The seventh-grade room was quite a distance away, so I went to where Brittany was. She was the most important person to me. I didn't care if I had to run all the way back through the halls to get to class on time. It was fun.

Kids in all grades were eyeing us up, as it was a surprise to everyone that Brittany and I were hanging off each other and talking before classes started every day. Keep in mind that no one else was in any kind of relationship in the entire school, so kids seeing a "couple" that wasn't there before really turned heads. People wanted to know what was up. Friends came up to me and inquired what was going on, so I proudly told them that Brittany was my girlfriend. I got a few high fives and a couple "you da man" comments, which made me feel like a million bucks. I was way up there on my high horse, and the only rough parts were when we couldn't see each other. We didn't have joint classes, but there would be times of passing in the hall to exchange notes and I love yous. It was young love at its finest.

Fifth through eighth grades congregated into one big hall for lunch. Normally, each grade sat in their own rows, and no one crossed over—until we came along. I would sit with Brittany at the eighth-grade table, leaving my seventh-grade class behind. There was no denying it anymore. The public could very easily see we were together. I think we both loved the attention and that feeling of being looked at as the "popular couple." No one else had what we had, and the only thing we wanted to do was be together.

And that's exactly what we set out to do. We were given one recess after lunch to go out and play and have fun. If we played kickball or football or whatever else, if you picked me to be on your team, Brittany was automatically coming with me. It was a great two-for-one deal.

We couldn't drive, we lived on opposite sides of town, and we didn't have smart phones. All we had was AIM, which was a great precursor to the texting we have now. We would chat as long as we could until we got kicked off from using the computer by our parents or siblings. We dreamed about the future and how we wished I could just skip a grade so that we could go into high school together. We talked about getting married, having a home with two kids (two boys, to be exact), and living happily ever after. I guess when you're thirteen, you think just about anything is possible, but the odds were very much stacked against us.

I liked keeping the relationship under wraps at home. I don't know when my parents knew that I was in a "serious" relationship with an "older" woman, but I couldn't contain my excitement when mom teased me about it. I was sitting shotgun with my mom driving us somewhere, and after the usual chitchat, she must have noticed my happiness and jokingly said, "What's got you smiling so much? You have a girlfriend or something?" I replied back, "Yeah, so what if I do?" I told her about Brittany, and she seemed happy for me, but I'm sure deep down she was worried about it; she had good reason for that. I had already been an uncle for seven years at that time because my brother Matt and his girlfriend at the time (now wife) had a baby girl at eighteen years young. I highly doubt my mom wanted me to break that record, and I didn't want to either. I just wanted to be with Brittany and have fun together.

The first real date that Brittany and I went on was a double date. I had to be dropped off at the movie theater by my mom (yeah, real cool), but when you can't drive and have next to nothing for money, you make do. I was over-the-top excited to see Brittany and finally have some together time outside of school. I walked into the theater, and there she was. All I could do was smile, walk up to her, and give her a hug. I felt very much like we had been together a long time. It was so natural being with her. We made our way into the seating area and found our seats, with Brittany on my right and her friend Katie and her boyfriend on my left. We enjoyed the movie, played a little footsie, and would nudge our arms together playfully. I also couldn't help staring into her green eyes when we looked at each other. She was so pretty. I thought I knew what love was. I thought this was it, and there was no way I wanted that night to end. I was happy. She was happy. It was perfect.

And then it wasn't. The movie ended, and we walked out of the theater into the lobby. Brittany wanted me to stay back in the hallway so that her parents or whoever was picking her up didn't see me. You see, she wasn't supposed to be out with me. Her parents said she wasn't allowed to date anyone, as she was too young. She gave me a hug and quickly said, "Goodnight, I'll see you Monday. I love you." I was a bit confused as to the abrupt departure, but I didn't think much of it. If her parents didn't want her to date, I really didn't think that was going to stop us from being together.

So, there I was after the best night of my life, alone, in the lobby of the theater, waiting to get picked up. Ten or fifteen minutes passed, and still no ride. I wasn't worried. I figured one of my parents would be there soon. Thirty minutes, then forty-five minutes went by, and the theater was getting empty. I was trying to figure out how the heck I would get home. An hour passed, and I found a payphone, but I didn't have any change to call home, so I started looking for loose change on the floor, but I had no luck. I think the people working in the lobby were starting to notice I was all alone when, finally, I saw my dad pull up. I quickly got outside and into the car, relieved that I didn't have to stay in the theater all night.

My dad's tone of voice sounded quite disappointed when I hopped in. I had just had a great night with Brittany, and I didn't think anything would ruin that until my dad told me that he and Mom were worried I didn't call to come be picked up, so they called Brittany's parents. Brittany was already home, and her parents didn't know I was out with her until they received that call. I got the "we're disappointed in you" speech when I got home (never a fun time). I felt sucker- punched. What just happened?

If that date had taken place during the time we had cell phones, where I could have easily sent a text or a call to have someone come pick me up, I don't think Brittany's parents would have known we had gone out. I had seldom, if ever, used a payphone. And in hindsight, if I knew how to make a collect call or was smart enough to ask someone for change so I could make a call, then the situation may have turned out differently. In either case, it was the beginning of the end to our relationship, and I was crushed.

I started blaming myself and felt like I had let Brittany down. If I had done this or that differently, then maybe we'd still be together, but we weren't. Everything was different after that night. There were no more notes being sent between us. There were no more *I love yous* as we passed in the hallways, no more lunches together, and no more dreaming of the life we were going to make for ourselves. How quickly it ended was very similar to how quickly it started. Our relationship only lasted a few months, but it took many more to recover from the letdown and disappointment. It was young love, it was dumb love, and it was a relationship with a high percentage of failure, but we didn't know that at the time. We lived in the moment. And for as much as it hurt when it ended, I wouldn't go back and not have those few months with Brittany.

It was a bummer of a summer, but life went on. Labor Day weekend came and went, and I was now embarking on my eighth-grade year. The memory of Brittany still ate at me. All I had to do was get through this year and make it into high school, and we could meet again. I had my doubts we could get back together, though.

Realistically, she was going to meet a lot of new friends, and I'm sure a lot of guys wanted to date her. I wanted her back. I knew I really needed to impress with grades and athletic accomplishments this school year. Her dad was one of my basketball coaches, so I figured if I could show him that I was a high-quality guy, I'd have better odds of being with Brittany again. I became focused on being the best that I could be.

I ran cross-country in late summer to make sure I was in great shape for soccer season (which we won the championship). I did very well running that season, best I had ever done. I was never the top runner, but I was consistently finishing in the top fifteen. I was recruited by the high school coach to become part of the cross-country team once I got there. I received a letter in the mail about how much the coach would love to see me on his squad. I didn't exactly know what I was going to do because that was also soccer season in high school, so there was a big decision to be made there.

It was coming up on deer hunting season again, I was fourteen, and it was October 2000, my eighth-grade year. I, along with my parents, my brother Mike, his wife, Kristie, and Sheena, my black Lab, headed out into the woods to look over our deer hunting area. We checked our hunting stands and trimmed back any overgrown vegetation that could impede a shot at a deer. We finished up with those duties and then headed to the swamp (where I was shot at a few years ago) to harvest some fern leaves for Kristie's mom. I was happily helping pick the leafy ferns along with everybody else while Sheena was running herself tired through all the vegetation. I would estimate we spent a good thirty minutes gathering the ferns until it was time to head back to the van and go home.

After no more than five minutes in the car, I noticed a bug crawling on me. I went to pick it off, opened the window, and flicked it outside. Then I found another one inching up my arm and another on my pants. In no time at all, I was finding them everywhere! It wasn't just me, either. Everyone in the car was finding these bugs all over them. Even though Sheena's fur was black, I could see what looked like tiny black spiders squirming around on her. It was a nonstop battle the entire ride home of finding and removing these little bugs from our bodies. They were very much the size of a grain of rice, if not smaller. I didn't know what they were, but my mom thought they were ticks. I had never encountered ticks before. Once we thought we had removed them all, no one thought twice about it except that it was rather gross and icky to have those bugs creeping around on us.

With 2000 coming to a close and winter starting to settle in, we were constantly getting walloped with snowstorms and cold temperatures. If you live in the Midwest, you know what I'm talking about. I've experienced twenty-five degrees Fahrenheit below zero with windchill of sixty degrees Fahrenheit below zero. I've been through snowstorms (or blizzards, as we call them) that can dump a couple of feet in no time at all. When those conditions roll in, everyone starts to wonder why we live in this area. However, for the most part, it's not too bad. At least there aren't any mosquitos when it is that cold and snowy.

My parents' house was on a cul-de-sac, and one of the neighbors hired me to clear snow for the winter. I didn't expect to be clearing both their driveway and my parents' driveway day after day while still going to school and getting homework done. It was nonstop for a couple of weeks where I would get up early to clear snow from the driveways, catch the bus for school, go to basketball practice, come home, clear more snow, get homework done, and then do it all over again the next day. It wasn't long before I was getting sick with some nasty head colds, but that was nothing out of the ordinary for that time of year. On top of that, I was experiencing pain and stiffness in my neck and lower back. I made a couple of trips to the chiropractor to try and straighten myself out. I regularly went to a chiropractor my whole life and didn't think twice about my new pain issue, as I was probably just overusing those parts of my body with all that was going on. I will admit, though, that it was tough making it to school and keeping up with everything at that time. Miraculously, I powered through it. I didn't miss any school, and I didn't miss any basketball practice or games. The constant clearing of snow got old quick, but I liked getting extra money to do with it what I pleased.

When you're fourteen years old, you feel a bit invincible, like you can do anything. However, I didn't realize how much I was actually running myself into the ground.

One good thing about the snow is that it makes for some excellent sledding conditions. There was a superb sledding hill in a park right by our house that not many people knew about, which my brothers and I frequented growing up. I would say there was a good foot of snow on the hill, and Mark, PJ, and I decided to go do some sledding. It was Christmas, so they were both back from college on break, and it was probably the last time we all went sledding there. We were having a good time gliding down the steep hill, setting up jumps so we could get some "air" on the way down. The only part that wasn't fun was that once you got down the hill, you had to walk all the way back up. Normally, it's not too bad, but with the snow being as deep as it was, it turned into a laborious excursion after you've gone up and down a few times. I felt fantastic, and we were all having a great time together, but all that exertion must have finally caught up with me.

CHAPTER 3

GOING DOWN

Nearing the end of our sledding excursion, my neck suddenly felt like an anaconda was wrapped around it. Every time I would try and swallow, it felt like razor blades were packed in my throat. The glands under both sides of my jawbone were swollen. I told my brothers I wasn't feeling very good, and I was hoping they would walk back with me, but they stayed behind for a few more runs on the sledding hill. I didn't want to go back up through the woods by myself, so I went all the way down to the bottom and got on the road so that I could walk back home up the giant hill. It was the same hill that was wicked fun and almost suicidal to ride down on your rollerblades, but this time, I had to go *up*. I was already tired, but going up that monstrous beast feeling the way I did took a toll on me. I managed to get back to the house, and luckily, Mom was there to try and fix me up. She could tell that I was not in the healthiest state, so I tried to explain what was going on. Mom got me some over-the-counter medicine to take, and I hopped in the shower to warm up. I had hoped the shower would help my throat not feel so raw, but any help was minimal. Mom was eager to help any way she could, and before I knew it, I had some Vicks VapoRub slathered on my neck and chest, which was then wrapped with a hot washcloth and then covered by another towel. I attempted to get some sleep, feeling like I was in traction with so much stuff wrapped around me, but by then, congestion was setting in, which made breathing very difficult. The next day wasn't any better. My head was hurting, I had chills, and my throat was still swollen and raw, not to mention the congestion, coughs, and sneezing. I honestly can't remember ever feeling this bad. It was like a common cold but ten times worse. I wasn't getting any better, so a trip to the doctor was in order.

I was never a huge fan of going to see doctors. Being poked and prodded was a bit uncomfortable, but with how sick I was, I knew I needed some assistance. According to my paperwork, my main symptoms were extreme fatigue, headaches, chest pain, runny nose, congestion, stomachache, and some slight ear ringing. The doctor ran some blood tests and discovered I had a low white blood cell count, high protein in my urine, and a panel for the Epstein-Barr virus came back negative.

My primary doctor wasn't able to diagnose me with anything concrete, so I was referred to the local hospital. The chest pains must have been a bit of a concern as an echocardiogram was ordered. Here I was, fourteen years old, hooked up to an EKG to see what my heart was doing. I have a family history of heart disease. My dad has had his fair share of heart bypasses. My grandpa and his brother all had heart surgeries as well. If your ticker isn't ticking too well or there is a family history of it, it's probably a smart idea to have it checked out just to be safe. The results came back normal, which wasn't a big surprise to me, but it was good to know.

More blood tests were issued. I don't believe anything came back conclusive, but I was diagnosed with a severe viral infection. I was told to go home, rest up, and I'd be fine in a couple of weeks. That was sweet music to my ears. I did not like being as sick I was. I missed a good week or so of school, as well as time on the basketball court. I needed to recover quickly so that I could finish up my final grade-school year on a high note.

The rest helped. A couple of weeks after the initial sickness, I was back in school, trying hard to get caught up on schoolwork. I took another week off from basketball so that I didn't have to exert my body, but after getting caught up, I was ready to get back to a normal schedule.

Whatever normal I experienced was short-lived. In school, it was harder to concentrate and think through problems than it was before. During basketball practice and games, I could tell I was getting tired a lot quicker than usual, and I was having pain in my knees that was never there before. I pushed through it as much as I could, but whatever was fighting me was starting to win.

One basketball practice in particular really stood out to me where I knew something wasn't right. It started out fine, but about halfway through, we were running sprints. We'd start at one end of the court and run to the free throw line and back. Then we'd go to half court and back, run to the second free throw line and back, and all the way to the end of the court and back. If you're not in shape, you don't last very long and get easily worn out. I was normally first or second on the team doing this drill. I was about halfway through, and the pain in my knees really kicked in. They were burning and throbbing. I had a hard time breathing and was exhausted beyond belief. I had to stop. I leaned up against the wall to prevent myself from collapsing on the floor. I could not for the life of me make sense of what was happening. I couldn't finish, and everyone on the team passed me by. The coach was just as shocked and confused as me. He knew I didn't slack off or sandbag anything. I told him how I was feeling, and he had me sit out the rest of practice. I didn't like watching from the sidelines, but there I was. It was really the first time I had felt like life was slipping away ever so gently, and there wasn't much I could do to stop it.

It felt like a cement truck had flat-out run me over, then backed up and hit me again for good measure. How great I used to feel playing soccer was now the complete opposite. It was unfathomable to me the state I was in. Basketball was now out of the question, and at school, I was increasingly absent.

February 2001 came, and I wasn't improving. I felt like I was stuck in quicksand. The more I tried to push through and get out of whatever I was going through, the worse I got. Sore throats, swollen glands, horrible congestion, achy muscles, colds, and exhaustion kept defeating me. My body was at war, and I was very much on the losing end of all the battles.

I went to one of my favorite places again to get checked out. That's right, the doctor's office. The doctor checked me over again just like what had happened a month prior, yet he still couldn't put his finger on any cause. We were throwing darts just to see what we could rule in or out.

The first time I had ever heard of Lyme disease was during this visit. The doctor wanted to run a Western blot test. (I guess my symptoms were fairly consistent with those of Lyme, but Lyme was also not very well-known in our area at the time.) We took a shot at the test, but the results came back *negative*. I found the original test that showed some level was at .14, but whatever that level was had to be greater than 1.00 to confirm a positive test. Even though I tested negative, I was prescribed the antibiotic Ceftin for twenty-one days.

I had some improvement after a few weeks. The cold-like symptoms went away, but I was still exceptionally tired. I made it back to school, but I was now significantly behind. I was glad to be back. Trying to catch up on that much schoolwork while still feeling run-down was not an easy task, but I did my best. My normal A and B grades quickly dropped into the C and even D range. Being in class, it was hard to stay awake. I constantly had my head on my desk with my eyes closed. My brain started feeling like there were waves crashing inside it, over and over again, just like it would on a sandy beach. That constant wave action was incredibly mind-numbing. Getting assignments turned in was now slipping away from being a top priority for me. I cared, but at the same time I didn't care about what grade I was getting, as long as I was passing.

Classmates, teachers, and family were now well aware I had something going on. In the beginning, I was given sympathy. I had never been one to fake being sick or want people to feel sorry for me to get attention. I would much rather be scoring baskets and getting good grades to get attention. Alas, my new reality was feeling like garbage for a few days, and then I'd have a great day where I felt everything was just fine and I could do anything. Inevitably, one good day would be followed by more bad days. It was a cycle I wasn't used to, but that's what I had to deal with. The up-and-down nature of my health was starting to wear on me emotionally and was also creating doubts about how others viewed me.

I didn't have a lot of fun things to look forward to during this time. I wasn't feeling well. I was missing school and falling behind. I missed playing sports, and I missed the high mountain that I used to be on top of.

One thing I did look forward to was watching the Milwaukee Bucks play. I never watched them play much basketball before, but they were doing very well that season and were making a deep run into the playoffs. Since I wasn't playing basketball, I figured the next best thing to do was watch it. Watching the Bucks play really opened my eyes to what it was like to play at a high level. I started to envision myself on the court, emulating what the professionals were doing. I really liked Ray Allen. He had a well-rounded game and a similar body type as myself, except I was a quite a bit shorter. I was fascinated by how fluidly he moved and how he could control his body as well as he did. I really wanted to get back on the actual basketball court, though it didn't look possible with how I was feeling.

I started doing half-days at school, which helped tremendously. I wasn't getting as exhausted as I had been, and I started to catch up on schoolwork. Having a little bit of a schedule, even at a reduced load, allowed me to get going in a positive direction. I didn't even attempt to play basketball for a whole month. I was still part of the team, however, and we had one last tournament coming up that I wanted to be a part of.

The basketball tournament was hosted by the high school I was planning on going to. It felt great to put that uniform back on. The team I was on still wasn't very good. We lost a lot more than we won. It was no surprise we were getting beat quite easily in the first game, so near the end, the coach put me in. I was angry and a tad apprehensive that I had missed so much time and opportunity. I simply went for it. I scored a quick five points and got a steal and a couple of rebounds before my body had enough. We lost the game, but I found that I could play at a much higher level than I had before. I attribute that to simply watching and learning from people who were better than me. I wanted more.

Thankfully, the tournament was on a weekend. I was tired the next morning, but by the afternoon, I was feeling better and ready to go for the evening game. If we won, we would continue, but if we lost, then our season was over. I didn't start the game, which wasn't unusual, so I waited patiently on the bench for my turn. The first half went by, and Coach still hadn't put me in, but midway through the third quarter, we were getting beat badly again, and my name was called. I was in, and I wanted to prove I could play. The high school coach was watching, so I needed to impress. I got the ball and brought it up the court while the other team was in a standard zone defense. I faked to the right, crossed back left, drove down the middle, and laid it in for two points. The fluidity in which I moved and the control I had without practicing for over a month felt out of this world. I was a different player. I was aggressive, and I wanted to dominate much like I did in soccer. After another great drive to the hoop for two and a steal, I was getting tired. I had the ball stolen from me as I crossed half court. I was too tired to chase after the guy who stole it. We had trimmed the lead down to make it a competitive game, so I was pulled out, and the regular starters came back in to open up the fourth quarter. Within a short period of time, we were down again, and there were only a couple of minutes left, so Coach decided to put me back out there. I kind of knew that this would be my last game in grade school, and I wanted to end on a high note. I started back aggressively again but changed how I scored by hitting a pull up three from the top of the arc. Not long after, I got a steal and assisted to one of my teammates who hit a three-point shot. We had six quick points but were still down by quite a few. There wasn't enough time to win the game, but I still played hard. On one of the last plays, we had an inbounds play where I was at the top of the three-point line and busted to the right corner, where I received the pass, set my feet behind the three-point line, and rose up and fired. It was nothing but net. I felt like Ray Allen. I had watched him do that play quite a few times. It was awesome, it was perfect, and it was over. I looked up at the scoreboard with my hands on my hips and saw we were going to lose with seconds left on the clock. I savored that moment. I believe that's why I remember it so fondly. I figured out that I could play this game and wanted to feel this type of confidence again on the court. I thought that if I could get healthy, I would have a shot at being really good at basketball.

The buzzer sounded. The game was over. My teammates were high-fiving me and telling me, "Great job, Boogie! That was awesome!" I never scored more than four or five points in a game before, but in this one, I had scored ten in a very short period of time. I would have loved to see what I could have done being fully healthy. Heck, even the coach afterward said, "Man, I guess you really don't need to practice!" I know he was impressed with how well I did, and that made me feel like a million bucks.

Unfortunately, feeling like a million bucks was short-lived. It was back to reality, back to school, and back to not feeling great. A million bucks turned into an old, beat-up penny on the curb that no one wants to bother to bend over and pick up. It was wild the day-to-day differences I experienced. How could I be playing basketball one day and then, a few days later, be extremely tired and in constant pain? I couldn't explain it. I missed a few more days of school, and by this time, I thought I should be more or less back to normal, but that was not the case. Not long after that, people around me started questioning if I was really sick or if I was just faking it. I remember one teacher in particular was frustrated with my situation and directed that frustration toward me. It made me angry that someone questioned my intent and sincerity of what I was going through. But at the same time, what was I going through? There was no answer to why I was feeling the way I was. I had been to the doctors, and that turned up nothing. I'm quite sure the teacher wasn't the only one doubting me. It didn't take long before I could feel the doubt from friends and family members. I didn't like that one bit, but at the same time, it was hard not to blame them. Heck, I even started having doubts myself about what was really happening. Bottom line, though, was that I knew I wasn't faking my symptoms. I had no reason to. I wanted to be in school. I wanted to play sports. I wanted to be with my friends. I wanted to get to high school on a high note.

The mornings were tough. Waking up started to seem like an impossible chore. At times, I was sleeping until two in the afternoon. My body was heavy, and it was difficult to move around without having pain shooting through my knees. I was most comfortable lying in bed where I could sleep and escape the little hell I was going through. That would last for a few days, and then I would be a different person. I would feel fine and be back in school. I was able to turn in most of my overdue homework, but I knew there were missing assignments and incomplete work, which were hurting my grades. One or two good days were then followed up with a week of agony. I had no consistency in how I felt.

With me showing very little improvement, it was back to the doctor. Another test was ordered, the same one as before, the Western blot. Shockingly (but not really), the results came back *negative*. However, this time I had a range of .15 instead of .14. The number still had to be higher than 1.00 to be positive. I matched the symptoms of Lyme disease, but with results showing negative, we were getting nowhere.

I was also going to the chiropractor to try and relieve pain during this time. The pain in my lower back, knees, and neck was becoming way too commonplace to ignore. I do remember getting relief, but it was short-lived. I was on a road littered with dead-ends and flat tires all around. I felt like I was running out of options.

March rolled into April, and I was now counting months of being sick versus just days and weeks. I continued to get worse. The pain and tiredness were already beating me down, and then came more cold-like symptoms. I had just gone through this junk a few months ago, and now I had to deal with it all over again. I had pretty much the same symptoms as before. The glands in my neck, just below the jaw, became inflamed, which made swallowing incredibly painful. Terrible congestion and coughing followed. There was no way I was going to school, so once again, I was in bed, simply trying to get better.

There were only a handful of weeks left in school, and track season was starting. I know I wanted to participate, but that was not going to happen. I had missed too much school and was not in any kind of physical shape to perform the way I would want to. Missing school was one thing, but missing a sport that I was good at and unable to compete in drove me crazy. Plus, how bad would I look if I went out and competed now and did quite well? The rumors and speculation about me faking would be off the chart! So instead of competing, I watched from the sidelines. It hurt a lot watching everyone else participate. If I had been healthy, I'm sure I would have done quite well. I always did.

I was up, and I was down, just like a roller coaster. The end of my eighth-grade year was quickly approaching. The weather warmed, and my body was on an upswing. It was a school tradition that the eighth-grade class took a field trip down into Illinois to experience Six Flags Great America. I had never been there. It's basically a huge amusement park with monstrous roller coasters all over the place. A few classmates experienced it before, and I was excited to hang out with my friends for one of the last times. The day started great, with an early morning bus ride that took a good hour and a half. We arrived safely, so now it was time to explore. We had chaperones along, but they mostly let us do our own thing. As long as no one got lost or hurt, there wasn't much to worry about.

Since I had never been on any wild rides before, a group of friends and I decided to start out on some smaller, less-crazy ones. I didn't know what to expect, but I got quite the thrill and adrenaline rush. It wasn't long before we went on all sorts of different rides. By the time the afternoon rolled around, we were all feeling invincible. It was time to hop on the Raging Bull. At the time, this was one of the more advanced ways to bring out the thrill-seeker in you. This ride took you up, down, and all around at super-fast speeds. If you didn't lose your cookies on this one, you can safely say that you can handle any ride out there. I remember getting strapped in and starting a slow chug up this incredibly steep ramp. I knew that once we hit the top and started going over, it was going to be intense. In a matter of seconds, we were free-falling at what had to be one hundred miles per hour (at least it felt like it). I was flung upside down, left, and right like a rag doll, screaming as loud as I could. It was invigorating, and then it was over. So, what did we do afterward? We got in line and did it again. It seemed like a great idea at the time, but after the second time through, I was not feeling right.

I was dizzy, shaking, numb, nauseous, and tired. The people around me could see I wasn't acting like myself. I sat out the rest of the rides and waited to get back on the bus to head home. I took a bit of a nap along the way, but after I woke up, I was still feeling gnarly. I'll never forget that feeling because I would feel that way again and again many more times. The only difference was that I wouldn't need the Raging Bull for it to happen. Thankfully, it was the weekend now, and I had a few days to recover from that excursion.

With only a few weeks left in school, I was academically behind. Feeling good one day and then terrible the next was impossibly hard to get used to. I was missing classes way too often and was in jeopardy of being held back because of incomplete work. I tried desperately to push through it. Mom brought me to school to pick up schoolwork that I could take home and do. I was shaking inside. I felt terribly weak. The Raging Bull factor was hitting me hard. This was one of the first times I started to break down. With classes being let out for the day, I walked in to gather my things. As I walked out of the classroom, I couldn't carry my backpack full of books and assignments. I was in pain, and I could feel my emotions competing against each other. I didn't want to feel this way, but I did. I didn't want to miss school, but I was. I didn't want to be held back, but I couldn't keep up. The harder I pushed, the worse shape I was in. I made it to the common area outside of the classroom and had to sit down on the floor by the railing overlooking the front entrance. Tears came to my eyes as I couldn't stop trembling. A classmate of mine, Ryan (the goalie on the soccer team), came over and helped me gather my stuff that had fallen out of my bag when I dropped it. I sat there awhile, broken. A few people came to check on me and offered nice words to try and make me feel better.

I stayed in that one position, staring off into the distance, waiting for this latest humiliation to pass. After what seemed like an eternity, I was able to clear my head enough to try and move. I struggled to get up. By now, it felt like everyone in the school saw me in my defeated state. Mentally, I was not used to being in this position. Physically, I was becoming a shell of who I once was. Spiritually, I was starting to raise questions about why this was happening. Emotionally, I was all over the map.

I missed around forty days of school my eighth-grade year. I know for a fact that I didn't have all my schoolwork turned in, and even if I did, it was failing work. How I made it to graduation, I do not know. If I would have been held back for a year, I would have ended up being able to legally drive a car to school by the end of the next school year. In a way, it would have been awesome to be able to drive in eighth grade. I could just imagine seeing the teachers' faces as I drove myself home from school. I then started to think of how awesome it would be to be driving as a freshman one year later. I think I would have been quite popular with everyone in my class.

Alas, that did not happen. I was allowed to graduate. Why? I don't really know. My body of work leading up to before I was sick may have played into it. I got good grades, never had any issues getting my work done, teachers liked me, and classmates liked me. I had everything going my way before I started to go downhill.

Even though there was no conclusive reason for why I was sick, even though some thought I was faking and doubted my sincerity, I made it through grade school.

It was bittersweet. I had gone to school with roughly the same thirty or so kids every day for the last nine years, and now we were all moving on. There were many different high schools in the area, so graduating meant that it was most likely the last time I would see some friends ever again. Pictures were taken, laughs were shared, and yearbooks were signed. I felt good and relieved. The stress of not having to complete schoolwork or get up early and push myself every day to get things done allowed my body to recover.

It was time to move on. The young and innocent years were coming to an end. A new horizon was fast approaching. I had three months before a new chapter would start. I knew that if I could regain my health, then I could still make something of myself. I had no doubt I would miss the friendships I had formed, but I was excited to find out who I was going to meet down the road. Time would tell what would happen, but I was looking forward to the opportunity. The summer of 2001 was about to shape the rest of my life.

CHAPTER 4

BUT NOT WITHOUT A FIGHT

Summertime was finally here. I could relax and get back on track, or so I thought. After a few weeks had gone by, I still had some pain shooting through my knees and back that I just couldn't seem to shake. I was still tired but nowhere near as bad as I had been. I considered that an improvement, and I wanted to keep moving forward as much as possible.

Moving forward wasn't easy. I didn't like how I ended my grade-school years. I felt like I had missed some good times and memories. I was fourteen, with my fifteenth birthday fast approaching. The world was moving faster and faster, it seemed.

It was the dawn of the internet age, and like most teenagers, I was quickly catching on to the new technology. The big rave was e-mail, but even better than that was instant messenger. If you grew up during this time period, you remember dial-up internet and the crazy noises it would make when it connected. "You've got mail" was one of the first things you heard when you signed in. Unfortunately, it never seemed to be good mail.

I chatted with a lot of the kids I was in school with online. It was awesome being able to stay connected with multiple people at the same time. It was exciting when you heard the "door opening" noise through your speakers to see who had just signed on. There were also chat rooms you could go into and talk with people from all over the place. It was a whole new world!

I stumbled into a chat room where people could talk about whatever they wanted. To identify yourself, you'd type in your age, gender, and location. It was simple, and you could connect with anyone in the room you had interest in talking to. As luck or fate would have it, there was a girl my age from Florida. Her username caught my attention because it had "Sheena" in it. (Sheena was the name of my four-year-old black Lab at the time.) I thought, *What the heck? Go on and say hi to Sheena.* So I did. Sheena responded back, and we struck up a conversation. It was so cool! I felt like a big shot that I was talking to a girl from Florida. Technology was awesome. We were one thousand miles apart but shared the same screen and could talk as much as we'd like. It was probably not the smoothest of moves to mention the fact that I was initially intrigued to talk to her because she had the same name as my dog. But she thought it was cute, so I had nothing to worry about. Sheena and I chatted on a regular basis. We had a lot in common, and it was super nice to get to know her. Her friendship would become invaluable.

I was over-the-top innocent about the internet. Who knew you could meet someone in a chat room who wasn't a creeper or a weirdo? I think I got lucky, or knowing what I know now, God was sending me an angel. Sheena was the first of the angels I believe were sent to help me navigate the coming years.

With only a few short months to prepare for high school, I had to start game-planning for what I wanted to do.

There was no doubt I wanted to play sports in high school, so I knew I had to get some training in. I signed up for a basketball camp and a baseball camp that was run through the high school I would be attending. It may not have been the best idea, considering my health situation, but with no official diagnosis, I had to push through whatever growing pains I was going through. My athletic ability wasn't going to get any better by sitting at home all summer.

Baseball camp was first. I was stoked to get out there and show what I could do. However, I quickly became intimidated by the size of the other kids I was competing with. It also seemed like everyone there had buddies they could team up with, and I was left desperately looking for someone I could partner with to do drills. It was not the best start to the camp, and it really didn't improve from there. After the first day, I was beat. It was difficult to make it to the second day, but I soldiered on. We started with infield ground balls hit to the shortstop and then making a throw to first. (I've done this countless times in the past with no problems.) I had a hard time reacting to the ball off the bat, and my movement was impaired. I attempted the throw to first base after gathering the ball up, but my arm strength was weak, and my shoulder started to ache. I knew something was off, but I didn't know what. We moved to outfield drills where we shagged some fly balls while drifting back, catching, and then "crow hopping" a throwback in. I had done these kinds of skills hundreds of times in the past, but after running through them a few times, I was gassed. I couldn't figure it out. The next day, I woke up and was so tired and sore that I didn't even attempt to go to camp that day. Camp was scheduled for seven days, but I only went to two of them. I was too drained and under the weather to put myself back out there. I was not happy with the situation, but I needed to get my body right, and soon.

I had two weeks off before basketball camp was set to start, and I was chomping at the bit to get after it. The time off had me rested and ready to go.

The very first day, everyone there seemed to be moving at light speed while I was stuck running through quicksand. I felt great the days prior, but that quickly turned. Running up and down the court was filled with pain, especially in my knees, and now I was getting bad headaches. I felt like throwing up a few times, and I was starting to doubt myself that I could make it through even the easiest of drills. The second day rolled around, and I was in a scrimmage pickup game. I took a few shots but missed them all. My vision and coordination did not seem to be working like they used to. It was frustrating that I could not seem to get it together. On a fast break down the court, I busted my butt past everyone and was fed a pass that looked like it was going to be an easy layup. The problem was that I didn't catch the pass. It went right through my hands, and the ball bent my right thumb backward. I was in terrible pain. The thumb swelled up. I got some ice, and then I was back on the sidelines watching. It wasn't where I wanted to be. I was getting down on myself at this point. How could I be letting this opportunity slip? Why was my coordination off? Was I just terrible at sports now? I couldn't make sense of it.

Free throw drills were about the only thing left that I could do. My thumb had swelled up so much that I had to start shooting left-handed. Oddly enough, I still made six out of ten and then seven out of ten. One of the coaches there was impressed, but that was about the end of it. I didn't go back after that day. I was sick again and in more pain than I ever had been. This was *not* the summer I had imagined. I needed some positive changes, and I needed them *now*.

Camps were over, and summer was not. I was worried that I wasn't at the health level I wanted to be. I did not want to start the next part of my life behind the eight ball. I needed a boost.

To make a few bucks, I normally helped my parents out at the local county fairs. I had been working at fairs in exhibitor booths since I was a little guy. My parents were in the residential fire alarm business, and having spots at the fair where they could advertise and get leads was part of summer life. Sometimes I dreaded spending ten-to-twelve-hour days working, but I didn't mind a little side money over the years.

The Waukesha County Fair was one of the last ones of the summer that I had to do. I was getting run-down from all the long weeks and weekends I was working. I had on-and-off headaches, pain in my knees, and my energy was on the lethargic side. It was starting to get more than a little annoying with how run-down I felt on a regular basis. I knew it wasn't normal, but it was starting to become part of my daily life.

The fair would last for a week, and it was commonplace to make small talk with the other vendors in the booths next to you. The booth to the left had a nice lady working named Kathy who sold vitamin supplements. I didn't think much about vitamins or how that could be beneficial. I was quite ignorant on the topic. I had taken Flintstones vitamins back in the day, and those were tasty. But other than that, I didn't think they did much good.

I eavesdropped a few times on conversations with customers who spoke to Kathy. I was intrigued when people would say that this product helped with this, or this product helped with that. There was always someone stopping by with a story about how these products helped them. I started thinking, *What if I tried some of her supplements? Could they help me?* I mentioned it to Mom, who was going to be there with me on the last day to check out her booth with me.

The final day of the fair came, and Mom and I went over to Kathy and inquired about what would be good for me to take. Kathy showed us this one product in particular, an antioxidant. I had no idea what an antioxidant was, but I thought, *Hey, it couldn't hurt to give it a try.*

The directions said to take it in the morning on an empty stomach. I was excited to give it a try the next day to see what would happen. I had to measure out a certain amount of powder with some water and mix up the drink. It was fizzy and tasted a bit like sour grapes, but all in all, it wasn't too bad. A few days into using it, I was getting some stomachaches, and a few urgent trips to the bathroom ensued. I remember Kathy saying that I may notice a few changes before an improvement was observed, so I stuck with it.

I was one week into taking this new supplement. I woke up and came down the stairs for breakfast. That may not seem like anything too dramatic, but my knees didn't hurt coming down the steps. I normally slept as late as I could if I didn't have anything going on, but on this day, it was 7:30 in the morning. Mom was having breakfast and had a shocked look on her face when I walked into the kitchen. She said, "My goodness, David, you're up early." I replied, "Yeah, so far my knees haven't hurt, and I actually feel good."

I felt a lot better after one week. The difference was amazing. From feeling the way I had been for the last eight months to now feeling great was just what I needed. I quickly wanted to make up for lost time. I needed to get back into shape, so I started running again. I don't recall having any issues after a few weeks of off-and-on running, and it was like I was a brand-new person. I couldn't wait to get back into a daily, positive routine, to push it, and to seize the upcoming start of high school.

For high school sports, I needed to get a "sports physical," so it was back into the doctor's office. Looking back through the notes I had from the evaluation, nothing out of the ordinary was found. I had some minor pain in my hips, which I attributed to my recent uptick in running and exercise. Otherwise, the doctor said I was good to go. Nothing was going to stop me now. I had quiet confidence that I was back on track, just in the nick of time.

It was decision time. Should I try out for soccer? I had a shot at being one of the best players around. I had heard the soccer coach wanted me on the team, but I never got so much as a smile or a handshake to sway me into playing. I was confident I could do well. Imagining my soccer prowess continuing was very attractive.

I also contemplated following in my brother's footsteps by trying out for the cross-country team. I was good at running, but I was better at soccer. However, the cross-country coach had written me a recruitment letter, asking me to be on the team, and I was appreciative of that. I saw the fun my older brothers had with running. It wasn't a glamourous sport, but you do get to meet a lot of people and have a lot of fun. I was also intrigued that the guys and girls trained together. I don't know of many teenage boys who wouldn't like to be around girls who were in shape and wore short shorts and tank tops. I hemmed and hawed with both sports in my mind, and I ultimately ended up going with running simply because of the friendships and memories I could make with the team. I'm sure I could have done the same with soccer, but there were no good-looking girls on the soccer team, just a bunch of sweaty dudes. So, with the decision made to run, I ran.

There was a weeklong cross-country camp at the end of August that was for incoming freshman, as well as the kids already on the team that I eagerly signed up for. A week of camping at a campground where we would train once or twice a day, and the remaining time was open for anything else. I was very much excited to meet some future classmates before school started. I felt like I was getting a "jump start" on everyone else, and I wanted to take full advantage of the opportunity. I was one of the incoming freshmen, but there were also sophomores, juniors, and seniors there as well. I knew a couple of the upperclassmen from grade school, as they were only two years older than me. It was nice to see some friendly faces right off the bat!

I got my tent set up when I got there and looked forward to the fun that was to come. The fun didn't start as quickly for me as it did for the upper classmen, though. The first night, I was fast asleep when I heard a ruckus outside my tent. I heard muffled laughs and then pipes from my tent clanging together. All of a sudden, I was covered up by my tent. The freshmen hazing had begun. I was a little upset, but I took it in stride the first time. I got it all set back up again in the middle of the night and was drifting back to sleep when I heard the same noise. I knew what was coming. My tent came down again! I was quite a bit agitated, but I didn't want to show any emotion, so I slept through the rest of the night with my tent knocked down on top of me. I was glad it didn't rain that night; otherwise, that would have been a mess. I laughed it off by the morning and hoped that they would leave my tent alone the next night, and they did. Thankfully, it was all fine after that.

We had early morning runs with the whole group. It was an awesome feeling running with everybody, and I really liked the team experience—lunches on the grill, hanging out by the bonfire, sand volleyball, girls in bikinis, ultimate frisbee, and laughs all around. I was having a great time. I felt great. The summer was coming to an end, but it really felt like my life was just getting started. I could hold my own while we ran. I was a better volleyball player than I knew (my team won the makeshift tournament), and I was outrunning people playing ultimate frisbee. I was a freshman, but I could compete with the upperclassmen. I was on the right track.

The summer was hot. One day of camp was especially warm, and after a morning and evening training, we headed to the lake. We had our fun playing around in the water, but Coach wanted us to burn off more energy. We set up a two-team relay race in the lake where we would run in waist-high water for about one hundred feet, tag someone, and continue until we had a winner. I was fast in the water and was doing just fine until my foot hit something in the water. I went down in a great deal of pain! I was the lucky dog who decided to kick a concrete cinder block that was secured to a buoy with the toes of my feet. I had a decent gouge in my toe that was bleeding at a good clip, so my fun was quickly cut short. I got bandaged up back at camp and hoped the next day would be better.

It wasn't. I woke up with terrible congestion and a horrendous sore throat that felt like what I had eight months prior, just not quite as bad. I didn't want to wake up when I heard Coach on the horn saying it was time to get moving. I lay there until someone came over to see what was going on. I said that I was sick, but whoever I was talking to said to come on and tough it out. So, I did. I got up, swallowed my supplements, and got on with it. It was difficult to get through my morning run feeling the way I did, but I managed. I couldn't look like a quitter this early in the game; I had to power through it. After the run, we had downtime until the evening, so I went back into my tent for a nap. By the time evening rolled around, I was doing okay for the most part. Another run was on the docket. It wasn't a hard run at all, but I was laboring through it. All the good vibes I had been feeling were quickly a distant memory. I was exhausted as we made it to the lake. A lot of people jumped in to cool off, but I stayed out and sat on the bench, feeling like crap.

I was out of it, dizzy, and wanted to throw up. I was staggering. My lips were numb, my hands and face were trembling, my head hurt, and I was in pain all over. I started to walk back to camp by myself, but I collapsed to my knees on the path. Two girls approached behind me, and I recognized who they were: the junior girls. My gaze must have said, "Help me" because I heard one of them say, "Boogie, are you all right?" I shook my head no, and they quickly took one of my arms and put it around their necks and helped me to walk back. Via Krista and Alanna, God had sent me two angels to get me back to camp. It was a moment I will never forget. As they carried me, I could feel the warm summer breeze as it gently passed through the trees and onto my face. The wind carried the sounds of laughter and music from up the road at base camp. "Here's to the Night" by Eve 6 was playing on the stereo. The warmth in my heart that I felt from those two girls was amazing. They didn't have to help me. They barely knew me. When we got into camp, I felt a bit like the big man on campus being a freshman with two junior girls around my arms. I was thankful they helped me, but I also knew something wasn't right. I sat quietly by the fire that night while camp shenanigans took place. Some guys tried to see if they could chug down a gallon of water, then we played random games, laughed, and had a good time. I was a lot more subdued than normal. I absorbed the surroundings as much as I could. Somehow, I knew that something about me was different. I don't recall anything else after that night. I don't think I fully understood what had happened until later, but the memory is so vivid and clear. That camp was a toast goodbye to what I thought my life was going to be like. I wished I could have replayed the first few days over many more times. I got a small taste of high school fun, and I hadn't even been to class for one day. Little did I know that would be the best time I had in high school.

It was not how I envisioned camp going, but there was nothing I could do about it. I had a couple of weeks before school was to start, and I needed to get healthy again.

Thankfully, I recovered with a little rest and downtime, and I felt optimistic that I could keep it that way.

As I started preparing for the upcoming entrance into my freshman year, I was 100 percent determined to seize the opportunity before me. I had so many recent setbacks that I was eager to get off to a great start and ride that momentum all four years. I knew I could do some great things. I knew I had talent, I knew I was smart, and I wanted to prove it.

I distinctly remember setting five goals two weeks before school started. The first one was to never miss a day of school. I didn't want to miss time, fall behind and be forced to catch up. I experienced too much of that recently. I knew if I could accomplish this first goal, the next ones would be a lot easier to achieve. Goal number two was to get good grades. I wanted As and Bs, and anything worse than, I felt, would be letting myself down. I was definitely a smart person. If I could stay on top of my classes, I believed I was more than capable of accomplishing that feat. For goal number three, I wanted to excel in sports. I wanted to be on the varsity teams early and often. I wanted to lead teams to state titles. I wanted to get a full scholarship to a great college. For goal number four on the list, I wanted to make a lot of great relationships with as many people as I could. I wanted to be well-liked and respected for being a great student athlete. The last big goal I had was to find that special girl. I wanted someone I could share in the success I thought I was going to have come my way. I wanted to have that girl cheering me on from the stands. I wanted that girl to pick up for school dances. I wanted that girl I could share graduation with. I had it all planned out. I simply had to set my plan in motion.

Before the high-school experience could take place, though, cross-country practice was beginning, and I had to start working my way up the ranks. I was off to a great start. I loved meeting and getting to know my teammates, and people quickly started calling me Boogie. I enjoyed my nickname. If someone called me by that name, I took it as a sign of respect and that they enjoyed having me around. I also really liked it when the girls on the team used it. It made me feel good. Practices were fun but also a lot of work. I continued to have pain in my knees and could not stop getting side aches or side stitches. Running with pain wasn't pleasant, but I also knew I wasn't in near the shape I needed to be, so I contributed it to growing pains. We would go long distances at times; eight miles was the longest I can recall, and we did that in under an hour. The pace was quick, but I got through it.

After a week or so of practice, the big day was finally here. I made it. I made it to the first day of high school.

I was anxious to start it off right. I had a neighbor named Joel who was a senior and lived down the street from me. I knew him and his family well, and he agreed to drive me to school each morning. How cool was that? Here I was, a freshman, riding to school with a senior. I thought it instantly added to the cool factor versus getting dropped off by a bus or by my parents. The school was buzzing with all sorts of people. It was much larger than grade school. It was easy to get overwhelmed. My initial thoughts were to just do my best to try and figure out my way around and not to look too lost and confused. I had classes all over campus, but after a few days, I settled into where I needed to go. I initially gravitated to people I had already known from grade school or from the cross-country team, but in a lot of instances, I had homeroom and classes with people I had never seen in my life.

The first week or two was very much a feeling-out period. I was seeing who I could be friendly with. I quickly made acquaintances with quite a few people, and I was really enjoying the experience. I was on top of schoolwork like a hawk. Anything that was assigned I made sure to keep track of in my daily schedule planner. No way was I going to allow myself to slack off or not pursue my classes to the best of my ability. In those first few weeks, I did that and was getting nearly flawless grades. I got up at six o'clock in the morning and made it to school by 7:30. Classes went until 3:30 p.m. with cross-country practice afterward, then I was home around six o'clock for dinner and homework. I settled into that routine in no time. I was happy with my focus and how things were going.

The first ever cross-country race was during the first week of school at a course and park I had run in many times before. I started on the JV squad, but I was confident I would be on varsity in no time. It was a great atmosphere to be in. Taking the bus to the meet and setting up our school "camp" was awesome. I remember being a kid at my brother's races in the past and wanting to be a part of that culture. And there I was, hanging out with the guys and girls on the team, having some laughs, stretching, and preparing for the race ahead. I loved running for the team.

I wanted to put on a good performance so when the gun went off to start the race, I was eager to be near the front of the pack. The first mile went by okay, but I felt like I was pulling a boat anchor behind me, so by the time the second and third mile came around, I was struggling. I had a hard time getting my breath; my shoulders hurt, my knees hurt, and my head was pounding quite hard too. I was looking for the finish line at one point, and I glanced over my shoulder to calculate where I could get my final "kick" in. When I did that, all I heard was Coach yell, "Don't look back. Go!" I got to the spot where I figured I could burn off any remaining energy and overtake a few more positions, but I miscalculated and was barely able to stride through the finish line. It was a bad race for me. I didn't feel like I performed very well, and I was a bit bummed out. I was surprised when I got a medal for that garbage performance. Apparently, finishing in the top forty earned you one. I didn't think I deserved it. I was used to being in the top fifteen, and this wasn't even the best of the competition. I needed to do better if I wanted to make varsity.

I thought things would start to get easier the more I got into the routine of school, practice, and homework. Out of nowhere, I got hit with a bad head cold. I was barely a week into school at this point, and it was not something I anticipated dealing with. I pushed through it without slowing down, and I didn't miss school. I didn't miss practice either, even though I felt terrible. There was no way I was missing anything.

I had another race with the JV squad, but it was even worse than the first one. My time was slower, but that was to be expected considering I was under the weather. Afterward, I was feeling extremely run-down, but I wasn't going to let it stop me, no way, no how.

I recovered and felt back to normal for a few days before I got hit even harder with another head cold. I couldn't believe it. Why in the world was I repeatedly getting sick?

With another race coming up, I didn't know if I was going to be able to make it, but I got myself out there. It was another bad run for me. I felt incredibly sick running through this one. When I crossed the finish line, I threw up. A race worker scolded me and said, "Come on! We don't do that here." And I thought to myself, *Hey, chill out! Do you think I did that on purpose?* I had never lost my lunch before, during, or after a race. It was a terribly unpleasant feeling. I started trembling, shaking, and feeling numb in my extremities after that race. I kept how I was feeling to myself. I wasn't going to complain, so I forged on.

The same pattern repeated: feel better and then get hit with another sickness. I had serious doubts that I could keep this pace up, but I wanted and needed to push through this. I thought, *Just keep going, and you'll be fine.* I still didn't miss anything, even though I probably should have with how bad I was feeling. I had my goals, and I was determined to accomplish them, no matter the cost.

I had another race, and I was really lagging behind everyone else and my normal pace. That boat anchor I thought I was pulling before while I was running turned into feeling like I was trying to pull the entire boat! I felt like a car that couldn't get out of first gear. Every step was a struggle, and every part of my body hurt. It was another bad performance. My times kept getting worse. To be on varsity, I figured I needed to be running under twenty minutes for the 5K run. I was close to that mark on my first race, but I was now running around twenty-one minutes. It wasn't looking good. When I finished that race, I made it back to our team camp where all our gear was, and I lay on my back for quite a while. I had teammates come up to me to see how I was doing, and I told them

I was just worn out and hurting. They told me to hang in there. It was the first time I shared that I was having problems. I eventually got up, but I knew the way I was feeling wasn't "normal."

Speaking of things not being normal, an event that forever changed the world happened: the terrorist attack on the World Trade Center on September 11, 2001. It was a day I'll never forget. I remember exactly where I was and what I was doing that day.

It was a typical school day. The weather was great, probably very similar to what it was in New York that day. My first-period class was my homeroom, where I could finish up homework if need be, and then it was on to English. Halfway through the class, the principal made an announcement over the loudspeaker. That wasn't anything out of the ordinary, but you could tell from the sound of his voice that something serious was going on. Do I remember exactly what he said? No, but the words *World Trade Center, Twin Towers, New York, explosions, planes,* and *fires* all sounded like a very bad situation. I have never been to New York City, so I didn't know what the World Trade Center was. I had no idea what the Twin Towers were at that point in my life, either. We all had questions, lots of questions. We didn't know what was going on. All we could do was pray for the people in New York, so we did.

Next period, the whole school had chapel. We filed into the auditorium, and everyone was talking about what was going on. We started to hear that it may have been a deliberate attack, and no one really knew who or what was next, if anything. The high school I was in was close to Milwaukee, which is a large city in its own right. *What if something happens here?* we thought. Everyone was on edge and wondering what might happen next. The school tried to continue as normal, but that just wasn't happening. I got to science class, which had a TV in it. The teacher had the news on, and we all saw the second plane crash into the second tower. It was surreal. The United States was under attack. You could hear the gasps from other students. We were all shocked by what was happening. It was real now. We saw it with our own eyes. We all felt a bit helpless because there was nothing we could do to help, stop it, or prevent it from happening here. We didn't know if a plane was going to come crashing into our school. All sorts of scenarios ran through people's heads. It was very much like living in a bad dream that I couldn't wake up from. As the news broke of another plane hitting the Pentagon and another crashing in Pennsylvania, school took a back seat. Everything stopped.

One of the most horrific images that came across the screen was when the first tower collapsed. The smoke and debris that ensued was immense, and you knew thousands of people had just lost their lives. We all held our breath and said a prayer for all the people affected. There wasn't anything more we could do.

I got home, and all I wanted to do was watch the news. I understood what was happening, but I couldn't figure out how and why something like this would happen here. This was my generation's Pearl Harbor. Life changed in an instant. The world was never going to be the same. When you're young, you feel a bit invincible. History was history. All the bad stuff that happened in the past wasn't supposed to happen now. I was fortunate to grow up during a time when it was peaceful. The only thing I had to worry about was being home on time for dinner. I commend those who lived through war and hard times. I always had food to eat and a place to stay that was dry and warm. I had good friends and a great family. I was free to do whatever I wanted. I didn't have to go through a war, a famine, the Great Depression, or any other major era where life was truly difficult. I'm thankful for that now. However, I don't think I was thankful at that point in time. I was living in my own little world, and I truly believed that what I was about to face next would eventually make me see things differently.

Life went on. School continued. There wasn't much else that we could do.

I found myself back at cross-country practice. We were doing sprints on the track to prepare for the upcoming runs. Out of the corner of my eye, I caught Brittany up in the stands chatting with another girl. I was lost with what I should do next, so I ran as fast as I could down the track. I found another gear, turned on the jets, and smiled at her as I flew past. I always wondered if she saw me or if she even cared at that point. I thought by running fast that she'd be impressed and would be swayed to want to say hi and see how I was doing. In hindsight, maybe I should have gone up to talk with her. It was nice to see her, even if it was only for a moment. I spent the rest of the day wondering about a lot of what-ifs. It was a game that I was a rookie in, but it wasn't going to take very long to become an expert. Not that I really wanted to be.

Homecoming was approaching. I was looking forward to the festivities, the dance, the football game, and having fun. Right at the same time when I was thinking about who I could go with, my coach informed me he wanted me to run varsity at an upcoming race in Minnesota. Me? Varsity? Why? It turned out that one of the guys who was on varsity wanted to go to homecoming, so it opened up a spot for one guy, and Coach picked me. I had a dilemma. The race and homecoming were on the same weekend. The situation got more complicated when I got asked to the dance by a girl I knew. She was cute, and I wanted to say yes, but I told her that I couldn't miss an opportunity to show what I could do. I chose to run a cross-country race rather than to go to the dance with a beautiful girl. What was wrong with me? I believe that if it had been Brittany, I would have said yes in a heartbeat. If I would have said yes to this other girl, I wonder what would have happened with my story. What if I did? What if?

After surviving multiple bouts of sicknesses and a few bad races the first month of school, I was feeling as good as I had in a while.

I was excited for the road trip to Minnesota. I was ready to get things under control and get a firm grip on driving myself down the paths I wanted to go. I felt that I had survived the worst of whatever I was going to experience. I had an excellent opportunity in front of me, and I was ready to take advantage of it.

I was all packed up and ready to run in the Roy Griak Invitational, hosted by the University of Minnesota and held at the Les Bolstad Golf Course in St. Paul.

The whole team of ten, plus the coach, packed into a van that was probably made for eight—five guys and five girls on a five-hour journey across the Mississippi River to reach our destination. The ride up was filled with lots of laughs and jokes. It was where I wanted to be, hanging out with the team. One of the most popular songs at the time was "Crawling" by Linkin Park. It came on multiple times on the ride to Minnesota. I had never heard of the band before, and it wasn't my normal genre to listen to, but it was catchy. Looking back, I can see the smiles on everyone's faces, but I can still hear that song coming from the speakers. It was a precursor that I didn't know of at the time, but it would all fall into place in the coming years.

We stopped at the Mall of America. I had never been there before. This place was huge! It was great checking everything out with the team, and the camaraderie that was forming was awesome. After a short time there, it was back to the hotel for a light run before dinner. It was exciting running through areas I had never been before. I felt great. My legs were turning over just fine, and I didn't feel sick at all. More importantly, I wasn't exhausted. I was invigorated. A quick shower to freshen up, and it was time to hit up a local spot for some food and fun. Since we didn't get to go to homecoming, we treated that meal as a sort of homecoming dinner. The whole team dressed up. I had on nice clothes and a tie. The girls all looked fantastic in their attire. I was savoring the good times. I was really looking forward to making the next four years great. The time to start making it great was going to be in the morning. With how I was feeling, I liked my odds of putting on a good performance. I couldn't wait to get after it.

The next morning, it was go time. It was September 30, 2001. The weather was great, a little cool with a mix of sun and clouds. You couldn't really ask for better running weather. The course was packed with people. There were teams from all over the place. It was by far the largest race I had ever been in. The adrenaline was starting to flow. I asked one of the girls on the team to take a photo of us five guys before we headed out to the starting line. Cam, Brad, Tom, Dan, and I represented the boys team. I looked extremely happy and healthy in that photo. I felt like I was heading in the right direction.

We went for a little warm-up run, which I normally dreaded because it always seemed to sap my energy, but this time it was the opposite. My legs felt fresh, my breathing was under control, I wasn't nervous, and I was focused. I quite honestly thought that I had finally pushed through whatever issues I was dealing with in the past. It was time to fly.

Getting to the starting line with a few hundred other runners was exciting, and the energy in the air was contagious. My teammates lined up: the two captains were side by side, followed by two of the middle classmen, and then there was me behind them, the last man standing, but I wasn't planning on being the last one to finish, not today.

The noise of the runners and people around quieted down as the race starter counted us down. Sixty seconds, thirty seconds, ten, nine, eight, seven, six, five, a slight pause, and *bang*!

The sound of the starter pistol sent a herd of amped-up runners flooding out into the open to quickly jockey for position. The crowd was roaring, and the cowbells were blaring. Man, this was exciting. I was pumped to be part of the race. I kept my eyes on the two captains. I knew if I could keep them in sight that I would run a great race. I passed my other two teammates within the first half mile. My legs were free. Finally, I was not stuck in first or second gear. My breathing was perfect and unlabored, and I had *zero* pain. It was absolutely wonderful to feel the way I did. It was almost too good to be true.

A couple of minutes in, and I could still see the backs of the captains. I was flying. I hadn't felt this athletic and in top form in quite a while. It was like I was back in my dominant grade-school days. As the first mile approached, I was faster than I had ever been for a 5K race. I ran a single mile in under six minutes before, but I had never done it for more than one. As I hit the first mile, I was clocking in a little over five minutes. I can still hear Coach yelling, "Boogie, what are you doing?" He had never seen me go that fast, and I didn't show any signs of that speed in the previous runs. I'm guessing he thought I was burning out my fuel and energy, but I was here to show that I belonged. I was humming like a well-oiled machine on cruise control. Finally, I had arrived. I felt like nothing was going to stop me. I was on top of everything I needed to be. I *knew* I was in control.

You know how car chases go in the old cartoons or movies? The fast car doesn't just stop. It slowly falls apart until it can't go anymore. You'll see the car smoking, parts falling off, oil leaking, and tires blowing out, but it's still grinding along as hard as it can until it simply gives out. Well, that visually sums up the last competitive race I would run for almost twenty years.

As mile one rolled into mile two, all hell broke loose on my body. At the time, I couldn't fathom what was about to happen. I mean, I felt fantastic only moments before.

Apparently, other plans were in store for me. It was like lightning struck me. I took a complete 180-degree turn for the worse. In the blink of an eye, I was in tremendous pain. My head was pounding, sharp pain ran up and down my spine, and my knees throbbed. Breathing that was once under control now had me gasping for air. The steady beat of my heart was now racing like that of a hummingbird. Every step I took was more arduous than the last. I wasn't comprehending what was going on. How could I be feeling like this? How could I go from feeling great to feeling horrible in an instant? If I took all the pain and suffering from the previous races I had run and rolled them into this one right now, it would fall short of what I was experiencing. I slowed down dramatically. As fast as I was that first mile, the second mile was by far the slowest I had ever gone. I was being passed by everybody. I no longer had the leaders in sight. It started not to matter. The only thing that mattered to me was to get through whatever the heck was happening.

I was tough and maybe a little stubborn. You could probably throw in foolish as well. Under any other circumstance, I would have stopped running, but I didn't. I had too much pride to quit. I wasn't going to let my team or the coach down. I had people counting on me to do a good job and to perform at a high level. By all accounts, there was nothing proven wrong with me. I had been to multiple doctors, and not one diagnosed me with anything conclusive. Perhaps if I had a definite answer as to why I was experiencing what I was, I would have stopped. I did not. I kept going and driving through the pain. I prayed to God that He would take this burden off me so that I could finish. In the distance ahead, I could see a tough climb up a steep hill. I could feel my body tensing up, even more knowing that the pain was about to be even more amplified. It was so hard to breathe, and I could feel tears come to my eyes as my legs were giving out while pushing up the hill. I was getting very disoriented. My vision was blurring in and out. I just wanted to collapse to the ground and die. I couldn't take it anymore. Mile two was ending. I had a little more than a mile yet to go. I was finished. I took my last few weak strides to the crest of the hill, and I could see the gradual downhill ahead of me. My pace had drawn to mere baby steps, as I was about to stop and fall to the ground, but my momentum got me far enough that I started heading down the hill.

The noise stopped. The pain was gone. I felt completely different. I didn't feel the need to breathe. A calmness like I have never experienced before gently flowed through my body. There was no pull on my body. Gravity had lost its grip. I looked down below me and could see myself making my way down that gradual decline. I was in a state of bewilderment and amazement. My eyes looked up, and I saw the brightest white light circled with a shiny golden glow. My body gently drifted upward toward the light. I was at peace. The savage, ruthless ordeal that I was experiencing was over. The state of bliss and serenity I was feeling was out of this world. There's nothing I can compare it to. I looked down again and was much higher up than my body was. I had a bird's eye view of myself and the rest of the course. I didn't understand why I was so high off the ground. It was literally an out-of-body experience. My eyes turned upward again, and I was surrounded by a gentle white glow. It felt like I was about to pass through the light. I had no control over what was happening, but I felt safe. I sensed that I was about to reach the pinnacle of this euphoria, then it was over.

I was pulled back down. It was like light speed how fast I was sucked back into my ravaged body. The noise returned. I could feel the pull of gravity again as I continued to run. The pain had disappeared. I could breathe, and my heart rate seemed to be back to normal. I had no idea what just happened. My mind could not process it.

I finished the last mile with no problems. It was as if nothing had happened. It was the slowest race I had ever run. I was a solid minute or two slower than what I had been at previous meets.

I was perplexed because I now felt fine. I was desperately trying to comprehend what I just experienced. I was flying high one minute, literally dying the next, and now here I was, finishing a race like I normally would.

I was disappointed in my performance. I didn't represent myself or the team well at all. I let down my teammates, and I'm sure Coach was second-guessing himself by asking me to run.

I can't recall much, if any, interaction with anyone on the team immediately following the race. I had just been through hell, up to heaven, and back to earth. I couldn't figure it out, and I didn't tell anyone about what I had experienced. I don't think anyone would have believed me. I didn't even believe it myself. I was trying to connect the dots, but I couldn't, so I did my best to simply move on and act like everything was fine. I had no reason whatsoever to believe that anything was seriously wrong. I figured that if there was nothing proven wrong, then I had nothing to complain about. I was taught not to complain. I was taught to be tough. And no one would believe me anyway.

Traditionally, before and after a race, we did a short, little run, one to warm up and the other to cool down. I wasn't sure if I wanted to do the cooldown, as I was still processing all that had happened, but again, I didn't want to wimp out.

It was just us five guys out for the cooldown, and immediately, the pain and suffering came back like getting hit by another bolt of lightning. The only saving grace was that the pace wasn't anywhere near what we would attempt in a race. Nevertheless, it was unbearable. I gritted my teeth, held back tears, and sucked up the pain as best I could. In my mind, I was begging the captains to stop. I was behind the other four guys, trying to keep up the best I could. It may not have been as intense as what I felt in the race, but after you've been tortured once, it's mentally worse the second time because you know it's going to hurt. I could have stopped, I could have quit, but I didn't. I wasn't going to let others see me fail or give up. Either I won mind games with the captains or God said, "That's enough," and we stopped the cooldown run shorter than we normally would. I fell to my knees and had my fists on the ground for stabilization. I was so happy to not be running anymore. The torture was over. I was looking forward to getting back to the hotel where I could rest and relax. I desperately needed it.

We arrived back at our rooms. The guys had their own, and the girls had one down the hall. I was content to just lay in bed, but everyone was headed down to the pool and hot tub. I figured I could handle that. Besides, a hot tub could be quite beneficial to relieve sore muscles. Plus, the girls in their bikinis? That was more than enough to get me out of bed on its own, even with being as tired as I was.

It felt a lot like running camp. I had been around the same group of people now for a few months and enjoyed their company. These were the kinds of memories I had hoped to make: being with the team, the guys, the girls, and having a good time. The pool was a bit cool for my liking, so I hopped into the hot tub. It wasn't long until almost everyone was in there, cracking jokes and loving life. We even had some sort of low-risk spin the bottle game going on. It wasn't anything crazy, but if a girl landed on a guy, he'd get a kiss on the cheek. Man, I was anxious. I thought a couple of the girls were awfully cute, so I was hoping one of them landed on me, and to my amazement, one did! I received a nice little peck on the cheek from one of the cutest girls on the team, and I was more than happy at that moment that I had decided to come hang out.

After spending a solid fifteen to twenty minutes in over one-hundred-degree water, I was starting to feel lightheaded. My hands and face were tingly and numb, and I was very much on the tired side of things. I excused myself from the tub and said I was going to use the restroom. I went back to our room and crashed into bed, disoriented, and figured I just needed to lay down for a while. I probably got thirty minutes to myself before one of the guys came in to see if I was okay. I said, "Yeah, I'm just tired." He said, "Everyone is going to watch a movie in the girls' room if you want to join." I wanted to, of course I did, but I also knew I needed to sleep. I got myself up and headed to the girls' room, feeling like crap, but I didn't want to miss out on the fun. They had a movie playing when I walked in, so I found a nice spot on one of their beds and crashed. I didn't even watch the movie. I was too exhausted. It would make for a cool story if I got to stay in the girls' room overnight, but either I got back to our room on my own, or somehow, I got carried back. I honestly don't remember. I wish I could have enjoyed that time more with everyone, but I was simply wiped out from all that I had experienced that day. I was still in a state of shock over what happened, but it would be a while before I was able to process it.

The next morning, we headed back to Wisconsin. I got to ride shotgun, and that was just fine with me. I wasn't as jovial riding back. I mainly stared out the window while fun and games were happening in the back of the van. I knew something wasn't right with me, yet I couldn't figure it out. I was hoping I could get back home, relax, and rest up for the upcoming school week.

It was good to be home. My dog, Sheena, was there to greet me, which always put a smile on my face. There was no school on Monday, and for that, I was very thankful. I really felt that an extra day to recover is just what the doctor ordered.

There was, however, a scheduled practice Monday afternoon. I thought long and hard about whether I should go or not. I wasn't feeling great, and if I pushed it too much that day, I might not make it to school on Tuesday. I had the coach's number and called. I left a voicemail saying that I wasn't feeling the greatest, and I would not be at practice. I wish I didn't feel the need to skip practice, but I simply needed to recharge my batteries from everything I had just gone through. I still couldn't comprehend what happened, but I wanted to move on and get back into a good routine.

Tuesday morning, the alarm went off, and it was time to get ready for school. I was a bit worried about how I would feel, and much to my surprise, I felt great. Dad was still sleeping, and Mom was out of town with my grandpa three hours away. Mom was normally up around the same time I was, but for this morning, it was just me and my dog, Sheena. I let Sheena out, got the newspaper, and had my breakfast while I read the sports and comic sections. I put my dishes in the dishwasher and was about to make my way back upstairs to freshen up and then head to school. I turned to walk out of the kitchen through the door by the telephone, and not one second after, I collapsed to the floor.

I went down like a load of bricks. I lost consciousness for a few seconds, and when I came to, the pain and exhaustion set in. It felt like I had sand running through my veins, my head throbbed, chills ran through me, and I just felt awful.

It only took me a few minutes to realize that I was in no shape to go to school, and I didn't know what to do. With Dad still sleeping, I called my grandpa's house, and Mom picked up. I told her what had happened, and I could tell she was worried about me. We decided that I should leave Dad a note that I wasn't feeling well and that I would be in bed and not at school. I literally crawled up the steps and into my room. My bed looked so inviting. I was 100 percent exhausted. I felt like I could sleep for days at a time and not get sick of resting.

So that's what I did. I slept and I slept. I was disappointed in myself that I was only a month into school and had already failed to meet one of my goals. This was not how it was supposed to be going. This was not what I had planned.

Instead of moving forward, I was quickly shoved backward. I didn't like feeling that I had failed. I couldn't help but feel like I had let myself down. I had no control over how my body felt, and that was the worst part about it. I had no choice but to deal with what was going on. There was nothing normal about how I was feeling. This wasn't something that was just in my head or that I was causing to happen or wanting to happen. I wanted to be in school. I wanted to play sports. I wanted to be with my friends and my teammates. I didn't want to be this exhausted, depleted, drained, or any other word that was never sufficient enough to articulate how run-down I felt. I could not process why I was feeling the way I was. It did not make sense, so I needed to find some answers, and soon.

SEARCHING FOR ANSWERS

Wake up! That was getting harder and harder to do. The next few days were a bit foggy, as I'm pretty sure I slept through most of them. I was hurting all over, drained, and not feeling like a fifteen-year-old should.

Mom got back home, and I was quickly in for more blood tests. She believed I had Lyme disease because the symptoms matched so well. A third Lyme test was done, and we got the results a few days later. The test came back again: *negative*. From the lab results, it looked like five bands of something were needed for a positive test, and I only had two bands. It didn't make sense to me or to Mom.

We continued searching for what could be causing my issues. I had a CT scan done, which I had never done before. Nothing out of the ordinary was found in my head (which, I guess, is a good thing). There were dead-ends everywhere every time we would try to find a cause for my failing health.

We were stuck with nowhere to go. I was frustrated with everything going on, and I know Mom was as well.

For the next couple of days, all I did was sleep. I was missing school left and right. With no answers being found, all I did was lay there and wonder what was going to happen to me. There was mounting pressure on me to get up and get to school. Every day I missed, the bigger the hole was getting that I was going to need to climb out of. I knew the slippery slope I was on, and I think Mom knew it even more. Things started to get a little tense. Nothing was proven wrong with me. Doctors couldn't figure anything out, and I'm sure people were doubting me. I was going on two weeks of missing school, and Mom came in to wake me up so I could at least try and make it to school. I was still gassed and felt extremely heavy. I wanted to get up and get going, but I was trapped in my own body. Mom started to plead with me to go to school, begged me to get up. I could tell she was having a hard time holding it together because her voice was cracking. "David, get up! Get up, David!" I just lay there. I felt bad because I felt bad, and I was feeling even worse letting Mom down. I was starting to get a little down on myself.

We went back to my pediatrician, and he diagnosed me with chronic fatigue syndrome based on how tired I was. I don't think there was any test that confirmed it, but it half made sense. I was fatigued, and it seemed to happen all the time, so that would make it chronic. Rest was ordered, so that's what I did.

I was bummed that I couldn't do what I wanted to do. I was wondering what my teammates on the cross-country team thought happened to me and what my other friends were up to.

One bright spot came when Mom said a call on the phone was for me. I had no idea who would be calling me, and it turned out to be Cam. He was one of the captains on the team and wanted to let me know that he and the team were concerned about how I was. He also said that they were all praying that I could make it back. I'll never forget that gesture. It was quite nice to receive that call, and it gave me a little jolt of happiness.

I ended up missing three weeks of school. After twenty-one days of resting, I got to a point where I felt I could attempt to try and go back.

To me, it felt like the first day of school all over again. A lot can change and happen when you're not in one place for that length of time. Friends and teachers were surprised to see me, and some thought I had died. I still don't know if they were joking about that or not. The walks to the different classrooms that used to be a breeze had me now catching my breath halfway there. I was routinely a few minutes late to class because I simply couldn't go any faster without being winded. My backpack seemed to be heavier than it used to be too, or I was simply weaker. I guess lying around for as long as I had allowed my body to atrophy a little bit. I had never experienced a loss in stamina or endurance as I had always been active. It was frustrating, to say the least.

Schoolwork wasn't coming as easily to me, either. The first few weeks I was on top of things like nobody's business. But now? My concentration was diminished, and I wasn't processing things like I normally could. If I could explain it, I would say it felt like the fluid in my brain was sloshing back and forth, and it would never stop unless I was sleeping. It was a nonstop assault on my cognitive abilities.

Each day I was at school, I could feel myself getting more and more run-down. I was dizzy most of the time, and it felt like I didn't have a whole lot of control over my body.

One time in English class, I was just minding my own business, sitting in the corner of the front row by the door. The room started to spin. I was feeling very warm. Nausea was setting in, and I could feel my heartbeat getting faster and faster. My body felt like it was under attack. My face was tingling and going numb. I could also feel that sensation in my hands. I would imagine this was similar to what a panic attack must be like, but I didn't really feel like I had anything to panic about. I was simply sitting in class, trying to get through the day. After a few minutes, it was hard to breathe. I watched the clock spin on the wall as I calculated my pulse. My heart was racing to the tune of well over one hundred beats per minute. I felt out of control, and I couldn't take it anymore. I quickly excused myself from class. I needed to find some water, a cool spot, and try to walk it off. The teacher came and found me wandering the hall a few minutes later. (I think she was genuinely concerned about me.) I was a bit emotional, and it was hard to keep it together. She let me sit in a small office area until class was over. I was able to calm down and get my body a little more under control. I hated how that felt. That kind of thing had never happened before. I did not know what to make of it. Honestly, it was a bit scary.

My sister-in-law, Kristie, knew of a doctor who was interested in seeing my recent test results for Lyme disease. I don't recall the name of the doctor or what he specialized in, but I thought it wouldn't hurt to have another set of eyes look at the results.

Mom faxed over the results to this doctor to see if he could make any sense of what might be going on with me. The doctor faxed back and on it, he wrote that the tests that I'd had done "validly and questionably show *no* Lyme disease."

Well, there it was, another doctor saying that the test results showed it couldn't possibly be Lyme disease yet failing to give any explanation as to what may be going on. Things were not looking too great for me at this point. I was struggling with school and still had no answers.

I started missing a few more days of school. I was falling further and further behind. I could hear the whispers. I could see the stares. People started to question if I was sick or if I was faking it. I'm confident that it wasn't just kids at school or the teachers that thought that way. I'm betting people in my own family started having those thoughts creep into their minds. I was angry about it then, but now, I couldn't really blame them. I may have thought the same way if I was in their position.

I was referred to an infectious disease specialist named Doctor D. I was starting to not like doctors at this point. This doctor suspected something along the lines of mononucleosis, but according to his notes, he wasn't expecting to find a whole lot wrong. He thought if I could just get over the colds and flu-like symptoms that I had been having, I would simply improve on my own. That wasn't happening. I kept getting worse.

I was tested for all sorts of goodies in October 2001. Tests showed that I had abnormalities in my urine (whatever that means), and hepatitis tests came back negative. So at least I was good on that front.

A new test for Lyme disease called the C6 peptide was just becoming available as a clinical trial but wasn't yet recognized as a true test to confirm Lyme. That test was ordered up just to see what it might say. The results came back a few days later. I was a little more optimistic with this being a new test that might shed some light on my situation. It turned out that I had just high enough levels to suspect that I was, in fact, dealing with Lyme disease.

A mostly positive result for Lyme disease, after so many negative results. What are the odds? Even though it wasn't a fully recognized test, the doctor was willing to treat me with the standard protocol at that time. I started on doxycycline right away.

I was thrilled, over-the-moon happy that we had finally figured out what the culprit most likely was. Some of the times, with Lyme disease, a person will get a bull's-eye rash to indicate they were bitten by a tick that carries the disease. I never had that. If I did, maybe I could have been diagnosed and treated right away. It would have saved me a lot of issues, time, and headaches.

When I got home, I called all my brothers up to tell them about the diagnosis. They were all happy that I might finally be able to get back to normal, well, as normal as I could be to them, anyway.

After my ten-day course of antibiotics, I figured I would be good to go. I was itching to get back to my full-strength level so I could catch up and salvage what I could of my freshman year.

I started to feel somewhat better. I was in school more often than I wasn't, but by no means was I 100 percent back to normal. I was done with running cross-country. Now, I was focused on catching up on missed assignments. I was behind by a good month at this point, and the mounting work to catch up was taking its toll on me.

I finished my ten-day course of antibiotics, and I had a follow-up appointment with Doctor D. I was hoping that I could continue on with the doxycycline, but I was told an emphatic *no*. Doctor D noted that I was "improved," which must have been good enough for him. Lyme still wasn't well-known at this time. The protocol for Lyme disease was a ten-day regimen of antibiotics, which should be sufficient to basically cure me. That was the general consensus among those in the know. I didn't know any better. Mom didn't know any better, so we had to go along with what the doctor said. Doctor D said to come back in six months to see how I was progressing, and that was that.

The rest was now in my hands. I had to power through whatever was about to come my way. I wanted to trust that Doctor D was right, that all I needed was time, and then I'd be fine. My body was telling me otherwise. I was conflicted in who and what to trust. The year 2001 was ending, and I had missed a bunch of school. I was starting to fall deeper and deeper into a hole that was becoming increasingly difficult to climb out of.

CHAPTER 6

FALLING BEHIND

First semester exams were on the horizon. I wasn't feeling the greatest, and I didn't know the material, so there wasn't much point in trying to take them. I do believe I actually attempted one, but I failed miserably. The small body of work I had done the first half of the year was basically for nothing. I lost all the credit.

Christmas break was coming up, and we had two weeks off from school. I was certainly looking forward to it. I wanted to rest up and recover as much as I could to hopefully salvage some of my freshman year in the second semester.

The break didn't exactly go as planned. I wound up getting wicked sick like I did the year before. It felt like déjà vu. My throat swelled up, and I developed chills, aches, and pains. I was so worn out that just walking up and down the steps to my bedroom would have me collapsing once I got to the top. I would lay there until I had the strength to make it to my room. This was not how I wanted or needed my time off from school to go. Things were not looking so great as we rolled into 2002.

One of my saving graces was that I would normally feel better late at night. I spent a good bit of time researching Lyme disease online. It apparently started in Lyme, Connecticut, around 1975, when a few children and adults experienced uncommon arthritic symptoms. It was later discovered that ticks were transmitting the disease by attaching themselves to people. (portal.ct.gov/DPH/ Epidemiology-and-Emerging-Infections/A-Brief-History-of-Lyme-Disease-in-Connecticut)

I know I had ticks crawling on me a year and a half ago, but I never recalled having one attached to me. The symptoms I had matched well with what was listed, and the Lyme diagnosis made sense to me. What I couldn't understand was how to receive sufficient treatment for it. There were no answers that I could find. However, thanks to the internet, I did find something that caught my attention: Lyme support groups.

I quickly discovered people from across the United States were doing the exact same thing I was. We were all seeking answers. It didn't take too long before I found people I could connect with.

Kelsey from Oklahoma was one of the first sufferers with whom I was able to bond. She was my age, and it was remarkable how easy it was to talk with her, or rather, type. We used instant messenger extensively to communicate back and forth. It felt fantastic to be able to connect with someone who was experiencing similar problems. It was a nightly occurrence that we would chat.

We both weren't feeling great, but having each other to talk about it was a lifesaver. Kelsey was another angel who came into my life at the right time. She was also a Christian girl, which only helped to deepen the relationship we had.

As school resumed for the second half, it was the same old story. I would go a few days, but then I was out for a week. I'd try a few half-days, but even then, my body wasn't having any of it. I was getting quite frustrated. I was way behind. The stress and pressure to try and catch up was not helping me recover.

I had planned on making a lot of new friends, getting good grades, and doing well in sports. I couldn't even make it through a day of school. Instead of making friends, I felt I was losing them. Old friends that I had moved on to new people since I wasn't there. Nobody knew what was really wrong with me. I hardly knew myself. I was looked down upon simply because I was now odd or different. "Why aren't you at school?" "What's wrong with you?" "You don't look sick." "It must be nice to not be at school." "Faker!" "I bet you're just wanting attention." Those were the kinds of things people said to me or about me. I quickly started to withdraw from people. I kept to myself a lot more and just simply tried to get through my day.

People I used to enjoy seeing or who I thought were my friends, I now didn't want anything to do with. I would get irritated with teachers because of all the work they wanted me to catch up on. I was months behind, so how in the world was I going to make up everything? If I were 100 percent healthy, maybe then it would have been possible, but I was far from that. For the record, I tried, but the mountain was incredibly high to climb. I pushed my body as much as I could. I remember getting quite frustrated at one project in English class. I was as sick as I could be, and the project was to decorate a brown grocery bag to fit a theme from a book we were reading. I thought, *Why in the heck am I putting myself through all of this just so I can complete a first-grade level project?*

My high-school experience was not going as planned, and I quickly started to hate it. I hated how I felt. I hated people who doubted me. I hated the snide looks and remarks I received. I hated that I was pushing myself as much as I could to only be learning about things that had zero carryover as to any kind of life skill that would be applicable as an adult. For the first time in my life, I was angry. I had scorn and hate in my heart that I had never felt before. I didn't like feeling that way. Looking back at it, it would have been hard to react differently. My whole life was getting flipped upside down and inside out. All the good and positive momentum I had was now a slow and painful slog. I was desperately trying to get myself out of the quicksand, but I couldn't escape, no matter how hard I tried.

Only a few things kept me from being 100 percent hateful at that time: my friends, Sheena and Kelsey, and my faith. Faith was important to me. I prayed a lot. God and I had quite a few talks. I would ask Him, "Why me? Why am I going through this?" I never got much of an answer.

My dog, Sheena, didn't care what I was going through. She was always happy to see me, play fetch, or go for a walk. Having someone or something that simply was always glad to see me no matter how I felt was priceless.

I talked with Sheena and Kelsey a lot through instant messenger. Sheena from Florida didn't have Lyme, but she had a strong Christian faith, which helped keep mine alive and going. Sheena had gone through some tough times, too. We talked about our different struggles, and we both used each other to simply listen. Sheena didn't have to talk to me, and I really don't know why she continued to. She was a beautiful Southern girl, super sweet and friendly, and could probably talk to any guy she wanted to. Here she was, one thousand miles away, had never met me, but still was there to chat when I needed to.

Kelsey was needed just as much. We definitely leaned on each other quite a bit. She understood what I was going through, and I understood what she was going through. It was so easy to talk with her. The connection we had was awesome. I'd talk about how I was feeling, and she would get it because she felt the same way. With her, I didn't feel the anger that I had toward almost anything and everything else. She was able to keep the door open enough on my feelings to let a little love and warmth in. It started to become a routine that we would talk every night and became the best part of my day.

Unfortunately, there were more hours in the day that I didn't talk with either Sheena or Kelsey that I had to deal with and get through.

I decided to make one last attempt at school to try and salvage my freshman year. I hadn't been in school for a few weeks. I took on a little less stressful workload to see what I could do. It was still difficult. It wasn't easy for me to come to school, a place that I always knew I was accepted and liked, to now being an outcast.

I had a hard time adjusting to being in class when the other students had been there the whole year. I simply tried to piece together what I could. I felt like I was playing checkers when everyone else was playing chess. I felt like a foreigner trying to navigate through a completely different country where I couldn't understand the language. I was so out of it and disconnected that there didn't seem to be much of a point in trying. I felt like crap. I wasn't looking so hot. I was down on myself and felt borderline depressed. I didn't know how much more of this I could take as I got to my seat in business class one day.

And then she walked into the classroom.

Abbie.

I only knew her name because when she stepped through the door and came into view, people were saying, "Happy birthday, Abbie!"

Who was this person? I had never seen this girl in my life. She walked in, and it was like one of those magical movie moments when the beautiful girl walks in the room, and everything moves in slow motion. She was smiling, laughing, and had a shimmering glow about her. I was mesmerized by her presence and felt privileged to be a part of it. The cold, windowless classroom now had a special warmth to it. Time slowed down, and in that moment, I was oblivious to everything I was dealing with. It was simply a joy to have her walk into the very room that I was in. For whatever reason, and I'll never figure out why, she took the seat right in front of mine.

Class proceeded, and I had no recollection of what it was about; all I knew was that I wanted to make some kind of impression on this girl to let her know that I existed. It was obvious it was her birthday from the multiple people saying it to her and the fact she had more than a few birthday balloons she was carrying around. How did everyone know who she was? How in the world did I not? Okay, granted, I hadn't been in school much for the last few months, but I figured I would have at least seen her before, but I hadn't.

I hatched a plan to pass her a note. All it said was *Happy Birthday, Abbie.* I printed my name at the bottom because I didn't think she had any clue who I was. I was nervous trying to get her the note. What if the teacher took it? What if she got it and didn't have a care in the world about me or what I wrote? *What if?* I thought. *Screw it. Just do it and see what happens.* The year already sucked. I didn't care if it sucked even more if I crashed and burned when I tried to get the prettiest girl in school to know who I was.

I gently tapped on her left shoulder, and she turned around with a little confused look on her face. I passed her the note. I think she thought it was from someone else and not from me, and she whispered, "Who's this from?" I replied cautiously, "From me."

She turned back to the front and still looked a little surprised. My heart sank when she opened it up and started to read it. I thought I was an idiot for trying to make an impression. I regretted my choice and immediately wanted to wear the invisibility cloak.

A few seconds later, she turned back to me, her blonde hair whipping around, and I'll never forget what happened next.

The sweetest, brightest smile I had seen in a long while greeted my eyes. She gave that little sweet "awe" that girls do and said, "Thank you!"

I immediately liked Abbie.

She didn't have to be sweet and nice in her response to me, but that was just the type of person she was. I was the fallen star, the weird kid, and she was the designated angel who got saddled with the task of being a caring influence when I needed it the most. I don't know how she got that job, but I'm glad she did.

School became a little more bearable after that. Knowing she was there gave me a jolt of optimism and something to look forward to. She didn't know me. She didn't know the hell I had been through. To miraculously have my butt parked in the seat right behind her was pure luck or divine intervention. She provided me with something that day that helped me move forward with a little bit of hope that things would be okay. She was another angel, but this time in the flesh.

I loved seeing Abbie at school. It was the best part of my day. One of my classes was by her locker, and she'd always smile and ask how I was doing. We never talked for very long, but the fact that she cared about me was what mattered the most.

I really wish her kindness could have cured me of whatever sickness I was dealing with. I made it through one more month, and there were only a few weeks left in the school year. With how bad I was feeling and how far behind I was, Mom and I decided to stop trying to force it and try again next year.

It was a fantastic idea for my physical health. I figured I could rest up and get my body right to try and see if I could salvage something from my high school years. Once that decision was made, I instantly got a boost in how I felt. The stress school was having on me was a heavy burden, and it felt like a little bit of the weight had been taken off my shoulders. I was cautiously optimistic that having an extended summer break would be a great benefit to me.

I would be turning sixteen soon, which meant learning how to drive. I was a bit later than normal in getting started with driver's ed, but it was something I wanted to be able to do. I figured if I could get through that, it would be a good sign for the upcoming school year.

I was quite confident driving. I had to have so many hours behind the wheel with a parent or adult person in my family, and it didn't take long for me to get the hang of it. The in-person classes weren't too bad, either. The instructor was relaxed and had a jovial attitude. I even remember a true story he told about someone who was driving to work and went to pass gas but ended up crapping their pants! I about died laughing when he told that story, as did everyone else in the class!

Halfway through the class, I began to get to know a few of the people who were there, and one girl in particular caught my eye. She was in great shape, had a good smile, and seemed like she was friendly. I wanted to get to know her a bit, and I caught her looking my way a few times, so I thought perhaps I had a shot. The next time in class, I would work up the courage to say hi and get to know her a little more. It was a very hot day, so I had on a tank top and shorts. I had slimmed down a bit from where I was, and my muscle mass wasn't as noticeable anymore, but I thought I still looked all right.

That girl thought differently. She had smiled at me the previous few times she walked in for class, but this time it wasn't happening. She started to smile, but when she saw me, that smile turned into a disgusted look. I believed she didn't like how skinny I looked. I could see what her mind was thinking. She used to think I was cute with a sweatshirt on, but now she could see more of me. At that moment, I became self-conscious with how I looked. I wanted to hide, but I had nowhere to go. I had to sit there and get through the rest of class.

I needed to get my now pale and skinny self back into shape. I didn't like the way she looked at me, and I didn't want it to happen again. It wasn't my fault that my body had atrophied. It was another reminder that my life wasn't going as planned. It was depressing.

I did end up getting my driver's license. I passed the written test and road test with flying colors. I loved having the freedom to be able to go somewhere at any time. It was also a nice boost to show that I could get through something again, as I hadn't been able to accomplish much of anything for a while.

As summer rolled on, I was feeling better than I had been. I started doing some light running and weight training, as I knew I needed to up my endurance if I wanted any chance of making it through school. I still wasn't feeling like a normal sixteen-year-old should, and I was quite certain that the Lyme disease was having some lingering effects. I had a follow-up visit with Dr. D to see if there was any more that we could do.

Dr. D noted that I was having a lot of tiredness and difficulty with concentration, which wasn't any surprise to me. I wasn't feeling terrible, just not that great, and I wanted to feel great.

I had a few different tests done. One was for the Epstein-Barr virus, which came back negative (not surprising). Another was for a Lyme titer test, which was also negative. The C6 peptide test was also done again.

The C6 peptide test came back positive for the second time. The range was higher this time versus the first time. Even with that result, Dr. D said it was normal, and no further follow-up was felt to be needed. He based that opinion on recent studies that showed only a ten-day round of antibiotics was needed to cure the Lyme. If I was cured, then why was I still not feeling well? He said that it may take six months to a year to feel back to normal. Even though my most recent Lyme test showed the Lyme was even *more* active than the first test, I was told to basically go home and see what happens. I didn't think his advice was right, and I realized an opportunity to get better a lot faster had been missed.

In the early 2000s, no one really knew what Lyme disease was, including the doctors in the area, let alone the long-term effects of it and how to treat it. Twenty-plus years later, there is a lot more the medical community understands, and more doctors know it exists, but it needs way more attention brought to it. There is still a debate going on how to treat it. Your best bet is to not get it at all, but if you do, get tested and treated as soon as possible. It took me nearly three years to figure out what was causing my problems, which is more than enough time for the Lyme to completely ruin your health.

I have a little love/hate feeling with what happened with Dr. D. If during the time I saw him I had been put on antibiotics for six months to a year (instead of ten days), I might have fared a lot better than I did. Instead, I think it agitated the Lyme bacteria. Because it wasn't killed off, it came back with a vengeance. I feel I could have been spared from the living hell that ended up coming my way afterward if there was more research about Lyme disease. That's the hate part about it because of the missed opportunity to get better faster. I faulted the doctors then, but I don't so much now. Dr. D was doing his job by following protocols and recommendations from the studies known at that time. He simply didn't know any better. Frankly, very few doctors at that time did.

The love side of it has taken me a long time to get to appreciate. Even so, I still don't know if I love it, but I'm grateful to be here now. I wouldn't be writing this story if I had gotten back to normal during the early years of dealing with the Lyme. I hadn't struggled enough, hadn't been chewed up and spit out enough, hadn't been broken down, laughed at, teased, disappointed, embarrassed, depressed, or hurt enough to be able to dive this deep into a story worth writing. I'm hoping these efforts can help someone else. If they do, I think I can grow to love what I went through.

Mom and I did quite a bit of research on Lyme disease. She probably printed out more stuff than I did. It was easier for me to talk to other people going through the same thing. I learned a lot from Kelsey, so I tried to reach out to more people my age I could relate to.

In another support group I found, I got to talking with a girl named Lori from South Carolina. Her experience with Lyme goes all the way back to when she was born. Lyme can be passed on through birth, and I don't think anyone really found out there was a problem until Lori was in her teens. We hit it off well. It was so nice to have another person to converse with who was dealing with the same issue I was. With so many people doubting I was sick or thinking I was faking it, the more connections I could make with other people like me was invaluable at the time. Lori was another angel. She was a consistent person I could lean on and talk with about anything.

As the summer rolled on, I noticed something funky going on with my eyes. They started to develop a film over them, and I would have to blink incessantly to get them to clear up. The issue was way worse when I had contacts in versus when I didn't. I had been wearing contacts since I was thirteen and never had a problem until now. It was frustrating already not feeling the greatest, and now my eyes were giving me trouble. Mom took me to see an ophthalmologist to see if there was any reason why I was having this issue. After getting my eyes checked out, the doctor said I had dry eye syndrome and gave me some eye drops to try out. I was also wearing gas-permeable contacts (the hard ones), and the doctor suggested I try soft lenses. I got a pair in and right away, this gunk covered the lenses and made everything blurry. Blinking would help, but it didn't last very long. It was quite annoying because I wanted to wear contacts as I felt I looked better that way, and I could see more clearly. I attempted to remove the contacts, but I was having a hard time. They were glued in there with all the junk in my eyes. The contact fitter didn't believe me that they were literally "stuck" in my eye, so she tried to get them out. She reached in with her fingers to attempt to free the contact, but even she was struggling. She was just as confused as I was with how well they were stuck in there that she decided to get a little suction cup tool to help in the process. With the tool, she got them out and was a bit shocked at the situation, saying that she had "never had a problem getting contacts out of anyone." I replied, "I guess there's a first time for everything. Maybe I'm just special."

The eye drops helped a little, but I couldn't wear contacts for much longer than a few hours after I had been accustomed to wearing them all day. I didn't like it, but at least I could wear them once in a while. The little annoyances were starting to be rather irritating.

With summer winding down, I was doing okay but not great. I didn't have a whole lot of stress, and I was able to do things on my own time, which helped a lot. I even did a little bit of running, as I thought of possibly trying to run cross-country at the start of the school year. I wanted to get back in great shape, but ultimately, it wasn't easy to recover from running the short distances I would go, and it sucked. I wasn't used to only being able to do things halfway. I did sign up for cross-country camp again because I wanted to be around the team, but I only went there for one day before I realized I was in no shape to compete. Everything was changing, and not for the better. I was down on myself that I couldn't do what I had easily done in the past. I was only sixteen and regressing, not progressing, at the point in my life where I wanted to be climbing the ladder of success on a daily basis.

With sports on the back burner, it was time to concentrate on academics. Labor Day meant school was about to start, and I wanted to be there to see how I could do. The prospect of being in school also meant I would be able to see Abbie again. I hadn't seen her for a few months. I had no clue what she was up to or if she would even remember me. Thankfully, she did. She was the one person at the time I looked forward to seeing. One of my classes was again right by her locker, so I got to see her briefly on a regular basis. It was always very casual between us. Her smile made me happy when I didn't have much to be happy about. She had a boyfriend. I think she would have been the type of girl I could have had a really good relationship with if I was at *least* normal, but I wasn't. I was far from it. I didn't want to mess up the little friendship we shared. Having her in my life on a small scale was enough to keep me pushing to get through the upcoming school year.

It was my sophomore year, but I was back in freshman classes. I was sixteen years old, but I was two or three years older than people I was in class with, which was a little awkward. I started back part-time with four classes in the morning: English, science, algebra, and a faith class. I didn't like getting up in the mornings, but I was able to get to school, and it started off okay.

During the first month of school, one of our neighbors knew of a doctor who would come see me at our house. I was a bit excited that a doctor was coming to see me on his own free will, so I looked forward to what he had to say. He looked over the tests results that we had and asked me some questions. He concluded that since I did *not* have the tell-tale bull's-eye rash that is typically associated with Lyme disease, he doubted that I even had Lyme disease in the first place. Well, that wasn't what I wanted to hear. I had multiple negative tests for Lyme, and one newer test that came back positive. That newer test had come back positive again with even higher numbers. This doctor believed I didn't have Lyme at all. What in the world? I wasn't sure what to believe, but I was quite certain I did have Lyme disease, even if it wasn't unequivocally agreed upon. He suggested that I might benefit from visiting a rheumatologist to run some additional testing.

It's just what I wanted to do, to go to more doctors. I was getting rather irritated and frustrated that there was no pinpoint diagnosis or treatment for what I was experiencing. I could see why people doubted me or thought that I was faking it. I didn't at the time because of how I felt, but looking at it now, I could see their point. In my mind, though, there was no way I wanted to keep going to doctors. I wanted to be in school playing sports. I wanted to get back to how I used to feel.

Back in school, I would have my good days and my bad days. I could go a couple of weeks and not miss any school, then I would miss one or two days. I have had a bit of trouble remembering a whole lot from this period of time, but thankfully, Mom wrote down some notes that have helped to get me through parts where I simply can't recall anything.

A month or so into sophomore year, yet part-time freshman year, I could tell I was getting worse. The tiredness was slowly dragging me down. My eyes were getting more and more gunky, to the point that wearing contacts just wasn't going to happen. I had pain in my back, more specifically in my lower spine area. I got another one of my typical Lyme colds, which caused me to miss a few days. I was tired and aching all over. My appetite wasn't great, and I was getting more frequent headaches. It was a slow spiral downhill.

I felt better on weekends or when I wasn't in school, and I would do things around the house. From the notes Mom has, I apparently cleaned a lot and made cookies but would then be worn out after doing that. I found that to be rather amusing.

When I was in class sometimes and even random times at home, I started to have some unusual sharp pains in my heart area and thought that couldn't be good. My heart would also just start racing for no good reason. I would sit there, and then feel it take off, which would cause me to have anxiety and feel very warm. It usually didn't last too long, but however long it did was more than long enough.

I wasn't making too many friends at this time either (in school anyway). I would rarely see the people who were originally in my class from last year, and I didn't know any of the newer kids. It didn't take long before people knew I was only a half-time student.

And since they saw me quite often and I looked fine, they would continue to pick on me. I kept hearing the same things as I did the year before: "You don't look sick." "Must be nice to only be here part-time." "Hey, there's the faker who's looking for attention." I heard the noise but did my best to ignore it. Kids can be mean, and it did bother me, but I couldn't do a whole lot about it, so I just did the best I could.

My best wasn't good enough. I was physically getting worse and worse. Mentally, I was upset, angry, depressed, irritable, and frustrated. It wasn't just the kids. Teachers made me feel the same way. I would say it was fifty-fifty for the teachers I liked versus ones I couldn't stand. And one teacher in particular made my blood boil.

This teacher knew I would be out for a day or two, and then I would come back and do my best to catch up. He would ask a question to the class and, even though I had not been present, would incessantly call on me to answer. Obviously, I wouldn't know what to say. If it would have happened a couple of times and that was it, I don't think I would have cared, but it happened every day.

I dreaded going into that classroom because I knew I would be called upon, and I knew I would be embarrassed because I didn't know the answer to his questions. He would say, "Mr. Bugenhagen" in a snarky accent that really emphasized the "ha" in my last name, kind of like how you would use it if you were laughing. It was annoying, and I knew he was doing it on purpose to get a rise out of me. One time when I knew he was going to call on me, I wanted to say, "How the *bleep* would I know?" I cleaned it up and begrudgingly said, "There's no way I'd know. I haven't been here." In a demeaning manner, he said, "Oh sure, sure. That's a good excuse." It seemed like the kids in the class were in his corner. I felt like a wounded chicken getting pecked by every other chicken in the coup until it would die. I was furious. I was reaching my breaking point for what I could take. It was one thing to absorb the physical ailments I was experiencing, and it was another to try and take the mental and emotional abuse. I purposely skipped that class a few times after that. I could not stand being in that environment. It was not healthy and not helping me heal.

After getting up early every morning and going to school for two months, my mind and body gave out. I missed quite a few days over the next month. I spent a lot of that time sleeping in and recovering. I felt the best in the late evenings. It would often be one or two in the morning and, on occasion, three or four before I would eventually go to bed.

I would stay up drawing, writing, and playing video games, but more than likely, I was up talking with Sheena, Kelsey, and Lori. My mind was most at ease escaping to chat with these three girls, and sometimes it would be all at the same time. It was fantastic. Sheena usually wouldn't be up too late since she wasn't sick and had school to get to. Kelsey and Lori were night owls like me, and we all felt the best at night. I think it was mostly because there was no pressure to get anything done. It was relaxing and stress-free. We could just chat and be in the moment. I would liken it to a drug, an escape from reality. We kept each other sane when everything else was trying to make us go crazy. We talked depression and the effects that come with it. We talked hope that we gave to each other, and that hope and common ground we shared kept us from unraveling.

Missing school wasn't what I wanted, but it did help me to recharge my batteries. I wanted to get back in the saddle. I had my schedule changed so that I could start school in the afternoon, which meant I could stay up later and get up later, which was a godsend. I felt much better doing it that way. I had significantly more energy and focus and was doing well in school, but I knew I needed to physically get in better shape, or I might not last.

Wrestling season was getting underway, and I knew wrestling was the best sport to do if I wanted to get in great physical condition. It had been four or so years since I last was out there on the mat, and even in my diminished state, I knew I still had what it took to be competitive. I also had some pent-up aggression that I wouldn't mind taking out on people. Wrestling is one of the few sports where you use raw strength and agility to make your opponent submit to you by being pinned on their back. I wanted to destroy people and beat them badly. That's what I typically would do back when I was winning most of my matches.

The first practice was after school, and we started with some jogs around the hallways in the school, which I thought was rather fun. My brother Matt showed up as well and was very happy to see me out there. He helped with the coaching, as he loves wrestling more than just about anyone I know. Once we got down to brass tacks and got on the mat, it felt really nice to be back out there. I was looking forward to getting some live action in.

I weighed in at a measly one hundred pounds, which was already fifteen pounds lighter than I was last year. I had zero fat on me. I was skin, bone, and muscle. Being sick, not having much of an appetite, and lying around most of the time caused my body to atrophy. During the period of my life where I should have been growing, I was shrinking. I was hoping to bulk up and get to a more respectable size, but I had to go with where I was at.

By the time we got to some live action, I was ready to go. Even though I was small, even by my own standards, I packed a lot of punch, and I surprised every guy who tried to wrestle me.

I quickly found out I could handle myself very well, but in a very limited amount of time. I would get exhausted after thirty seconds, which didn't bode well for a real, live match, as periods would be two minutes long, and there were three of them. There was no conceivable way I could last a whole match without falling apart and passing out from exhaustion. The only thing I could do was pin my opponent in thirty seconds or less. That was my plan until I could muster up some more endurance. In hindsight, this was an extremely stupid idea. If I could go back, I wouldn't have even attempted to wrestle, but it makes for a good story!

There were about two weeks of practice before live matches were to take place. I was in school and making it to practice every day, trying my best to stick with it. At one practice, I was tangling with one of my teammates who I routinely could handle, so I was taking him down and letting him up and taking him down again, for fun and practice. I started getting tired, which caused some sloppy form on my part, and I ended up with a twisted, banged-up right knee. I was in terrible pain. It swelled up quickly and turned black and blue. I couldn't put any weight on my right leg, so Matt picked me up and carried me into the trainer's room to get checked out. I was fearing the worst. Maybe I tore something and wouldn't be able to wrestle anymore.

I got plopped down on a table and, low and behold, I saw a familiar face. It was Brittany.

She was a trainer's assistant and was in charge of fixing me back up. She was still as beautiful as ever, and I was a skinny, stinky, sweaty, busted-up former version of myself. I was shocked but happy to see her, as awkward as it was. I didn't know what to say. I wasn't expecting her to be there. There was no, "Hi, how are you?" or "It's been a long time." There was no chitchat. She was professional and handled things accordingly. She wanted to get the swelling down in my knee, so it was into the ice bucket with my leg. She handed me a rubber thing that I had no idea what it was and said, "It's for your toes so they don't freeze." I replied, "Oh, that's good to know, thanks!" I was in pain, sick, and tired as I let my badly bruised knee soak in that ice-cold water. I don't recall if we said much more than what we did, but as I watched her, I knew our lives had gone in opposite directions. We had our moment in time a few years ago that made me feel on top of the world. After it ended, though, it began my slow fall back to earth, and now it felt like I was getting buried under it. She was a junior now and had a bright future. I was a sophomore acting as a part-time freshman, with no foreseeable light at the end of the tunnel. I was desperately trying to get back to that cloud-nine feeling that I used to have. Sitting on that table, with my leg starting to go numb from the cold, I knew there was nothing more between us. It sucked. It really hit me hard how far I had fallen behind where I thought I would be at this point in my life. To think that just a short while ago, she and I were on the same sentence and chapter of the same book seemed unfathomable. I haven't seen or spoken to Brittany since that day, but I'm sure she's a great nurse somewhere out there if I had to take a wild guess.

I invested in some super-padded knee pads after that. As I transition into more of the story, there was a wrestling tournament in about a week, and as long as my knee was feeling okay, I wanted to give it a go to take out some frustration.

The weekend rolled around, and I would normally be asleep until noon, but my early morning alarm clock changed all that as it pumped out the theme song to *Rocky*. I was getting in the zone to see what I could do at my first ever high school wrestling tournament. I weighed in for the 112-pound weight class at 103 pounds. For each weight class, you must be at or below that weight. You can't be above it.

A Saturday tournament consists of three matches throughout the day. I knew that I would have to win and win quickly if I wanted to make it to the end. I was feeling great for the first match, confident I could take on my opponent. As I strapped on my headgear and shook the hand of the guy I was about to do battle with, the referee blew the whistle, and it was game on. In my head, I knew I had to get to it, and I did. I quickly dove in for a single leg takedown and got on top. I loved doing the half Nelson move, so I put my right arm under his right arm and wrapped it up over the back of his head. I used all my strength to drive him over onto his back. I squeezed as hard as I could to essentially bury him on the mat with my weight and heard the referee slap the mat and blow the whistle. It was over. I did it. I executed my plan to perfection. I pinned my guy in under thirty seconds. It was incredible!

Unfortunately, I couldn't physically get myself off my opponent. It felt like I had sand in my veins again. I had no strength left to move. My brother Matt came out quickly and helped peel me off the guy and get me on my feet. The referee took my hand and raised it in the air to declare me the winner, but I think I only succeeded in hurting my body as I was extremely worn out. I still had two matches to go. I didn't think there was any chance I could go on.

Luckily, there was about two hours between my first and second match. I made my way to our team spot we had in the bleachers and took a quick nap. I was out in no time. I woke up with about twenty minutes before my next battle and felt absolutely terrible.

My head hurt, I was super nauseated, and I was exhausted, not to mention that I was in otherworldly pain. I tried to walk it off, but it just got worse and worse. I was near tears as the pain was throbbing throughout my body. I felt like I was going to throw up. I quickly hobbled to find a bathroom. I got in there with nobody else around, which I was glad to see because I was a mess. I got into one of the stalls and closed the door. I collapsed to the ground and had to hang on to the toilet to keep myself upright. I was panicked with how miserable I felt. I literally thought I might die. I had flashbacks to that Minnesota cross-country race with how dire of straits I felt I was in. I wanted to desperately scream out for help or for someone to call 911 because I thought this was it. This was how I was going to die.

Just as I was about to keel over, it felt like my whole body had a demonic release, and all living hell dumped into my stomach. I convulsed and threw up so hard, it felt like death was escaping my body. I could not stop puking my guts out. It was wave after wave to the point where I blacked out on the floor. I came to with tears rolling down my face.

I surprisingly felt a lot better. I flushed death down the toilet, walked out of the stall, washed up in the sink, and got myself back out into the gym. I grabbed some tic-tac mints from my bag, as I'm sure my breath was just fantastic. I was due to wrestle in just a few minutes. Talk about a quick turnaround!

Nobody knew what I had just gone through ten minutes earlier, but I was a new man, fuming with adrenaline.

I stepped out onto the mat to face my next opponent and knew this guy was going to get his butt handed to him. The referee blew the whistle, and it was on again. The kid tried a quick shot into my legs, but I reacted perfectly with my favorite move, the "cowcatcher." His shot into me was a little too slow and allowed me to get my right arm under his left and my left arm over his right. I caught him and turned him violently onto his back. He had no clue what hit him. The referee quickly slapped the mat and blew the whistle. I had won again! It took all of ten seconds. I was so pumped I jumped up, and Matt caught me as I flew through the air. I had a fleeting moment of pure perfection that I had been craving for such a long time, and it felt great! How in God's green earth I was able to have that turnaround from thinking I was about to die moments before to dominating an opponent as well as I did is beyond me.

There was one match left.

That match would decide who would take first or second place. I was accustomed to winning tournaments in my earlier years, so I felt right at home with a chance to be the champ.

I did not have the same energy as I had for the second match, but I figured I had enough in the tank to be able to get it done quickly. A quick handshake with my opponent, and again, the whistle blew to get the match started. I could tell right away this guy was as strong as, if not stronger than, me. The seconds passed by, and with each one, the hopes of me winning went way down. I blocked a few of his shots and tried to turn him, but he was much harder to push around. I could feel my energy depleting at a rapid rate. The 75 percent health I started with quickly dropped to 25 percent. Over a minute and thirty seconds in, I was gassed. I tried a quick single-leg shot and tried to pull it into my body as hard as I could. The blood drained from my head as I squeezed every drop of energy I had into trying to take him down, but it simply wasn't happening. My fuel reserves were at zero. I collapsed down to the mat and was out like a lightbulb. The referee quickly stopped the match as he realized I was in trouble. The next thing I knew I was on my back, looking up at the lights as people hovered over me. I didn't know if I was alive. Everything was blurry and muted. After a few minutes of lying there and getting checked over by coaches and medical staff, I was helped to my feet. I shook the hand of my opponent and was helped off the mat.

Technically, I didn't lose the match, but I was unable to continue. The blackout I had didn't last for more than a few seconds, but it was enough to know I couldn't go on. I didn't like that I had lost, but I left it all out there, literally. Second place wasn't too bad for how sick I was, and I thought that if I could just get some stamina, I could do very well with wrestling.

Surprisingly, I was back in school the following week and made it through the practices to be in line to take the mat again. For the life of me, I can't recollect a single thing about my fourth match. I know I had one, and with the notes I had written down in my planner, I can confirm it. I believe this was about the time that my cognitive ability really started to decline. I apparently won the match with a pin in less than thirty seconds to improve my record to three and one on the season. Why I can't remember that win bugs me, but there's not much I can do about it except forge on!

Now on to match number five. It was a dual meet where we traveled to another high school to have a one-on-one battle. There was only going to be one opponent for me to take on, and I wanted to do my best to help the team bring home the victory.

My health was okay that day, but not great. I could feel some lethargy settling through my body. Again, I had to try and win as quickly as I could, or else it would be near impossible to come out on top. As I walked onto the mat for the showdown, I had a weird feeling that this wasn't going to go very well. I zoned in as best I could in the eerily quiet gym. The referee sounded the whistle, and it was game on. The noise from the bleachers started to amplify. My opponent was quick and strong, and it didn't take me very long to realize this was going to be tough to get through. I couldn't take him down. My reflexes were not what I was accustomed to, and I was quickly behind. I struggled mightily to stay off my back as he tried to turn me over. I was hanging in there the best I could, but I was getting exhausted.

The horn sounded, and I had made it through the first period. I was given an option of what position I'd like to start in, so I chose to be on top to see if I could quickly get my opponent pinned. I couldn't keep him down for more than a few seconds before he scored the reversal. In the blink of an eye, I was staring at the ceiling, fighting with all I had to have a chance to make a comeback. I scored a break in the action when I started bleeding.

I had braces on my teeth at that time and, in my struggle, cut my lip. I needed those precious seconds to rest and get some water in me. The stoppage in play wasn't near long enough, and I barely made it through the second period.

At this point, there was a slim-to-none chance I was going to win, so I just held on as long as I could. As the third and final period got underway, I was on the verge of blacking out again. In the back of my mind, I had the stubbornness or pride to not let both of my shoulder blades fall flat on the mat. I had never gotten pinned in my life, and I wasn't about to let it happen now. I could hear the yells from my team's sidelines to keep fighting and not give up. I knew I was going to lose. I felt like a helpless piece of prey being ravaged by wolves. The lights above were blinding, and I was not accustomed to being able to see the rafters of a gym. The strain and torque that I put on my body to keep from getting beat was extinguishing any fire I had left. The crowd was roaring profusely for the referee to slap the mat and end my misery, but that also gave me reason to not give in. I hated losing, and I hated letting people down. When that horn sounded, I heard the crowd groan in disgust. They were shocked that the referee didn't slap the mat and say I was pinned. I can still feel that strain and feel how close it was. All your shoulder blades need to do is touch the mat for a brief moment, and you're done. I didn't give up. I was a fighter.

Matt helped me up to our team's sideline as I was a kneaded piece of wet dough struggling to hold myself up. I was nauseous, dead-exhausted, and in pain. I sat behind the bench with my back against the wall as the rest of the night continued. I remember Matt looking over at me a few times to see how I was doing. To be honest, I felt like I was dying a slow and painful death. If the building were on fire, I don't know if I would have had the energy to get up.

It probably appeared like I was a bad teammate not sitting on the bench to cheer on the rest of the guys that night. I was so out of it and in a daze with no energy to move. I felt like a limp, boiled noodle. My face and hands were tingling and numb. I can liken the feeling to being in a shockwave after a bomb goes off. The noise was muffled, lights were a blur, and everything was out of focus.

I don't know if we won that night or not. All I know is that I felt like the grim reaper was chasing after me as we hit the showers. I don't know how I got into the locker room. I believe I may have been carried there.

Showering in high school wasn't very glamorous. It's normally just an open room with multiple shower heads. It's really gross to not shower after you've been sweating and rolling around with another human being trying to beat the snot out of each other. I felt like dog dirt and thought getting cleaned up would help. There I was, butt naked in the shower, with cold water running over me, when I heard a teammate say, "Boogie, man, what's up with your back? It looks like you have red scars or scratches all over you!"

I turned around and was confused because I think I would have noticed if my skin was all scratched up, but the guy said, "Look in the mirror," so I did.

What I saw was horrifying. I had what looked to be claw marks from being mauled by a tiger or a bear all over my body. Everyone then started commenting on it, and I had no idea what to do or say. My teammates thought it was actually scratches from my opponent, but they weren't. My skin wasn't damaged or cut. It was almost like a sub-dermis type of red striping. It didn't hurt, but I looked like Tony the Tiger with red stripes instead of black. No one knew what to make of it. Since it didn't hurt, I finished getting dressed and went home. By the next morning, the striping had pretty much faded away, but I was beat and had no energy for school. I wish I had taken a picture of what my body looked like. I seriously looked like I had been attacked with a knife and had been cut and stabbed repeatedly. I had no clue why that happened or what it was from. I don't even think I mentioned it to Mom at the time. It wasn't normal, but since it went away so fast, I didn't think much of it. It wouldn't be until five years later that I discovered the cause.

Life was starting to suck more and more. I was done with wrestling. I couldn't continue to put my body through that kind of torture. It was stupid to attempt to wrestle in the first place and even more stupid to keep trying to suck it up and push through everything. I again missed a week or two of school because I was so worn out after my most recent ordeal. The harder I tried, the worse things got.

The new year of 2003 was here, and I didn't have a whole lot to celebrate. The year 2002 hadn't been very kind to me, and I wasn't sure how 2003 was going to fare. I was in the same boat as I had been, simply searching for answers.

With me not getting any better and increasingly falling behind in school, I became convinced to try out another doctor. This one was a rheumatologist about three hours away in Marshfield. My sister-in-law, Kristie, had a sales meeting with a different doctor there at the same time, so she drove my mom and me to the hospital. I didn't like the car ride. It was cold outside, and I wasn't optimistic about my chances of a whole lot of good coming out of this trip. I couldn't help but think my life was slipping away from me as I stared aimlessly out the window.

The initial visit with Dr. W was full of questions, reviewing past tests, procedures, and figuring out what could be done now. Dr. W seemed to know a good bit of what she was talking about, but I got the vibe that she didn't believe it was Lyme disease from the get-go. I got the impression that she believed Lyme was easily treatable and that chronic Lyme disease did not exist. Both of those would be incorrect.

The C6 peptide test that previously showed there was a small indication of Lyme but not enough to give a firm diagnosis was quickly dismissed. She mentioned that even though the C6 peptide test showed there was *something* related to Lyme going on, Dr. W said that a positive C6 peptide would be highly unusual with a negative Western blot. Well, I had a handful of negative Western blot tests, so in her mind, it was nearly impossible that it could be Lyme disease.

One of the most popular tests for Lyme disease was the Western blot, so I donated more of my blood and was tested again. I was a little confused why she wanted to have me do that one since she already believed there was zero chance it would be positive. We did it for what felt like the hundredth time just to see what would happen.

Previous results showed "Lyme bands" but not enough of them for a positive diagnosis. This Western blot came back negative, which I didn't really expect any different result, though I hoped it would have. Ironically, a "band" that was detected in previous tests once again showed up on this one. It was still there! I didn't understand at the time, and really still don't, as to why a Lyme band would show up at all if I didn't have it. A pregnancy test doesn't say you're only partially pregnant. You either are or you are not. I understand that certain criteria needed to be met when diagnosing a disease, but I believed that if something was present, that meant it was there. I'm not smart enough to know if a "Lyme band" can randomly register on a healthy person if they were to have the same test done on them as I did. If that's the case, then I could see why a positive diagnosis would be difficult. My opinion as a sixteen-year-old at the time would be that if a healthy kid has a major decline in health, has all the symptoms of Lyme disease, *and* there is laboratory evidence that *something* Lyme-related is present, you dive in and try and figure it out.

It would have been interesting to have the Western blot test done at different points in time over the last couple of years. Would the test have been positive when I had raging cold and flu-like symptoms? Would I have tested positive after some of my wrestling matches when I felt like I was going to die on the mat? Would there be *any* change in the test results if I could have had my blood tested when I was dying during my last cross-country race and had a hundred symptoms raging all at once? What would an autopsy show had I died at that race in Minnesota? Would the cause of death be Lyme? I have a feeling the results would have been different had I been tested when the Lyme was raging versus when it wasn't.

No, I wasn't feeling horrendously bad at the time I saw Dr. W, but Lyme ebbs and flows. Sometimes I felt pretty good. In a lot of ways, that was the hard part about it. I could live, but I couldn't live how I wanted to or how I should. If I pushed too hard, I'd get knocked down. If I stayed low-key and eliminated stress or exertion, I could get through the days, but living only half a life wasn't what I wanted. The mental side of things was definitely taking a toll on me. I was set to go back to Marshfield in a couple of weeks to see what this doctor would recommend.

I was not looking forward to the follow-up with Dr. W. I knew the results were negative for Lyme already. It was even colder outside for the three-hour car ride to the hospital. Mom was hoping for the best. I was predicting the worst.

Even with that prediction, I couldn't foresee what would happen next.

We made it to the hospital and into the room where Dr. W would discuss the next steps. I simply wanted to go home. I knew it would be a pointless trip and a big waste of money. I didn't like doctors before, and I was about to dislike them a whole lot more.

Dr. W came in and sat down. The sense I got from her was cold and uncaring. She discussed the lab results, admitted that some levels were higher than they were on previous tests, but it wasn't enough to produce a positive Lyme test. We had a controlled argument over the results. A lot of frustration was spewing over. How could a test go up, show there was something there, and still there was no concern that it was Lyme? There was nothing Dr.

W could do to help me. She was adamant that it wasn't Lyme. Multiple tests over multiple years were *negative*. She stated that chronic Lyme disease can't and doesn't exist, and if I somehow did have it in the past, the treatment protocol I had would have eliminated the Lyme.

Why then was I still feeling as bad as I did? Why couldn't I get healthy? Why was it that every time I pushed it, I got worse? I had no control over how I felt. I told Dr. W that I was being truthful in how I felt and that I just wanted my life back. I came to this doctor in hopes of finding answers, but all I got was frustration and disappointment.

At the end of our follow-up session, some of the most spearing comments that made my mom and I fume and be on the verge of tears then came from the doctor. She said that she would recommend that I go to physical therapy for assistance with a conditioning program (remember, I was a very good athlete until I got sick). She added that a *psychological evaluation* would be appropriate. She didn't think I was as concerned as I should be about my level of function and that I was simply missing school without an adequate reason. All that translated in my head was that she thought I was faking it and that I wanted attention. It was exactly like the negative comments I heard in school, but worse. Kids didn't believe me, teachers didn't believe me, family didn't always believe me, and now doctors didn't believe me. It was messed up. It was depressing.

It took a good bit of restraint on my end to not step up and take a swing at her. I could not believe what I was hearing. Mom was just as upset as I was, but we just gritted our teeth and said, "Thank you for seeing us, but this has been a waste of time coming here."

Lyme and other tick-borne related diseases were not understood well at that point in time, and they still aren't.

I had lost so much respect for the medical community as a whole. I had been poked and prodded, had blood repeatedly drawn, and had endured test after test, and there was still no direct answer to why my health was unraveling. I couldn't even find a doctor who believed I was dealing with anything "real."

Life went on, though, and so did school. I was handling the part-time student thing the best that I could. I had stretches where I'd be able to stay in class for a few weeks in a row, but inevitably, I would then miss one, two, or three days a week. Coming back after missing a few days was a tough ordeal. I'd need to make up missed assignments and deal with the people there. I saw the stares, I heard the whispers, and I knew the rumors. I was looked at differently because I was different. I could hear all the negative comments that had been thrown my way many times before as I passed through the halls. The gossip of me having any and all weird diseases made some people keep their distance from me. A lot of the kids simply thought I was a part-time student because I wanted people to feel sorry for me or that I wanted attention. But that was never the case. I just wanted to be who I thought I was going to be, but I was a million miles away from that person.

I also didn't like getting harassed. I remember one time I was just minding my business at my locker and some punk upperclassman who I didn't know spun me around so that I was facing him. He picked me up under my shoulders and slammed me up against the lockers. I didn't flinch. I was already particularly perturbed that day and simply gave this guy the death stare. It was my way of saying, "Put me down, or I'll use whatever strength and energy I have to beat whatever I can out of you!"

He wised up and put me down. I continued to glare at him as he walked on down the hall, and I never saw him again. A girl who was there asked if I was okay. I just nodded and went about my day. I was extremely angry and agitated on the inside, but I kept a cool appearance on the exterior. I didn't want to show that the ridicule was getting to me.

There was a mental battle in my mind on a regular basis to try and keep my sanity. I was doing the best I could, but the environment was hostile. I was very much a loner outside of a few friendly faces. Seeing Abbie was the brightest part of my day, but that was a very small percentage of the time. The rage and anger kept building like a stoked fire in my mind. I was worried what might be the last thread to unravel before I snapped.

I knew I was depressed. I believed I had every right to be. I didn't want that to be the case.

I started missing days at school for reasons more than not feeling physically good. I was missing school because I hated myself and a lot of people around me. I hated the position I was in. I was on a slippery slope. I knew that I couldn't get through school by just being a part-time student. It would take me eight years to graduate at that pace. At no fault of my own, I had fallen into a giant hole. I was sick and tired at trying my best and getting nowhere fast.

Faced with despair and impossible odds, the devil started to creep into my mind. The sadness turned to anger, turned to depression, and then turned to thoughts of how I could die and how I could stick it to the people who had a hand in pushing me in this dark direction.

Driving alone became a constant fight of whether or not to push the accelerator to the floor and cross the center line into oncoming traffic. I would drive in silence, alone with the demons in my mind. What was the point of going forward? Who would really miss me if I was gone? How did I end up in this mess? Why did God allow all these troubles to be cast upon me?

Many times, I would see an approaching semi in the distance, and the thought of only having to slightly pull the wheel to the left and all my problems would be over tantalized in my mind. A simple action could end it. No one would really know how or why it happened. Did I fall asleep? Have a medical emergency? Get distracted? Vehicle malfunction? There would be more questions than answers. The thought of it being over, consumed me. It was so easy to gently pull to the left and face death head-on. I felt like I was ready to do it numerous times. As I would stare at the oncoming flashing headlights and hear the blast of the distinctive sound of a big rig horn, I wanted to feel the impact and then nothing, to feel nothing.

I pulled back right. I pulled back right over and over again. As much as I hated life, I hated giving up and giving in. I knew my family would miss me. I knew some people would wonder what happened. I knew Sheena, Lori, and Kelsey would never know what became of me, and I couldn't do that to them. The thought of someone giving Abbie the news of my tragic "accident" and hurting the one girl who showed me compassion and kindness in real life was a stronger thought to keep living than it was to let go completely.

I soldiered on, though I would continue to battle against the demons of my mind for quite some time.

Spring was coming around again. I did enjoy the warmer temperatures and the break from the ice-cold grip that Mother Nature can have on Wisconsin.

School was still school; at least I was there more than I wasn't. My health was "okay," and mentally, I was "eh." Knowing there were only two months left in the school year brightened my outlook a bit. I tried to make the best of it.

Boys' golf was a spring sport at school. I desperately wanted to play on the team and get some normalcy and fun back in my life. I loved competition, and golf is one of the best sports because it's just you versus the golf course. Whoever plays it the best wins. I was really good at chipping and putting because that was something I could do at home. I was only half-good at the other aspects of the game, so I decided to give it a shot. I figured it would be a lot easier on my body than wrestling. I had hoped it would help get my mind focused on something completely different from school and the demons I had in my mind.

There were some driving range sessions and a few practice rounds to see who would make what team. A top player would play nine holes in the thirties or low forties to be on varsity. The worst of the rest would play on the junior varsity team. I was excited to play the practice rounds at courses I had played in the past. I felt it gave me a good advantage, and I scored decently. I was averaging forty-five for nine holes. Not quite good enough for the big leagues, but I thought I had a good chance to get there if I could stick with it.

I didn't know anyone on the team. Almost two years of being in school, and I still didn't know very many people. One guy I got along with well and who seemed to be friendly and accepting was Rich. He was an easygoing guy like me. We formed a bit of a friendship. It was fun for me to have a buddy on the team and at school who I felt had my back. Rich was a tad better at golf than I was, but we both got stuck on the JV team, hoping to work our way up.

On the golf course for my first individual match, it was a bit nerve-racking. I wasn't sure if I could play as well as the other kids. I remember I shanked my very first tee shot into the weeds on the left. I was praying that I could simply find it in the garden salad that I hit it into so that I didn't have to take a penalty shot. Luckily, it came to rest in a playable lie, and my second shot, I nailed up toward the green. My normally sound short game let me down as I chunked my next shot, but then I hit a decent one and ultimately made the putt for a bogey. For some reason, I only remember that hole. As the match played out, the other kids were a lot like me. They could hit some good shots, but that was quickly followed by an atrocious mess. None of us were scoring that well, and since it was JV, scores weren't always accurate. It didn't really matter if you took a seven or an eight on a hole. Sometimes it was hard to remember how many hacks you had, and penalty shots weren't always played by official golf rules. If this was varsity and a big tournament for state, that would have been a different story. Every stroke mattered at that level. That's where I wanted to be, but I found myself quickly running out of gas after a few holes. I was tired and worn out, my body hurt, and my game reflected it. In the few matches I played in, I don't think I even broke fifty on nine holes. It was rather embarrassing because I knew I was better than that, but my body wasn't allowing me to perform how I wanted. I could be good for a little while, then the wheels would just come off, and I would lose any momentum I had.

Golf wasn't going the way I wanted or the way I thought it could. I hit some amazing shots, but I was never consistent enough. I still wanted to try and be better, but in all honesty, I wasn't good enough or healthy enough to seriously try and compete at a higher level. I believed that I had the ability under healthier circumstances.

Not a whole lot ever went right, and disappointments were a daily occurrence. I was starting to get used to things not going the way I wanted them to.

After a month of playing golf, I got the news from the coach that I no longer could be on the team because I was a part-time student.

I wasn't surprised when he told me. It didn't bother me. I wasn't mad. It was almost like I expected something like that to happen. Deep down, I believe it did hurt, but it would have been a lot worse if I was performing well.

I would have loved to have been 100 percent and competing at the highest level, but I was nowhere near that. In the end, it was another thing being taken away that I couldn't do because of my health.

I had already failed at my goal to not miss a day of school. Now I failed at being able to excel in sports. I was failing at keeping, maintaining, or making new relationships, and I was not even close to being as popular or well-liked as I thought I might be. I didn't have the best grades either. I was almost halfway done with high school, but I wasn't even an eighth of the way toward completion. I certainly wasn't popular with the ladies. I would have loved a special girl to lean on, but that was a pie-in-the-sky dream at that point.

On all fronts, I was falling short of what I wanted to accomplish. The reality of my situation was really starting to hit me. I was getting lapped by everyone and being left in the dust. My classmates would, in a few short months, be starting their junior year. I hadn't even finished my freshman year credits.

The last month of school, I missed five days. I was getting sicker and sicker again, with new symptoms emerging.

My mind, or my brain, started to give me issues. I had always been a whiz with numbers and math, but now simple addition and subtraction was starting to become difficult. I often felt like my brain was a jumbled mess. It was a relentless assault on my psyche. It got to the point where even signing my name on worksheets was a battle. I couldn't remember how to write certain letters without some serious thinking.

One of the weirdest and scariest symptoms was the sudden stabbing pain in my chest or heart area. It seriously felt like someone would randomly come up behind me and plunge a knife straight into my chest. The pain was lightning-quick and extremely painful. It would knock the wind out of me and crumple me to the floor. It happened a few times walking to or sitting in class. Kids and the teacher would sort of gasp or really be startled when I would grab my chest, pound the desk, and gasp for air. It was very unpleasant, but it was over in a matter of seconds. In some ways, I had hoped my heart was giving out and I could just die from one of these attacks, but it was always a short-lived pain. It was random and scary. It would happen at school or at home and sometimes when I was driving. I couldn't control it, and no one could explain how or why it was happening. It was just another nail being struck into my coffin.

I made it through my "sophomore" year, but I was still behind.

I had only completed a little more than half of what I needed to for my freshman year classes. I really looked forward to the summer break. I needed those three months to rest and recover. If there was going to be any attempt at getting back my life, I needed to be healthier. The pressure was mounting. I had no clue what I would do if I couldn't salvage my high school career. I needed answers, I needed a plan, and I needed help.

CHAPTER 7

DISCOVERY

I had recently turned seventeen. I was coming up on three years of being off-and-on sick. Some days, I darn near felt normal; other days, I had been near death in that stretch. The wild ups and downs and twists and turns had definitely thrown me for a loop. I again felt better without the burden of school or having to do anything on a regular basis. My job was to rest up and improve my well-being. The newer symptoms I picked up at the end of the school year were still prominent. The shooting pains in my heart area, the cognitive issues, the pains in my neck and back, and the tiredness weren't improving like I hoped they would. I was stuck between a rock and a hard place. I needed help, and I needed answers.

I heard a new term that I hadn't come across before: LLMD, or Lyme literate medical doctor. Lori mentioned it to me to try and find one of those if there was one available. I didn't know those types of doctors existed, so I was intrigued if there was one in the area versus flying to the East Coast.

Around the same time and out of the blue, Mom had a connection through a Lyme group, and that person connected us to a Dr. B down in Illinois. Illinois? Just where I wanted to go. It was roughly a two-hour drive there. I was hesitant to agree to meeting with this new doctor. I was intrigued, though, that she knew about Lyme disease and sounded like she could be one of those elusive LLMDs.

I talked it over with Kelsey and Lori that I had a chance to meet with this doctor, and they said to go for it. It couldn't hurt to at least have an initial consultation. I figured this doctor had to be better than Dr. W.

I agreed to go. The new, scary symptoms I was having helped to make that decision. If I could find a doctor who was willing to work with me, maybe in a few weeks or months, I'd be back to normal.

The ride there was smooth. I had to pay a few tolls and navigate into a place I'd never been before. Mom was with me, as she always was when I went to see a doctor. I'm sure we talked about what we were looking for with this Dr. B. We half-expected it to not be of benefit, but we had to try. I didn't have many other options at this point. We went in cautiously optimistic.

We arrived safely and made our way into the little office building. The doctor was on the second floor. It was a small office, definitely not like the big hospitals I had been in before. It felt cozy.

The receptionist was nice, and we felt welcome. It was make-or-break time. Was this doctor going to work out? Or was it going to be another Dr. W experience all over again?

We got seated in the exam room, and a few minutes later, a knock on the door sounded as Dr. B walked in.

She smiled at me and had a genuine warmth about her. She appeared to be the exact opposite of Dr. W right off the bat.

Dr. B took a sincere interest in *listening* to me and hearing my story. She wanted to know everything. I thought, *Why aren't all doctors like this?* All the ones I had been to couldn't add up anywhere close to this doctor's honest desire to help and try to find a solution.

After a few minutes of speaking with Dr. B, I liked and trusted her. I started to get a good feeling that maybe I could discover what was really going on.

Dr. B wasn't your typical doctor. She wasn't content to just run a test and throw some drugs at the problem. She was a big believer that natural remedies could be just as effective as drugs, if not more. She really liked the supplements I was using and encouraged me to continue taking them since that was the only thing offering some relief over the previous years.

She knew that a lifelong drug regimen wasn't the way to go, and I told her if that's what she thought I needed, I wasn't going to have any of it. It was nice that a doctor was on the same page as me for once.

Dr. B wanted to start me on some additional natural products to start things off. One that I fondly remember and half dreaded was a liver flush. It consisted of twenty large, honking pills and a lot of water. I'm not sure if I had to do it every night, but it was quite often. I would get out a cereal bowl and fill it with the pills and head off to the computer to chat with the girls. I figured that it would take some time to choke those pills down that I might as well have some company while I did it. I don't recall seeing too much benefit from doing the protocol, but a cleaned-out liver probably wasn't a bad thing.

Dr. B thought that it was at least plausible I had Lyme disease or some sort of coinfection going on, so she ran multiple labs to see what would happen. The ever-popular Western blot came back negative. Babesia came back negative. Bartonella also came back negative. Another test called the Lyme Dot-Blot, not surprisingly, was negative.

The result was negative again across the board. The frustration was maddening.

We did a live blood-cell analysis that was quite interesting. I had never had one done before, and it was fascinating to see what my blood was doing. From the results, they asked if I ever had a concussion. I answered, "Yeah, why?" Something in the analysis showed there was some kind of information in my blood that indicated a prior head trauma. Either that was a good guess, or the analysis was correct, but I was half-dumbfounded by that. The test also showed that my blood cells were vibrant and in good condition and one of the better results they had ever seen. I attributed that to the supplements that I used because one of the main benefits to them was that it helped get oxygen to my cells to make them perform the best they could. I had not only a personal testimonial that natural things can work but also visual proof that it was helping my blood cells. I will always be adamant that supplements (good supplements) can be very beneficial. God gave us fruits and vegetables and all sorts of things to be good for our bodies. Taking a concentrated mix of God-given food just always seemed like a smart idea. I will also always believe that without what I had been taking, I very well may have been dead by now or, at the very least, be in much worse shape. I would almost venture a bet that the Lyme tests in the past would have come back positive if I wasn't using the supplements. Of course, I can't prove that, and we'll never know for sure, but it is interesting to think about.

A newer Lyme test was in a clinical trial and had just become available that Dr. B wanted to test out on me, as she was quite certain I had it. We just couldn't confirm it. It was some sort of DNA-based test that could somehow be a possible way to diagnose Lyme. I don't believe it was FDA-approved at the time, but it couldn't hurt to draw a little more blood and see what it said.

It came back *positive*, or at least positive enough to be diagnosed as Lyme disease. "This test was only used for clinical purposes and should not be regarded as investigational or for research." That's what the sheet of paper that had the results said anyway. At the end of the report, though, it said that "a diagnosis should not be based on laboratory tests alone. Results should be interpreted in conjunction with clinical symptoms and patient history."

I understood it wasn't a 100 percent FDA-approved test that showed it was Lyme, but a clinical test showed *something* Lyme-related was there, just like previous tests did before. Something was there that shouldn't be there. This time, I had a competent doctor who had seen multiple Lyme patients, and based off that test, my health history, and current symptoms, I finally had a doctor believe what I suspected all along: I indeed had Lyme disease.

Lyme *positive*. Doctor diagnosed. It was surreal. It was scary. It was the right diagnosis. Chronic Lyme disease *does* exist, and anyone who says it doesn't is wrong or misinformed. I'm living proof of that. It had been nearly three years since I initially started getting sick until this positive diagnosis. I had been put on the ten-day protocol to eradicate Lyme in the past. That *did not* work. Lori had the disease her whole life. I knew it could be passed through childbirth. Other doctors had no clue. Dr. B knew because she cared to learn. She cared to listen and connect the dots and realized that all her patients with very similar symptoms and conditions *could not* be faking or were needing a little psychological help because of how the disease strips away our energy and ability to fully engage with life. We weren't crazy, and we weren't seeking attention. We were seeking answers. She knew there was a reason, and that reason was Lyme and the coinfections that can come with it. It's part of why it's difficult to figure out, diagnose, or treat. Throw in the coinfections, and you have all sorts of weird things that happen to people. It's a terrible, tricky disease to comprehend, and just when you think you do, up pops a million other things to learn about it. It's downright tragic, and the worst thing about it is that it gets swept under the rug because too many people in the position to help just go along with the same old mindset that Lyme is supposed to be easy to diagnose and treat with a simple round of antibiotics. That *might* work if you catch it early. It can lay dormant, and you'll remain symptom-free or have mild symptoms until you go through something traumatic, like giving birth, being in a car accident, or running yourself to the ground, as I did many times before.

I finally had a little victory, a little vindication. I was really looking forward to getting started on some treatment and to hopefully get back on my feet and be ready to rock and roll in a few months because I had a whole lot of catching up to do if I was going to make it through high school.

Even though I didn't like antibiotics, I was willing to give them a try, along with everything else I was doing. I started on doxycycline and Ceftin. I had to be careful being out in the sun with the doxycycline; my skin would burn so easily while I was on it. It only took a time or two to figure that out the hard way. I also felt the most benefit on doxy, so I just tried to remember to not cook in the sun too long and wear appropriate clothing or have some sunscreen to help me not fry.

A very interesting thing happened a couple of weeks after I started on the antibiotics. As I was getting into the shower, I noticed something weird on the back of my upper right arm. I was a tad flabbergasted as what it could be. What did I get into in the yard? What bit me now? I took a closer look and also showed Mom. We took a picture to show to Dr. B so we could ask what her opinion might be. It became very obvious that it wasn't just any sort of rash or bug bite. It was the notorious red bull's-eye rash that you can sometimes get after you've been bit by a tick. You don't always get that rash as I noted before, and somehow mine appeared *after* starting treatment. It was crazy!

The best thing I could come up with was that I never got the bull's-eye rash in the beginning because I was a healthy individual. Symptoms didn't appear right away. They took a while to manifest. I had Lyme disease, but it had laid dormant until I overexerted myself, became overworked, or got stressed out. The more I pushed myself, the more it agitated the Lyme, and it burrowed itself deeper. The Lyme bacteria is also shaped like a corkscrew, and it uses that shape to dig in and hide. Once I had some different antibiotics stirring things up inside me, then the Lyme was more or less brought to the surface, and out popped the bull's-eye rash.

I now had the symptoms, a positive test, a doctor-confirmed diagnosis, belief from other Lyme people, *and* the bull's-eye rash. There really couldn't be much more evidence to support what was going on. I took a picture of it just in case someone ever doubted me in the future. No way was I ever going to let a different physician tell me it was all in my head.

It felt great to finally feel like I was heading to a destination with the correct directions versus guessing which road to choose. The heavy weight of the naysayers was slowly starting to roll off me. I was looking forward to having a fun summer and starting to heal.

An interesting opportunity came up. My brother PJ was studying in Spain and had a two-week break. My parents wanted to have a little tour of Europe during that stretch of time. I was hesitant to go, as I didn't know how my health would hold up. I was feeling decent with my regimen of things I needed to take. I figured I had missed out on a bunch of things before, so I didn't want to miss out on a trip like this. I packed up my bags, and off we went.

I had never flown on a plane. I had never been out of the country, except for Canada, but I don't really count that. I was eager to explore a different continent and see what life was like across the Atlantic Ocean.

It was the height of summer in Spain when we arrived, and it was hot. It was a dry heat and felt fantastic to me. We spent the first couple of days exploring Barcelona. It required a lot of walking, but I surprisingly held up just fine. I didn't have many cares in the world. I was relaxed and stress-free. I was simply able to enjoy life and experience the fantastic opportunity at hand.

My first memorable experience of being in a foreign country was the differences in the food. The first meal in Barcelona was shrimp scampi. I loved that dish, and I was excited to see how the Spaniards made it. When my plate was placed in front of me, I couldn't believe my eyes. There were other eyes looking at me! Apparently, they don't use shrimp that's been in a bag. They use shrimp that was fresh caught with zero processing. I was a bit grossed out, but I found a way to pick at it to get at the tasty bits, and it was more than edible. I get a kick out of that now. I was definitely caught off guard.

We rented a car and drove all the way north to the English Channel and stopped at many places along the way.

Normandy was one of my favorite stops. I felt it was a privilege to be standing on the same beach where the United States stormed that very same spot not many years before. The blown-up cement bunkers were still there, and the crater marks still had their imprint on the land. Knowing so many people had lost their lives on the ground we were walking over very much gave me a somber and appreciative feeling. As if that didn't leave a lasting impact on me, visiting the cemetery where thousands of white crosses were spread out as far as one could see did. I understood what happened but was uncertain of why. I mean, I was just a know-nothing teenager. Looking back on that time and now knowing more of the details of what took place, I can value it more. To be between eighteen and nineteen years old and leave everything you know to fight to the death on land you've never been to against tremendous odds of surviving is almost incomprehensible. I wondered why all that carnage had to take place. Why would people feel the need to order other human beings into that kind of living hell? It was difficult to comprehend. I understand the situation more now; with sin and evil in the world, anything can happen.

I was seventeen years old at the time, and to think that if I lived during that era, I could have possibly been in that situation makes me very thankful I wasn't. It also makes me very thankful for the freedoms that I enjoy now. Everyone should remember what happened and where we come from. If you have the chance, visit a place like that and truly soak it in. You'll live a much more appreciative life.

Moving on, we headed for Paris. I don't think we intended to drive *into* downtown Paris, but we ended up in this crazy mess of traffic without knowing where we were going. How in the world we didn't get into an accident is still a mystery to me, but we made it to our destination safely. A day or two spent checking out the Eiffel Tower and the Arc de Triomphe were some of the highlights. Seeing the Eiffel Tower lit up at night was particularly amazing. The food was great, people were friendly, and figuring out where to go with just a map and our street smarts was an adventure in itself. We drove in a car called a Picasso, which was some sort of minivan. It wasn't pretty, but it got the job done. On the highway, we were going at a decent speed when, out of nowhere, a Ferrari flew by at what I'd guess was 150 miles per hour. It was the strangest experience, as if a bullet had shot by. We were all a bit shocked by the ordeal, as well as impressed. I had always loved fast, exotic cars, and now I really wanted to get one of my own.

While traveling around on planes, trains, boats, and buses, you get a lot of time to think and pray. I did that quite a bit. We stopped at many of the old churches over there. It was surreal how old some of them were, and I couldn't help but feel like I was attending church services on a daily basis.

I prayed that my health would hold up. I prayed that I could get my life back on track. I prayed that I could get through school when I got back home. I prayed for a fresh start and a clear mind.

I prayed for the strength to help me do the things that I needed to do. I prayed and prayed.

Between praying, different modes of transportation, food, and sites to see, one of the best parts about traveling was interacting with the locals. From my experience, people just want to go about living their lives in peace. The people there were happy to have tourists come so that they could share their culture. We had to ask for directions a few times, but even though we didn't speak the same language, locals still pointed us in the right direction. It was nice to see there was a lot of good in other parts of the world.

Over time, though, memories of where you've been fade, but experiencing the moments with the people closest to you tend to stick in the mind a bit longer. Our journey concluded with taking a car ferry across the English Channel into London and flying back home from there.

I got through the trip without any major issues, and it wasn't long before I was back at home, safe and sound. I was glad I went but couldn't wait to see my dog Sheena again and chat with my online friends about my trip.

There wasn't much time before my third attempt at high school would be upon me. I was cautiously optimistic. I had a doctor in my corner, so I thought I stood a good chance this time.

I was going to attempt to take on a full schedule in my valiant return. I would be full time with very little room for error at this point.

One helpful but embarrassing thing was the handicap sticker Dr. B was able to get me so that I could park right next to the school building. I needed every little perk I could get to limit the stress I was about to endure. The fact that I wasn't going to need to walk a quarter mile just to get into the building every day was a big win for me.

The only problem was that now I had another target on my back for people to attack me. The first day I pulled into that handicap spot, I was so happy to not have to walk as far as I normally would have to. It was immediately easier on me. Unfortunately, that was short-lived. As soon as I got out of the car, locked it up, and starting walking into the building, I heard the heckle. "Hey, you don't look handicapped! You can't park there, loser!" Maybe they didn't see the sticker hanging from my rearview mirror, but I doubt it. I didn't know who it was. I tried to shake it off. It wasn't the start of school that I wanted it to be.

I was supposed to be a junior by now. I was old enough to be a senior. I was in sophomore classes, but I hadn't even finished my freshman year. What a messed-up puzzle I had to try and piece together.

I'm glad I was able to find an old notebook to map out what I had going on for classes because I didn't recall much, if anything, about my schedule.

Apparently, I was in a geometry, Spanish, and religion class, among a few others. Not only did I not remember these classes, but I also didn't know who my teachers were. Nor did I recall any of the kids in my classes. It's a blank mystery that I'll probably never figure out.

I made it through the first week. It was an accomplishment that I hadn't been able to do for two years. It was tough, but I was holding it together.

Then week two came around. The teasing about the handicap sticker carried on. I could feel myself wearing down physically, but more so mentally and emotionally. The stress I was going through was real. I didn't have that in the summertime, but I was more than making up for it now.

By the middle of the third week, I was brutally sick with the same sort of cold or flu symptoms I had been getting every single year once I started back to school. I couldn't believe it. I missed the rest of the week. The wheels had already started falling off. I knew this type of sickness all too well. It would start in my throat, then my glands would swell up, and it felt like I was swallowing razor blades again. The congestion was horrendous, and the tiredness was never-ending. I was already tired for the next day when it hadn't even begun. That's how worn out I already was. It was maddening.

I was out for a week. This wasn't the start I needed, but it was the hand I was dealt.

I cut my schedule down to part-time again. I started getting to school in the afternoon. I didn't have to worry about being teased about the handicap sticker because everyone was in class by the time I got there. It was very awkward getting to school and having to press a button to identify myself so that I could be let in. I always felt like I was bugging whoever had to answer the door. In my mind, I always thought the lady would be thinking, *Oh, here comes that weird boy again who is always late for school. Why doesn't he just show up on time?* I felt like an inconvenience, on top of already feeling stupid and alone.

I had a study hall period where I could attempt to catch up on schoolwork, but I could tell my focus and concentration wasn't always cooperating. I know I tried to catch a little shut eye more than once because on some days, I was just too tired to do much except exist.

A familiar face with me in that study hall was a girl I'll call Holly. I knew her from the cross-country team my original freshman year. We used to have a little friendship going before everything went south with my health. It was awesome to see her again. She was a little bit of sunshine to brighten my day. I passed her a note one time to see if she'd wanted to go out because I had always liked her. I didn't have much to lose and figured why the heck not. If we could be an item, then maybe people would get off my back a little bit, and I'd have something to look forward to at school.

I wasn't surprised when she passed on me. I mean, why in the world would she not? I had nothing to offer. She was really sweet about letting me down, though, and was happy just being friends. I respected her choice. I wasn't disappointed. I was used to things not working out. Holly still liked me and was nice to me after that, so there was no love lost. At least I had someone around who I saw on a regular basis who seemed to care at least a little bit.

The only other girl I really cared about but didn't see a whole lot anymore was Abbie. We didn't have classes together, and we rarely would pass in the hall. The boost that she gave me last year just wasn't the same as our paths kept drifting apart.

My friend Rich I would only see occasionally as well, but there was no way I was going to be on the golf team to hang out more consistently. Abbie and Rich were the two people I liked most at school, but they had their lives going forward, and mine was going backward. We were going in opposite directions.

I really wanted to feel better, but that wasn't the case. The stress of everything wore on me heavily. I wanted to keep going, but my health wasn't allowing it. I thought being under a doctor's care and being under proper treatment would have allowed me to be healthier. My body did not like the pressure to perform and was giving out on me. I pressed on as best as I could.

It was a Friday and a gorgeous day outside. A few hours to get through, and I could start my weekend, a weekend where I didn't have the stress of school. I was looking forward to it.

The first class of the day was geometry. The only thing I recall was how I was feeling, and I knew something was different; something was off. I kept thinking about getting through it, and then I'd have two days off to rest. My chest felt compressed, and my heart was fluttering. I was lightheaded and dizzy, and my hands and face were numb. I kept having waves of emotions crash into me, and I wasn't sure which way was up. I kept getting progressively less in control of how I was feeling. I couldn't calm down.

My next class was speech. I was supposed to give some kind of talk in front of class that day, but I was in no shape to do so. I approached the teacher privately in the hall, already visibly shaking, and told him if I have to talk in front of class, I'm going to collapse. Surprisingly, he accepted my request to sit this one out. I excused myself to pace the hall, get a drink, and try and relax.

I couldn't.

I trusted one teacher, Mrs. H. She was my algebra teacher the year before. I went to her classroom before my study hall period and let her know that something wasn't right. The bell was about to ring, and she told me to try some deep breathing and try to get through it. I didn't want to leave her room. I felt out of control and lost. She pointed me in the direction I needed to go. I eventually made it to study hall.

As I sat there, I was fighting back tears. My body was burning on the inside. I was nauseous, hurting, and trembling. It felt like my body was being ravaged and raped by tiny demons inside me. I had never felt such erratic feelings. I liken it to my last cross-country race where I should have died, but even this was different. I wasn't exerting my body, but my body reacted like I was. I didn't know how much longer I could hold it together.

The period was up, and I again walked past Mrs. H's classroom. I looked at her, shook my head, and mouthed to her, "This isn't good." Then I walked to my last class of the day, which was biology.

My world was falling apart. I felt like a juggler trying to keep the balls moving in a precise manner, only to see them start crashing to the ground in front of the whole crowd. I was a little baby deer being chased by a pack of wolves. I was a bleeding bait fish, struggling in the water as sharks grew closer and closer. Whatever was happening to me, I wanted it to stop, and I wanted it to stop now!

I took my seat in class and, through the tears in my eyes, saw a guy I knew, and he could tell I was having a harder than normal time. I read his lips, "What's wrong?" I shook my head in disgust and mouthed back, "I don't know."

The bell rang, and everyone was taking their seats. I couldn't take it anymore. I didn't care what would happen next, I had to get out. I grabbed my bag and walked out of class for the last time.

I was stumbling off the wall in the hallway. Everyone was in class except for me. I wanted to find a spot so I could curl up and die. I hated the way I felt at that moment. I was so perplexed and confused. I made it to the steps, and about halfway down, I collapsed. My body gave out. No one knew where I was. I was alone and shattered. I couldn't stop crying. I had trouble breathing, and my head was spinning. All the anxiety and stress and sickness and death spewed out of me like a dam bursting. If you could imagine what it's like to throw up through your eyes, that's what it felt like. As I lay on the floor, I wanted to not be there anymore. I was done. It wasn't worth it. The pain and suffering to make a grade was not worth this torture. Trying to be liked and have friends wasn't worth the hell I kept trying to put my body through. The harder I tried to get through school, the worse it got.

I lasted three weeks in my junior year.

Fifteen minutes passed, and surprisingly, nobody witnessed the train wreck of a mess I had just gone through, so I pulled myself together. I wanted to grab my stuff and walk out. Looking back on the day, I would have felt better if I did that.

I slowly walked back to Mrs. H's classroom. I could see her teaching as I stood outside the door. *What can she even do for me?* I thought. I didn't know where anyone else was who I trusted in the entire building. She saw me through the little thin piece of glass, and we locked eyes. She noticed the dejection on my face and stopped class to come out and check on me. I collapsed in her arms. I was trying to hold back tears as much as I could. She shook me a bit to help me snap out of it. I was like a limp noodle. She shook me again and told me I needed to get to the school office and asked if I could make it there. I stupidly said yes. For some reason, that's where I went instead of just leaving on my own.

I made it to the office where I called Mom and let her know I wasn't doing well. She came and picked me up, even though I had a car at school.

It was finished. I was done. I got my car later that weekend. I wasn't going back to class. No way was I putting myself through that again.

Now I know that being on medication for Lyme combined with stress can cause an adverse reaction. It's called a Herxheimer reaction. I later would call them Lyme attacks because that's exactly what it was.

I didn't know what that was at the time, but it was the first one I had. It's basically a revisit of all your worst symptoms all at once. The Lyme doesn't like getting agitated from the antibiotics, so when it dies off, it flips you the middle finger and ravages your body one last time on its way out.

I went back to Illinois to see Dr. B.

I had recovered from my latest lovely experience, and I was en route for my latest monthly visit to see what the next steps would be.

I let Dr. B know about the Lyme attack that I went through, and she wasn't surprised that it occurred, so I at least felt a little relief to hear that it wasn't uncommon. I still didn't like that I went through it, though.

Since I was out of school, I could concentrate more on just getting better. We kept switching up the antibiotics to confuse the Lyme as much as possible. Some antibiotics I tolerated better than others. I didn't like being on them because even though they were killing off the Lyme, they can hurt my immune system in other ways.

I won't bore you with the details of how much or how long I was on different antibiotics. Frankly, I wouldn't be able to tell you anyway. I do know which ones I was on, though, and they include metronidazole, amoxicillin, probenecid, minocycline, Zithromax, and tinidazole.

It was quite the list. One of the side effects of a medication I hate the most was an aluminum taste I constantly had in my mouth. Eating was difficult because nothing tasted good, and when nothing tastes good, you don't want to eat. I wasn't in a position to lose weight, so I don't think I stayed on that med for very long.

There was talk about possibly giving me a port. Basically, I would have a tube inserted into me, and any drugs could then be sent straight into my heart. Lori had one of those, so I knew what it was all about. The other option would be to come in every two weeks to have an IV administered. I chose the IV over the port. The port just seemed a bit too scary at the time.

The IV I was on was Rocephin. It was nice that I could come to the clinic that I knew versus going to a big hospital to have it done.

It was an eye-opening experience. The clinic had a living room of sorts with a bunch of recliners that were mostly filled every time I was there with other Lyme patients. I saw firsthand the devastation that it can do to people. People came in with walkers and wheelchairs. Some were in a lot of pain while others seemed to have cognitive issues. I actually felt blessed and a bit grateful I wasn't in some of these people's positions. I believe that I could have been or would have been in a lot worse shape had I not been taking the nutritional products at the beginning of my illness. At the same time, I wondered if I had not taken the supplements, would I have gotten sicker faster and diagnosed sooner? Lots of what-ifs can be played for anyone in any situation. I wasn't immune to that game.

There was one girl I remember who was there at the same time I was. She was younger than me and in really rough shape. She was confined to a wheelchair, so the nurse had to pick her up and carry her to the recliner for her treatment. It was tough to see. No kid should have to go through that.

Lyme didn't discriminate. There were old and young patients, men and women, and boys and girls. It didn't matter what you looked like. Anyone could get it.

It was about that time that I learned people could die from the complications of Lyme disease. It wasn't hard to believe, as I had been on my way there once or twice already.

I didn't want to get worse. That was a big fear of mine. It didn't take much for me to get knocked down. All I had to do was exert myself, and I would be bedridden. I could handle life as long as it was easygoing and stress-free. I couldn't handle stress, I couldn't handle a normal schedule, and I couldn't live like a normal teenager should be able to. Some days, I would feel great. I could do a lot that I wanted, but then I'd be down and out for the next week. I paid dearly for trying to have one good day because it was always followed by a bad week or two. It wasn't possible to function at any level like that. I tried my best to stay positive, seeing how bad it could be made me appreciate the good days I had when I did.

After a couple of IV treatments, I developed scar tissue buildup in a major vein in my left arm. It started in my hand, and it went all the way to my shoulder. The vein became hard and stiff. I could put my fingers on it and feel the rigidity of the tissue that had built up. It hurt like heck just to move my arm. It took almost a good month for my body to break down the buildup and allow me to freely swing my arm around again without feeling like my arm was tearing off. It was just another issue to deal with, and luckily, it only happened once, but once was enough.

It was weird being home while all the people I knew were in school. I missed it, but I didn't at the same time. I was a bit of an insomniac before, but now with the different drugs I was on, the night became my best friend.

Luckily for me, I was not alone. Bedtime used to be eleven or midnight. Now it was one or two in the morning. Lori and Kelsey were right there with me, late night after late night. We leaned on each other like crazy. As bad as the day could have been, the tranquility of a dark, quiet house at night with the company of people who understood the situation balanced out my emotions.

Kelsey had a boyfriend, but she would always want to check in and see how things were going. I felt very lucky that even though she had a special someone in her life, she still gave part of herself to me. She didn't have to. I think with how well we understood each other and could relate to how each other felt, it was needed. Unless you've been through it or something similar, you can't fathom the loneliness, isolation, and difficulty of dealing with a disease that even doctors didn't know much about, especially when you're still just a kid.

Lori was single and an hour ahead, as she was in South Carolina. Sometimes I felt bad because if it was two in the morning, it was actually three o'clock where she was. She was even more of a night owl than I was.

They both had been dealing with Lyme longer than I had been. They both had been able to manage their lives around school better than I could.

I think if I would have gotten sick in fifth grade or the middle of my junior year, things would have been different. Transitioning from grade school to high school and then being hammered with Lyme threw me into a downward spiral that I couldn't correct in time to catch up and recover.

If getting sick happened in fifth grade, I think I would have had more sympathy and understanding and less pressure and expectations put on me. At the same time, if I got nailed with Lyme disease in the middle of my junior year, people would have seen my work ethic, grades, athletic accomplishments, friends, maybe a girlfriend, and they would hopefully have given me the benefit of the doubt. I don't believe I would have been teased by students or picked on by teachers. I don't believe friends would have bailed on me. I believe there would have been more people willing to help versus people who were willing to jump on the bandwagon to take me down and watch me helplessly fail. There's no way to know what could have happened, but I'd like to think

I would have fared better if all this took place at a different time than when it did.

Without the support from Kelsey, Lori, and Sheena online, I didn't have anywhere to escape to. Without Abbie and Rich being friendly to me, I would have had a lot more hate, anger, and rage built-up inside. Having them care and show kindness and compassion toward me when they didn't have to exemplify the good type of people they were.

I had been out of school for a couple of weeks and was feeling back to my normal, not so great, but good enough self. For some reason, I wanted to go back to school, just not back to class. Even amongst the annoying people whom I despised, there were still enough people there who I thought would be nice to see.

Homecoming was on the docket, and the Friday before that weekend, there was always a pep rally. I think part of the reason I liked that atmosphere was because I always pictured myself on the other side of where I was. I was supposed to be the popular kid who was well-received by the crowd. I wanted to be the guy people were high-fiving. I wanted that walking-on-air feeling. Instead, I watched other people be in that moment while I was an onlooker from the stands. It ate at me, no doubt. I also knew I tried my best to keep those dreams alive. It was an internal battle to not be depressed by the situation.

My mood brightened when Abbie came out. She was a cheerleader, and her smile could light up any room. When the cheer squad completed their routine, Abbie saw me in the crowd, smiled, and gave me a little wave. I smiled and waved back. I doubt my reciprocated gesture meant as much to her as hers did to me. I appreciated her kindness. She didn't have to be kind, and that's what made it special.

Holly was also there and in the running for homecoming queen. I hadn't seen her in a few weeks, and we were able to have a small, pleasant chat after the festivities were over. I don't recall if she won that night, but I felt a little win that I got to see and talk to people I liked and who I thought cared about me. That was one of the better moments of my high school career, and I wasn't even enrolled in classes anymore. Go figure!

I saw Holly a few more times when I'd go to her basketball games. She was the only reason I went, as she had always been nice to me. I could not have cared less for the other people in the crowd. There were people there who didn't even know who I was because they hadn't ever really seen me consistently over the past three years. I was just the kid who was there one day and gone the next.

At one of Holly's basketball games, there was this doofus kid who kept trying to bug me. We had a class together the previous year, so I knew who he was, and he thought it was fun to ask stupid questions and try and get a rise out of me. I ignored him as much as I could. I wasn't giving him the time of day. That's how I tried to deal with the negativity surrounding me. He then escalated things by stealing my hat and running off. I was livid. He was a pudgy, slow kid and even though I was sick, I was still fast and strong. I chased after him, and he took off into a small hallway. I quickly pursued him and was on him like a lion attacking its prey. I jumped onto the back of him and tackled him to the ground. I was about to start beating on him as hard as I could, but then I restrained myself. I grabbed my hat, gave him a *don't mess with me again* look, and walked back to the gym.

I knew I had anger and rage inside me. I kept it subdued and under wraps as much as I could, but that encounter made me realize those feelings even more.

I didn't go back to school for any reason for a few months after that. I didn't see the point. It wasn't worth it to me anymore to maybe have a small chance that I'd get to have a fleeting good feeling from seeing someone I liked. Odds were that I'd just get more depressed and feel even lonelier. It was a tough time to be a teenager, and it was only made more difficult because of what I was dealing with. I dealt with a lot of bad feelings that came along for the ride with this crazy disease.

I struggled with deciding to add this next part to the book. I went back and forth a few times on it but ultimately decided that opening up on the subject could help somebody else in a similar situation.

The mental side of things and how the devil can get into your mind and plant seeds of doubt and despair are real. I believe the majority of people who have had their lives chewed up, spit out, and turned upside down have felt the weight of inadequacy pile up. I didn't feel the way I wanted to feel. I didn't look like I thought I should at this point in my life. I couldn't do much of anything without risking permanently disabling myself. I've had too many experiences where I pushed too much and almost paid for it with my life.

I mentioned earlier on in the book how the Columbine massacre was one of the more significant stories that stuck in my mind and impacted me quite a bit when I was younger. It was one of the first bigger news stories I can remember from my childhood. You couldn't turn on the TV and not see coverage about it for weeks. It was an unprecedented event, and it was incredibly shocking that something like that happened in a high school.

I knew about the shooting and most of the details, but it didn't make sense to me at the time. I was only twelve years old when it happened. I was a happy-go-lucky preteen with my whole life ahead of me, full of optimism and hope. People liked me. I had goals, dreams, and aspirations.

How could two kids do that to their classmates?

What happened to them? What caused their minds to steer them into that direction, to take that kind of heinous action and perpetuate it onto people they knew?

It was terrifying that I had something in common with those two kids.

In some weird, sick, twisted way, I could relate to them.

The situations in which we arrived at a similar way of thinking and cognitive ploys were no doubt different. Wanting to have the satisfaction of getting even, plotting revenge, or some sort of vindication against a person or group of people, I felt, was unfortunately similar.

I feel incredibly guilty, sad, and sick to my stomach that I must admit I had thoughts of taking hostile action against people at school. There were some people there I really did not care for. There were many who made me feel inferior, stupid, and isolated.

I contemplated many times how or what I could do to get back at the people who increased or fueled the anger and hatred that was fuming inside me.

That's when the Columbine massacre became relatable.

I was already in and out of the grips of depression and having suicidal thoughts, so the jump to thinking about taking other people out instead of myself wasn't much more of a stretch.

Bullets flying, bombs going off, people running, screaming, and pleading for me to stop the carnage. I thought about how I would do it. How could I pull that off? Could I even get away with it? Would I take myself out before someone else could take me out? When could I do it and where?

My mind was the devil's playground. I've never told anyone I had these thoughts. I kept a lot inside. I've told select people almost everything about me. There wasn't much left that someone wouldn't know. These thoughts, though, I kept under lock and key.

I believe it would have been good to talk with someone about what I was experiencing and thinking. But how do you tell someone that? You don't get much deeper and darker. How would someone respond when you opened that can of worms on them?

I kept it to myself. I kept a lot of feelings and emotions to myself.

Thankfully, those terrible thoughts never even came close to realization.

A formal plan was never mapped out, weapons were never possessed, and materials or supplies to do anything of major consequence were never obtained. I wouldn't have even known where to start. I only had the thoughts.

I knew those thoughts were wrong. I knew those actions wouldn't have solved anything. I knew that because of how I was raised and the biblical Christian views I was taught. That was the biggest reason as to why I would not and could not act.

I had faith in God. It had waned over the course of my sickness, but I still held onto it. It wasn't easy. I wanted so many times to let go and just let the devil use me and my mind for his purposes.

But I couldn't do it. I couldn't lose 100 percent of my faith and hope that God had plans for me. I also couldn't stand the thought of the hurt I could cause to the small group of people I did like at school. Abbie would be traumatized for life. Rich wouldn't be able to figure out what, how, or why. The people I was closest to would forever have questions and doubts about so many things. Abbie's innocent smile was something I did not want to be responsible for removing. She may not realize how much of an angel she was to me until she reads this. God put her in my life so that I could see some light in a dark world. Her kindness toward me, even with the little amount of time we interacted in school, kept me alive.

It doesn't surprise me at all that other people struggle as bad or worse than I have with mental health situations. It's not inconceivable to me that some people can act on the visuals of their minds.

The devil tried to get me. The devil will go after whoever he feels he has a chance to corrupt.

I'm not immune to sin and evil. I really wish the thoughts I had could be erased. However, I know my sins are forgiven because of what Jesus did for me. The amount of sin debt I have accumulated could never be repaid by anything I do. Through Christ alone am I forgiven and have the gift of eternal life in heaven. It's an amazing gift, one that anyone can have.

So, how did those two kids at Columbine kill their fellow students? What made them think the way that they did? The short and easy answer is this: sin and the devil got to them.

The devil is crafty. He's brought down many victims. That's why it's important to stay on guard and watch your step.

A few ways that helped my faith stay strong growing up were when Mom and I would say prayers before I went to bed every night. As a family, we prayed before our meal at dinner. I was taken to church as a kid. I attended a private Christian school. I learned about God and the Bible. With those actions being instilled in me when I was young, the teachings and lessons that I learned ultimately impacted my decision-making and moral compass. I pray that I'll always have that guidance.

Faith and trust in the Lord were difficult for me to have over the coming months and years. Being isolated and away from the things I wanted to be participating in made it worse. It was a constant battle going back and forth between feeling positive to then wanting to jump off a cliff. There were nights where I would spend hours and hours praying and pleading with God to help, to send some sort of sign to let me know I was being watched over.

I had lost my health, my dreams, my friends, and my happiness. The only thing I could really do was hold onto my faith.

My routine would be to get up when I felt like I was ready, have breakfast, play with Sheena dog, chip some golf balls, maybe do something productive like clean the floors, get worn out, take a nap, play video games, have dinner, and then finally get to the late night where I felt the most comfortable. There wasn't much that I could do while I was trying to recover, but I tried to do *something* on a regular basis. I had a difficult time adjusting to operating on two cylinders when I knew I had eight. Some days, it felt like I was on all eight, but then it would be four the next day and then back to two after that. There was no consistency in how I would feel, and that was the most frustrating thing about it. I appreciated the good days because I could have fun and enjoy life a little bit. On the flip side, when I felt bad, which was the majority of the time, I couldn't figure out how I had just felt so good the day before and why I couldn't *stay* feeling good.

In some ways, I felt like God was punishing me for something, but I couldn't figure out what that might be. Every day, it was like being put through the ringer and tested to see how much I could take before I broke. I felt like I broke many, many times, but I always woke up the next day. There were days where I wish I would never wake up. I wanted God to simply take me, to get me out of the misery that I was in.

Misery loves company, though, and without the company that I had on late-night chats online, I don't think I would have made it. Kelsey and Lori became even more important. They were my escape. The understanding we had between each other was priceless. We knew exactly how one another was feeling, and the relief in knowing that I wasn't alone in this struggle was worth its weight in gold. The hours between eleven at night and two or three in the morning were my favorite. That was the only normalcy I felt in my teenage years. I don't know how we could carry on chatting back and forth that long, but we did. My typing skills became advanced, which has been helpful in putting this book together. It would be a mighty struggle if I had to one-finger every key.

The year 2003 came to an end, and 2004 was underway. But a different year brought the same sickness, the same problems, and the same routine. Trips to the doctor happened monthly. I felt I was improving at times simply because I didn't have the stress of school, but I couldn't sustain or put together multiple days in a row where I felt I could operate at a high level.

It had been about four months since I had been in school for actual studies. I kept in touch with Rich the most. He came online one night and said he had some bad news. A guy who was on the wrestling team had passed away. His name was Chris, but everyone called him Jags because of his last name, Jagodzinski. I didn't know him that well. I didn't know *anybody* that well from high school, so the fact that I knew who he was shocked me. Matt and PJ knew him as they had coached him on the team. He had already graduated and was in his freshman year of college when he suddenly passed away.

I went back to school for a basketball game and got there as classes were letting out. You could tell the seniors and some of the juniors who knew him were very saddened by the news. I found Rich to try and make sense of what was happening or how Jags had died. He was really a good guy whom a lot of people knew and liked.

In some weird way, I wondered, *If I was the one who had died, would people have even known or cared?* I thought I would have been well-liked and popular in high school. I mentioned before if everything that happened to me would have happened in the middle of my junior year, I think there would have been a lot more support. The timeline with how bad things got and how quickly they did never allowed me to carve out a place in other people's lives to really have them know and care about me.

I felt bad for Jags. I felt bad for myself. In a lot of ways, I wish it had been me and not him who died.

The funeral was that weekend, and I wanted to attend. Matt and his wife Jenny were there too. We sat next to each other in the pew at church. I couldn't believe how many cars and people were there to pay their final respects. The church was full. You could feel everyone's sadness. Jags impacted a lot of people in his shortened life, and people seemed to have a hard time coming to terms with why he was taken so soon.

The service started, and underneath the pastor talking, you could hear muffled sounds of people crying. I was holding up just fine, wondering why things happen the way they do. Why did God take Jags when He did? I couldn't understand it. I just tried to remember that God was in control and that I may never fully understand why things happen the way they do.

About halfway through the service, I felt my heart rate start to get higher and higher. Out of the blue, my face and hands began to get tingly and numb. My breathing was labored, and I was starting to feel lightheaded. I sat there for a few minutes, trying to get myself under control. I started to shake internally, twitch externally, and felt like I might pass out.

I had nowhere to go. I was in the middle of a church pew with people packed in on my left and right. It was a Lyme attack. My nerves felt like they were being fried, and my eyes started to water. I *had* to get out of there. It felt like I was in my last biology class again, where I just got up and walked out to go have a breakdown. I couldn't fall apart in the church. I did not want to make a scene and disrupt the service and have people be concerned about me. I wasn't going to be a distraction. I sucked it up, but I couldn't sit there any longer. I composed myself as best as I could, got up, and quickly pushed my way to the left and into the back of the church.

I got to an area where no one was, collapsed to the floor, and began shaking. I was numb all over as tears rolled down my face. I was extremely tired and wanted to fall over and die. I could not control anything. I relate it to being extremely drunk.

After a while, I slowly started to relax and calm down. The service had ended, and people were coming by. No one really knew who I was. Matt found me and came to check on me. He had seen me fall apart a few times on the wrestling mat, but I don't know if he really knew what I went through at the time. He just knew I wasn't doing well. He helped me to my feet, and we proceeded to a cafeteria where there was some food and drinks.

I remember being uncomfortably hungry after my body was finished being ravaged and tortured. A bite to eat was definitely needed to refuel. I started getting back to a more normal state, well, as normal as I had been, which wasn't that great.

As I was finishing up a drink, I saw a familiar face approach me. Holly was walking toward me. I recognized her smile right away. She was bubbly and bright, the type of girl who was easy to like. It made me feel good that she came up to say hi and see how things were going. We hadn't seen each other in a few months, and I could tell she wasn't expecting that I would be there. She was thrilled to see me but concerned at the same time because I wasn't at school anymore.

I told her the truth, that things had been quite rough, and I had just gotten through recovering from a Lyme attack. She didn't really understand much of what I was saying, but I could tell she was empathetic to what I was going through. She felt bad I couldn't return to school this year, and I had to tell her that I didn't think I would be coming back ever again. As we were about to part ways, she gave me her number so that I could call her up if I wanted to talk about stuff. I was shocked. I had never gotten a girl's number before. I wasn't even trying. I didn't take it as a sign that she wanted to date or go out. I took it that she was a nice person who cared about me. Besides, I had already asked her if she wanted to go out and got declined. There was nothing that made me believe she was being anything more than friendly.

A few days later, I gave Holly a call. I have no recollection of what we talked about, but somehow, it was decided that she would come pick me up, and we'd go out for dinner.

It was surreal when she showed up in her little Toyota Camry. I had always imagined having friends over from high school to hang out, party, swim, and so on. Unfortunately, she was the only friend who was a girl from high school who was ever at my house. I was happy she was there but sad at the same time when I thought about all the missed social experiences I thought I was going to have.

I gave her a quick tour of the house, and she was enamored to see the indoor pool (most people are). After a little chitchat, we loaded into her car to go to a local restaurant.

The ride there was unique. It was the first time I was alone in a car with a girl. I remember thinking how good it felt to be with someone of the opposite gender to go and do something together with. I felt very lucky, and I appreciated that she took time out of her life to spend a little time in mine.

I didn't know what to order at the restaurant. It wasn't anything fancy, just a small buffet-style place. I settled on the spaghetti, but it wasn't as good as Mom made it. I wasn't really there to eat, though. I was there to talk to Holly, and she was there to talk to me.

I wasn't used to face-to-face talking with someone for any length of time. I was used to typing and really being able to think about what I would say before I would say it. It wasn't long into our meal and conversation that my hands and face started to tingle and go numb. When your face is numb, it's harder to speak. My speech became mumbled and stuttered. It was embarrassing, but I got through it. I realized that connecting with her about what I had been experiencing was next to impossible. She wasn't Lori or Kelsey. To no fault of her own, she couldn't relate. My whole life the past couple of years had been about sickness and not knowing what I was sick with. There wasn't much more I could talk about. Bless Holly's heart that she even tried to understand. I was relieved that she drove because I was dizzy and shaky after dinner was through. I may have looked fine on the outside, but on the inside, I was trying to control a demon of a disease from ravaging through my body. I did not want to have a breakdown in front of her. I didn't want her to worry about me. I wanted her to like me for who I was and not the sorry, sick person who was in front of her.

We got back to my house, and she gave me a hug and wished me luck on getting better. I was hoping she could have stayed around a little while longer, but she was headed to her job, and I didn't want to make her late. As she drove away, I waved goodbye. I knew my life would have been so much better if I wasn't sick. I couldn't help the way I felt. I wished I could just wake up and it would all be a bad dream, but that wasn't happening. All I wanted after that was to get back into my comfort zone with the girls online I knew I could say anything to. With them, I didn't have to worry about being misunderstood or unrelatable.

The next few months were filled with a bunch of the same. It was back and forth to the doctor every few weeks. No school, less stress, and flip-flopping between happy and depressed. At times, I was content to just sit back and watch my life go by. There wasn't much that I could do about it. I needed to heal, but I also needed to figure out how I was going to get out of the mess I was in. Online learning would have been helpful during this time period, but the internet was still new and *very* slow. If you wanted to watch an hour-long presentation, it would have taken five hours just to get through all the loading and buffering. I know I could have found some time in there to learn something if it was available. I do remember printing off some information about how a car engine works, but that never got me very far.

My eighteenth birthday was fast approaching. I was coming up on four years of dealing with Lyme disease and all the mess that came with it. I couldn't help but think how fast the time went, even with how slow it felt with the four walls of my room constantly surrounding and closing in on me.

Instead of having mostly awful days, I was starting to have a fair balance between good and bad. I would have mini-Lyme attacks quite often. I tried very hard to not let those consume me. I still got stabbing pains in my chest. My back and neck would go out far more often than they should. I don't think I really realized it at the time, but progress was being made. When my birthday arrived, I made a goal for myself, which was to improve in some way every single year from now on. I was hoping it was a goal I could somehow accomplish, but with my recent history of failures and disappointments, it wasn't going to be easy.

An interesting opportunity came about. The nutritional products that had helped me also had a business behind them. Now that I was officially an "adult," though I didn't feel like one, I could start my own business. I thought selling supplements I believed in would be something I could do. I had a very good testimonial on how the products benefited me, and I knew they could help other people if they gave them a chance.

I started attending some local meetings and trainings to figure out different things I could do. I was excited I could potentially make some nice money while helping people live better lives. In a way, I thought that maybe this was the reason I went through what I had up until this point. I don't think I ever would have come across this option otherwise. To help people and make money, all I had to do was share my story.

I did that. I did it a lot. I thought what I was doing was the best thing since sliced bread. I felt optimism that I hadn't in a long time. I had everything that I needed to get going. I had a sales receipt pad, a business calendar, and business cards, the whole nine yards. I was learning what I could about the products I was using, and it made so much sense to me why I had gotten the results I did. I was getting good stuff into my system and giving my body a lot of what it needed to fight off what it could. I honestly think I would have died at some point if I hadn't been on what I was. I had a very high belief factor in what I was trying to help people with.

My mom was on board and was one of my first customers. She knew me better than anyone at that point when it came to my health, and she saw the difference it made.

It was definitely more difficult than I thought to get other people I knew to get started on the supplements, but I wasn't discouraged. I knew I was going to make a positive impact on people.

One of the first bigger chances I had to share what I had with people was at a Lyme support group that took place at Dr. B's office. I brought some products with me, as I figured I'd have a few people who wanted to begin a supplement program. There were probably ten or so people at the meeting. I knew a lot of these people were not feeling well. I could just see it. Introductions were made around the room, and people shared a little bit about their stories with how they had dealt with Lyme. There was a need in the room that I thought I could fill. I was probably the healthiest one there, and I was thrilled when I got to share one of the ways that I felt that I had gotten better.

I felt very comfortable explaining things I had gone through and how I felt because everyone could relate. The people there were nodding their heads in agreement when I would say that I went through this and that. I felt I was connecting very well with everyone in the room. I got to the point of sharing with them what I used to help improve my health and saw a lot of their faces light up. It was like I was in possession of a magic potion, and they all wanted to know what it was. They asked, "How do I get the supplements?" I replied, "Well, I have some in my car if you want to try them out."

Then it turned to, "Well, how much are they?" I let them know what the cost was. I thought I would sell out all the stuff that I had and I would have to ship the rest to people. Unfortunately, since the price wasn't dirt cheap, people immediately clammed up. I knew the products weren't "cheap," but they were worth it. I tried to explain it costs less than a dollar a day to have very beneficial nutrients getting into their bloodstream quickly and effectively. It didn't seem to matter, though. No one wanted to try them. No one wanted to invest in their health. I was thoroughly confused and dejected.

As we were wrapping up, one lady did come up to me and asked if she could buy some products from me. I lit up like fireworks on the Fourth of July. I said, "Of course, I'd be happy to help!" She wrote me a check, and I gave her the product. It was my first real sale. I was floored that I had a chance to help someone, and hopefully they would have great results like I did. I couldn't wait to hear how this person was doing in a couple of weeks.

I gathered my things and was about to head back home when the lady who hosted the meeting wanted to talk to me. She worked in the office, and I liked her a lot, so I thought that my second sale of the night was coming.

She had a disgruntled look on her face. I knew something was on her mind, but I couldn't imagine what it could be. She said, "I'm glad you came to share your story and experience, but next time, please don't bring up the products you're using. This is a support group, not a place to *sell* people stuff."

I was caught off guard and felt sucker punched. I said, "What do you mean?" She repeated, "Please refrain from trying to sell to people. It's not the place for it." I nodded like I understood and said, "Okay, not a problem."

I heard her point, but I didn't like it. I wasn't trying to "sell" anybody anything. I was trying to "help" with how I had been helped. I thought the purpose of a support group was to share with other people your experiences and things you have found to deal with your sickness. If someone else had brought up something they felt benefited them, I would have gladly listened. I would have welcomed people's success stories. We were all going through the same thing, and we were all looking for ways to improve. What was I supposed to do: just sit there and complain about how life sucks and have a pity party? I wanted to get better. I wanted my life back. If I could, I wanted to help others get their lives back. That was what I wanted to do. I never said I had all the answers. I just knew what had worked for me.

The support group fell apart quickly after that initial one. I followed up with the person who bought from me initially, and she said she used it for a few days and didn't feel anything, so she stopped using it. I told her that's not how it's supposed to work. You have to give it an honest try for a few weeks or a month at the minimum. I never heard anything more from her. It was disappointing. I thought I could really help someone out, but it was as if she were searching for a magic potion that you take one time and you're cured. I never gave that impression, or at least I hope I never did. You have to make positive changes and keep at those things that are beneficial for the rest of your life. I really wish there was something you could do once and be better, but that's a pipe dream. The only way to make improvements stick is to be disciplined and consistent over the long haul.

I was rather bummed out that I was experiencing negativity and pushback so quickly over trying to help people. I kept at it, though.

I wanted to help the Lyme community, I talked with so many people about my experiences and how I had found a few things that had helped me. I thought for sure I could help someone out there. No matter what I did or said, though, no one cared. Even people I was close with who had Lyme couldn't be convinced to give the supplements a try. I didn't have the money to spare, but I got to the point where I would give some away for people to try. Still, nothing was working. I knew people who were sick with Lyme for ten to twenty years longer than I had been and were still struggling. It was like pulling teeth for anyone to give me or what I had to offer a chance.

All I wanted to do was help. It's all I could do at that point. I was accused of just trying to sell people "snake oil" many times. I wasn't in a good state of mind to be able to handle this much rejection and disappointment after all the letdowns I had already had to deal with. I knew my heart was in the right place, and that almost made it worse. I thought I had found something I could do to make a beneficial impact in the world, but the only impact it was having was making me more and more depressed.

Summer was coming to an end, which meant school would be starting soon. It was supposed to be my senior year. I gave it some thought about attempting to go back. I wasn't feeling bad, but I also knew that I didn't have the stamina to hold up for a full year. It was an easy decision to just let school finally not be an option. It wasn't worth it anymore. There was no way I was going to put myself through the torture I had before. The harder I tried, the worse things got for me. It made more sense to try and do things at my own pace and work my way back somehow. I didn't know what I was going to do. I just knew my high school career was officially over. If it wasn't for a few good people I had met there, the last three years would have been even more depressing.

The goals I had set and that I was determined to make happen never came to fruition. The dreams and accomplishments I thought I would obtain would not be realized. I was pushed further and further off the pedestal that I thought I had a solid leg upon.

I felt adrift in the expanse of the ocean. I was at the mercy of the water and the waves.

HOW LOW CAN YOU GO?

I wish I could have all my lost time back. I had a lot of time on my hands. I wasn't in school. I wasn't working. I had no plans of doing either one.

I still wanted to help people with supplements. I would go through phases of thinking I was making traction and being able to make it work to then feeling like a worthless pile of garbage. I started to half figure out why I couldn't get anything going with business, which was because I was a nobody. I had no previous selling skills, no degree behind what I was talking about, and certainly no plethora of connections who trusted me or my opinion. I stayed on that vicious cycle of ups and downs for a long time. At that point, it was my only option that I felt I could enjoy and be successful at. The more I failed, the more depressed I became. I'm sure people could start to see how downtrodden I was, which isn't the most idealistic quality to portray when trying to be a difference-maker.

My eighteenth year of life was not off to a good start. I tried to make it better. Lori became more prominent in my life. She became my crutch I could lean on. We talked just about every day online. When it was just her and me talking, nothing else mattered. I could share with her my thoughts, feelings, failures, and shortcomings. And she stayed connected with me no matter what. She was fantastic to have in my life. I just wished she lived closer.

I missed having personal contact. I missed seeing the very few friends that I had. I missed seeing Abbie, but her life went on without me, and I'm sure she could handle the fact that I wasn't around. I wondered if she thought about how I was doing or what I was up to.

Holly and I at least had some recent in-person contact, and we'd say hi on AIM from time to time. I looked in the student directory to see where she lived. I thought that if I was in the area, I could stop by and say hi. I saw people do that kind of stuff all the time on TV, and I didn't have any other good ideas of how to connect with people, so I waited until I had the opportunity to try that method out.

A couple of weeks later, I was coming back from a meeting with a rare customer, and I knew I'd be driving by Holly's house. I didn't see any harm in stopping by and saying hi, so I did. I saw her dad outside mowing the lawn as I pulled up. I got out of the car and asked if Holly was home. He said, "She's inside. Go ahead and knock on the door." Her mom answered, and I introduced myself. She remembered who I was, as I had met her before. A moment later, Holly came down. She was surprised to see me and asked what I was doing there. I said, "I was in the area, and I thought I'd stop by to say hi since I hadn't seen you in a while." She looked a little confused or rushed and replied, "Hey, it's good to see you, but I have to leave for work in a few minutes. I'll try and catch up with you later online, okay?" And that was that. I went home. I was happy to see her, and I wished we could have chatted, but I understood she had a life of her own. I didn't expect her to wait on me.

Not too long after that, school was already a couple of weeks in, and I was wondering if anyone cared that I wasn't there. I hesitated back and forth on whether I wanted to show my face there or not. There was a guys' basketball game taking place, and I ultimately decided to go. I wasn't sure who I would see. There were definitely some people I didn't want to see, but I thought if I could run into Abbie, Holly, or Rich, that would give me a little boost.

I got to the parking lot. It was already dark outside and a little cool, but not too bad. I remember looking up at the lit school sign and hearing the noise from the band in the gymnasium and thinking, *Man, this went fast. It wasn't supposed to be like this.* I was already bummed out before I even got into the building. I walked on the path between the walls of the school with my head down. I got inside and decided to make a quick detour to where my locker used to be. I tried the combination, but it had been changed. I walked the halls and visualized the faces of the kids as I made my way around. I went to where Abbie's locker was, and as I got closer to it, I could see her smiling face and her sweet voice saying, "Hi, David, how are you?" Before I went into the gym, I visited the stairwell where I became shattered and broken. I started to get quite emotional remembering everything I endured. It didn't seem fair to me. I felt wronged in so many ways. Having the school to myself with the lights dimmed and the halls quiet felt like I was at a funeral giving my final respects. I knew this part of my life was just about at the finish line. I wasn't going to have the storybook ending that I wanted. This time next year, the kids in my class would be in college and moving forward with their lives. I felt like I was still stuck in freshman year.

To make the drama worse, I made my way to the gym where the game had already started. I didn't even sit in the student section because I wasn't one. I sat by myself as the game was going on. I scanned the crowd and watched as people went in and out. I recognized some, but I had no idea who most of them were.

Halfway through the game, and on the other side of the court in the student section, I saw Holly. She was with her friends, having a good time. I was also seeing what looked like a possible boyfriend she had by her side, so I didn't even bother to say hi. I didn't want to interrupt their good time by coming up to her and bringing everyone down to accommodate the "weird kid."

I started to feel extremely down on myself. I was the outsider. I was the nobody. After seeing and being around the crowd of people I barely knew, and who knew me even less, I realized that I didn't belong there anymore. I left before the game was over. High school was nearly a complete failure. I tried so dang hard to make it work, but it wasn't going to happen no matter what I did.

The drive home, I was trying not to break down, but I was fighting back tears. I didn't care if I made it home that night. I didn't want to make it home. I felt that my life was over and there wasn't anything to live for.

I didn't even go online that night to talk to my usual friends to help sort through things. I was home alone, and I wanted it to be over. There was light rain outside on a gloomy night. I thought about what would happen if I took more than the recommended amount of the drugs I was on. I didn't even hesitate as I popped three or four more times the amount I was prescribed. I went to bed hoping that I wouldn't be awake in the morning.

Unfortunately, but also fortunately, I woke up.

As far as I know, there weren't any adverse side effects of taking as many pills as I did. I was disappointed, but at least the sun was shining, and my dog Sheena was happy I was there to let her out. My mind was a little clearer. Sometimes a little sleep and waking up can give one a better perspective. I wasn't giddy and upbeat by any means, but at least I wasn't too far down in the mental sewer.

A few days later, I was online talking with my usual friends when I saw Holly sign on. I waited a few minutes to see if she would stay online before I said hi. I don't remember exactly what was said, but I got shut down fast. I have no way of knowing, but the person who typed back to me said he was her boyfriend. He stated that I was "freaking her out" because I showed up at her house, and then I "stalked" her at the basketball game the other night. He told me to stay away and not contact her anymore. I quickly tried to apologize and explain I was in no way stalking her or that I had any intention of making her feel uncomfortable.

It didn't matter what I tried to say. Holly was gone, just like that.

I don't know if it was really her boyfriend or if it was her pretending to be, but either way, I got the hint that any friendship we had was over.

I was shocked, disappointed, and crushed. However, I wasn't surprised. I wasn't surprised that another letdown just occurred. I thought I had a friend in real life. I didn't think I did anything wrong or overstepped any line. I just wanted to have one friendship work in real life. I didn't think that was too much to ask. I honestly believe Holly cared about me, but my circumstances made her uncomfortable, and she didn't know how to handle that. It was easier for her to walk away than to try and understand. I don't blame her. I was messed up, but it hurt. There was nothing I could do.

It was becoming all too common to absorb letdowns and disappointments. I kept a lot inside. Thankfully, Lori was there to lean on that night. Without her, I think I would have spiraled down the drain again.

Tick, tick, tick, tick. The seconds of the day would go by slowly. I had the house to myself a lot of the times, as Mom and Dad were working at various shows around the Midwest. I helped Mom get things prepared for their excursions. It was interesting when they were gone. I could do whatever I wanted. I could have had parties on top of parties. I could have been doing all sorts of things to get in trouble, but I didn't. For one thing, I didn't have any friends who would want to come over. For another, I wouldn't even know what to do or get to cause any sort of mischief. I always tried to make sure the house was cleaned up before they got home. It was the least I could do, and I know Mom appreciated it. I really didn't get lonely because I had my dog Sheena there with me. I started letting her sleep in my room with me. She was a great companion to have around. Having her to take care of helped to keep me halfway responsible with my actions.

Dad belonged to the local fitness club, and Mom was able to sign me up at a discounted rate. Since I wasn't in school, I figured I could try and ease myself back into some sort of shape. I didn't have to worry nearly as much about overexerting myself, as I didn't have any other responsibilities. I could rest and recover as much as I needed to.

I had an initial consultation with a personal trainer to help me get set up and familiarized with the different machines. Dory was her name, and I instantly liked her. She had short blonde hair and was in really good shape. I didn't know what her age was, but I knew she was older than me. Her personality was easy to get along with, and I felt very comfortable going over things with her. She had me do some sort of fitness test on a stationary bike. I was feeling good that day, so I didn't have any issues pedaling through the progressions. She took my blood pressure and monitored my heart rate. I was wishing the nurses I had could be as cute and nice as she was. I really took a liking to Dory. I would see her every time I went to the gym. I made sure to figure out her schedule so that I would be there when she was. I didn't make it into the gym on a very consistent basis the first few years, but Dory would be a constant, important factor to me as I moved forward.

I couldn't find a whole lot of positive consistency, and I was still more down in the dumps during the day versus at night. I didn't drive to too many places. I mostly stayed at home. I would chip golf balls, watch sports, play video games, play pool and darts against myself, or just daydream. I didn't love my situation, but I didn't hate it. I just sort of drifted through those days and let them take me where they would.

The medications I was on definitely contributed to my ups and downs. Some of the drugs helped more than others. I didn't like taking them, especially when they would leave a bad aftertaste or suppressed my appetite.

I still dealt with the piercing pain in my heart area that would drop me to the floor when one of those zingers hit me. My back and neck would go out more often than they should. I would be laid up for a week or two at a time if a really bad one came upon me.

I was living life as easy as I could, but I was still having problems physically and mentally as well as spiritually.

There were many talks with God, asking Him to help me figure out what I should be doing and to send some sort of sign.

I remembered a part in the Bible where Jesus prayed so intensely that His sweat turned to blood. I felt I was at that point after what seemed to be an hourlong back-and-forth marathon of prayer and Bible reading. My mind and soul were at odds with each other, trying to find some reasoning for how I got into this position in my life. I was perusing random verses to find *something* to help me make sense of it all.

I was also playing with a hunting knife in my hand. I would open and close it, twirl it around between my fingers. I was in pain, but I thought if I caused new pain that I could forget the old. I was angry. I was frustrated. I felt trapped with no way out. I took the knife and plunged it into the Bible. It barely got through the hard cover. I then did it again and again and again. I was beyond consoling at that point. I didn't care about myself. I ended up running the knife across my wrist and watched the blood pour out. I lifted up my arm as the blood drained to my elbow, then let the blood drip onto the cover of the Bible I'd just punctured.

I remembered then that after Jesus bled from praying all night, He knew He was on His way to be innocently crucified to pay for everyone's sins, even though we didn't deserve it.

I felt a little glimmer of hope and comfort.

In a way, I felt like I was just an innocent kid, at no fault of my own, who had this immense burden thrown at me. This curse of Lyme I was saddled with was no doubt terrible, but the duty that Jesus had of suffering and dying innocently for people who despised Him was beyond comprehension. The love and mercy God had for me and everyone was starting to come into view.

"For by grace are ye saved through faith; and that not of yourselves: it is the gift of God: not of works, lest any man should boast." That verse from Ephesians 2:8–9 hit home. I couldn't get into heaven because of anything I had done. The only reason I have forgiveness and a place in heaven is because of what Jesus did for me. I began to accept that fully and understand that on my own, I was nothing. In the beginning of this book, I wrote about Job and the experiences he went through, and it all started making sense.

My battle with the Lord was over. I saw His point. We live in a sinful world, and because of that, bad things happen to good people. Good things also happen to bad people. Life isn't fair. Life is tough. Life is scary. Life is a constant battle. I didn't have it all figured out, but I knew I had God on my side. That was the little glimmer of hope that I needed. No matter how bad it got, even if I died (which I still wanted to many times after), I knew I'd be in heaven. The fight would be worth it in the end. I would rather struggle my whole life and have the gift of heaven than get everything I want in this world and forfeit my seat at the table in heaven. I always had faith, but I understood it a lot more now.

It was the start of the humbling process. I hated it. It was still difficult to understand, and I don't know if I'll ever fully have the cognitive comprehension to figure it out. I knew one thing, though, that God was on my side, and that was a great feeling.

Being at home, the time seemed to go by slowly. Out in the real world, it was flying by. I was now turning nineteen, which meant I should be ending my senior year and graduating from high school. That wasn't happening for me, but it was for everybody else.

I had no major reason to attend the graduation ceremony. I didn't qualify to be there. If I went, would anyone even care that I was there? With being away from school for a whole year, I was out of everyone's mind. People almost forgot about me when I was gone for a couple of months, so with a whole school year going by, I was confident I wasn't going to be very popular.

I went anyway. I thought maybe I could get some closure. I liken it to attending a funeral again. It doesn't feel like the end is really happening unless you see it end with your own eyes.

I remember it being a really nice day outside. I found a place to park and made my way into the building. One of the first people I ran into who I recognized was the teacher I despised the most. I was expecting some sort of snarky remark like I would get when I was in class. I could feel my blood pressure rising. To my surprise, he was warm and friendly and said that it was good to see me. I was a little taken aback, as I wasn't expecting that at all. I think he realized the crap I was going through was real, and he genuinely felt bad about my situation. It was nice to have a little peace with him so that I didn't have to carry a negative viewpoint anymore of our past encounters. The white flag was raised, and I felt a lot more positive about him personally.

At the very least, showing up did some good. I wasn't sure how the rest of the day would go.

With the ceremony about to start, I made my way into the bleachers of the gym. I was by myself, so I didn't have anyone to sit by. I climbed to the top of the seats and found a spot that wasn't too crowded. I didn't recognize anyone.

Music started playing, and all the students who were or should have been my classmates walked in. It was hard to tell who was who because everyone had a blue cap and gown on. It started to sink in that this part of my life was over. It went by fast, and I felt a little sick over it. I couldn't help but think I should be down there enjoying this day to the fullest.

There were some speakers who got up to say a few words, words of encouragement, words of brightness about the future, and taking the opportunities in front of you the best that you can. That's how I felt four years ago when I started high school. All the people in blue down below me were headed to different lives. I was the lost kid in the bleachers with a very bleak outlook for the future.

It was time for everyone to get their diplomas. As names were called, I didn't know very many of them. Once the announcer got into the B last names, I started to get a little anxious. Maybe my name would be called? Maybe it was all just a bad dream? I had quite a few thoughts go through my head.

What really hit me hard was that my last name was directly in front of Abbie's last name if you go in alphabetical order. It only showed up once in the freshman school directory. The directories after that never had me listed in the same class as her. If I would have been graduating, we would have been right next to each other: me and Abbie. The one girl from my crazy high school experience I really liked and felt I had a good connection with. We would have been next to each other. The odds that she was the one girl from class I always looked forward to seeing, who was friendly to me when she saw me, that gave me hope. The odds we would have been next to each other was crazy to me. I got a little emotional when I heard her name called and saw her walk across the stage. She was my angel. I thanked the Lord for her and asked Him to watch over her for me.

My name wasn't called before hers like it could have been. My name was left out. I didn't graduate. It wasn't because I didn't try. I knew I tried the best I could, but sometimes things happen, and we don't understand why.

I heard a few other names called of people I knew. It was great hearing Rich's name called. I was happy for him, but I didn't even know who the majority of the kids were anymore.

With it being so nice outside, everyone gathered in the common area of the campus. Families were coming together to give hugs and congratulations. Friends were high-fiving, smiling, and having a good time. There were a few tears that I saw, tears of happiness and sadness because a lot of the kids knew they may not see the friends they had ever again. I wasn't naïve to the notion that friends you meet in school will always be your friends. Coming from grade school to high school, friends I had didn't always stick. I knew it wasn't going to be any different now. I knew a lot of the faces I saw that day I would never see again.

I looked around to see who I could see. I found Rich and stopped by to say hi. Rich was the only guy I really considered a true friend. I had a feeling that our friendship would stick around for a while. He was going to college not too far away, so we had a better chance of hanging out in the future.

I then saw Abbie from a distance, surrounded by friends and family. I didn't want to barge in and take that time away from people who knew her more than I did. Of course, I wanted to go over and chat for a while, but it didn't seem like a good time to do so. I was also very hesitant because I didn't want to seem like a stalker or creeper like I had been accused of before by Holly and mess up another friendship. The thought of that happening with her terrified me. I was content to just let it be. If we were meant to stay in each other's lives in the future, then we would be.

People started to clear out, so I figured I would too. As I was heading back to my car, I saw Abbie walking in the same direction as I was. When she looked my way, I waved to her. She saw me, smiled, and waved back. How we first met felt very similar to how we said goodbye. She impacted my life for the better and brightened my world. I'm glad I met her. I wished we could have had more time together. She was going to do just fine without me, and I was going to have to be okay with the memory of her kindness, warmth, and smile. There was no turning back the clock, no going back in time. High school was over.

CHAPTER 9

HEADING SOUTH

The summer of 2005 had begun. I wasn't a freshly graduated high school student. I wasn't on my way to any college. I existed, and that was about it. I felt like the world was flying by at a thousand miles per hour, and I was in the slow lane, getting passed by everyone and everything. I wasn't depressed, but I was depressed at the same time. My health was better, and I felt stress-free, but the mental side was eating at me. I didn't know what I was supposed to do. I had spurts where I would feel productive, then I would crash and burn and be bedridden. I wasn't living and progressing. I was stuck in the mud and slowly decaying.

Lori kept me afloat. We chatted all night, every night. Kelsey was still a big part of my life, but we didn't talk nearly as much as she had a boyfriend to keep her more occupied. Sheena and I would still talk on occasion, too. She was in college already, so her studies and friends took up most of her time.

Having Lori to communicate with was a huge lifeline for me. She understood the feelings and different varying symptoms of dealing with chronic Lyme disease. We were both sick with the same disease. We both had days where everything was just fine, and then we'd have days where we felt hit by a truck.

Honestly, I don't know what we always found to talk about on a nightly basis, but getting to know her more everyday always gave me a good feeling. We both needed and craved that.

I really started to love Lori simply because she meant a lot to me. There wasn't a lot we didn't know about each other after chatting for three years. It was incredibly easy to talk to her. If I went out of town for a few days and didn't have internet access, I couldn't wait to get back to talk to her and see how she was doing. A bad day was always made better because of our relationship.

I began wondering what it would be like to hear her voice on the phone. I started figuring out how far it was from Wisconsin to South Carolina. I wondered what it would be like to meet her. I wondered a lot, and I think she did too.

Our conversations started getting more emotional. We said things like, "I'm glad you're in my life" or "I don't know what I would do without you." The familiarity was there, and the feelings were starting to intensify. It was obvious to me that we liked each other and cared deeply for one another. At the same time, having never met and being a thousand miles away, it was crazy that we were at that point. Something had to give.

In July of that year, my brother Mark and his wife, Lisa, were heading on vacation somewhere and wanted me to house-sit their place while they were gone. I, for sure, didn't have a whole lot going on, and a week or two of just doing whatever was fine with me. I could watch movies, play video games, and, most importantly, I could chat with Lori.

It was just the house and me. It was rather nice. If I was tired, I could sleep. If I wanted to go somewhere, I didn't have to worry about telling anyone where I was going. Being nineteen, I probably could have gone to different places and done many different things, but I didn't. I kept it simple. I didn't feel like I was nineteen and an adult. I still felt like a little kid in many ways. The grocery store was the craziest place I went to. I drove around town for the fun of it. More often than not, though, I was just hanging out at the house.

I felt very free in my conversations with Lori. I didn't have to worry about anyone interrupting our conversations or looking over my shoulder to eavesdrop on what we were talking about. After a few days, the feelings were getting more and more intense. I knew I really liked her, and I was sure she liked me too; otherwise, why would we have been keeping up this routine for so long?

We both were starting to gush over each other a little more, and neither one of us backed down from it. It was a natural progression of a relationship, albeit a long distance one, but it all felt right.

One night, we were chatting like we always did, but it got to the point where I felt like she wanted to take a step forward, and I did as well. Hesitancy ensued. After some back and forth, I just went for it and asked her if she thought or wanted to take a step further with our relationship. I honestly didn't know what that step was going to be. I just knew I wanted her to be more involved in my life.

Her answer wasn't exactly what I wanted to hear. She admitted she had feelings deeper than she was letting on but wasn't sure if it was a good idea to take it that far.

I started to feel like a noose was wrapped around my neck, and someone had kicked the chair out from underneath my feet. I was hanging high and dry, gasping for air.

I felt my heart start to race and a deep panic rushing through my veins. I started thinking the worst, which was losing Lori completely. I thought that maybe I'd just made a huge mistake. I had lost lesser "friends" I knew I would be okay without. I didn't know what I would do if I didn't have her. She was my lifeline.

The thought of not having her in my life was like a dark cloud swallowing the little warmth of light I had burning.

I went from being on my high horse to being bucked off and buried in the dirt. I didn't know where to turn. My world was crashing down.

I didn't want to know what life was like the next day.

An internal demon took over as I grabbed my antibiotics and some vodka from the shelf and did my best to make sure I wasn't going to come back.

I started out slowly. I didn't like the taste, but after a few swigs, it went down easier. Each shot I would take was coupled with a pill. It didn't take long until the room was going in circles.

I could see and hear Lori sending messages, but I started to not respond. I was becoming numb and dizzy. I was getting warm and lightheaded. The feeling of nothing was euphoric as I managed to ingest more of the toxins into my system.

It got to the point where I felt like I was floating. I got up out of the chair, and the whole room was spinning in circles. I didn't know where I was or what was happening anymore.

My body succumbed, and I collapsed to the floor.

I was out cold. My body shut down. It was over.

It was the deepest sleep I had ever been in. I didn't move or change position on the floor. I woke up face down at the bottom of the steps that I had apparently tried to walk up. The sun was up, and I heard birds chirping. It was an extremely peaceful morning. As I lay there wondering where I was and what the heck happened, I felt a calmness overtaking me. It felt like I was being held and told that it was going to be all right.

It was a short-lived moment. As soon as I started to move, so did my stomach. Adrenaline shot through my body as I bounded up the stairs into the bathroom, opened the toilet seat, and spewed my guts out. It was a constant wave of gag reflexes that had me begging for mercy.

Once I got all the toxic soup out of my system, I was feeling better.

And then the thought of how Lori was doing came over me. *What had she said last night? Is she worried about me? Is she gone forever? What are we? Are we anything?*

I was nervous as could be when I went back to the computer to see if she had left any messages.

She did. She was very concerned and worried after I stopped responding. She said she had been holding back so many emotions and just wanted to hear from me, to know that I was okay.

I was relieved she still wanted to speak to me. I replied to her that I had a rough time with the thought of losing her. I at least wanted her friendship. I needed her in my life.

She needed me, too. She didn't like the thought of losing me.

The messed-up, crazy night turned into a day of beauty. Both of us were feeling a deep connection that we wanted to explore more. I, for one, was extremely thankful that I didn't lose Lori the night before. We made plans to actually *call* each other on the phone that night versus chatting on the computer.

It felt like a first date of sorts. The deal was that I would call her after nine o'clock to get the ball rolling, and then she would call me back because I had free incoming calls, and she had free nights and weekends. (Side note: We didn't have unlimited calling back then. We had to figure out how to best use the service plans we had.)

I was more excited than nervous to hear her voice. There wasn't a whole lot to worry about because we already liked each other, so I figured once we got talking, it would feel like we had been doing it forever.

And that's exactly what happened.

I dialed her number, and it rang twice before she picked up. Her voice was sweet, and she had a cute laugh with a little bit of a Southern accent, which I really liked. She thought I had a Northern accent, which I'm not sure what that sounds like, but at least she didn't hang up on me over it.

We talked for a couple of hours that night, and I couldn't imagine anything better in that moment. I could feel her smiling through the phone, and you couldn't get me to stop smiling as our conversation carried on into the early morning hours. The joy we both felt that night was out of this world. I had someone who cared about me, who could understand me without fear of being alone with my thoughts.

We didn't have to use AIM that much anymore. We upgraded to the cellphone and actual voice conversation. I liked it, and so did she. We kept it quiet between us in the beginning. It was like we had a little burning ember in a pile of tinder that was just beginning to smoke. We wanted to let that little ember grow into a nice, little fire before we started to let people in on what was going on. Having Lyme disease brought us together. It felt like a magic carpet ride that we had found each other.

Lori was about to start college, but we always found time to talk. I wasn't doing much of anything except trying to feel better, which I was. Without the stress of school or work, my body could rest and heal. Physically, I felt 50 percent better, not great, but not bad. Mentally and emotionally, I had improved significantly, and I owe that to having Lori as a constant part of my life now.

We kept things going strong after a few months, and thoughts of how and when we could meet in person were in the works.

She let her parents in on who I was and our plans, and to my surprise, they were excited to meet me.

It was my turn to let my parents know the situation. Mom half-knew about Lori already and that she was someone I talked to a lot. She could also see the phone bill with countless calls to and from South Carolina. That part was hard to hide since Mom paid the bill.

I let Mom know that Lori and I were interested in seeing each other. I showed a picture to Mom of what she looked like, and to my surprise, Mom thought that would be a doable thing.

I expected pushback from either Lori's parents or mine, but there was none. I think both parents saw what we had gone through and wanted us to experience some happiness for once.

So, there we were, excited and filled with anticipation of how, when, and where we would meet. We planned things around Lori's schedule. I was free to meet anytime, but with her being in school, we needed to wait for her classes to be on a break.

We settled on a week visit after Christmas. I was going to take a plane ride into Charlotte, and she'd pick me up there and then drive us back to South Carolina. Charlotte was the closest and cheapest airport to get to, and I figured a good two hours in the car would be a good time to figure out who we really were. I didn't have a ton of money in the bank, but I bought a necklace for Lori if I felt everything was going in a good direction.

Christmas had come and gone, and the new year of 2006 was fast approaching. It had been a cold few weeks, but I was on the verge of heading south, where it was a lot warmer, and to finally meet Lori face to face.

I had to wake up early to get to the airport. There was no direct flight to Charlotte, so the plane had to make a stop in Detroit. As I got to the airport, I started to have some doubts about what I was doing. Mom and Dad helped me to get checked in, then I was all alone figuring out which terminal I needed to be in. It was really starting to sink in that there was no going back now. I knew I was taking a little bit of a risk going to meet a girl I'd never met before. I just hoped she would be there to pick me up.

When you fly to Detroit from Milwaukee, as soon as you reach altitude, you immediately start going down to land. It's a very short flight. I arrived safely and then had to find the next terminal to get to. The Detroit airport was massive. I found where I needed to be and was anticipating how the next few hours were going to change my life.

The flight to Charlotte took a couple of hours. As we were coming in for landing, it was weird seeing green on the ground and not white. It was a different world. Where I just was, it was freezing and snowy, but down south, it was still mild and green. It was a little jolt to the system, but it was one that I didn't mind. I typically would feel better in the warmer air, so I was looking forward to a week where I didn't have to bundle up or worry about clearing snow.

Once I arrived, I knew I was now only a few minutes away from being with Lori. She knew when I was arriving and where to meet me. I found my bags on the carousel and patiently waited in the seating area.

I arrived on Northwest Airlines. I double-checked that I was in their part of the airport and anxiously waited for her to arrive. I was nervous watching people move in and out of the airport. Every time I saw a younger female, I had to figure out if it was

Lori or not. *What if she doesn't look like her pictures? What if she doesn't show up? What if she does show up and immediately turns around after seeing me?* I double-checked the time. It was fifteen minutes after I was supposed to arrive, so I figured I'd see her at any moment.

The baggage area was getting more and more empty as each minute went by. I started to feel alone and concerned that I may have to figure out how to get back home if she didn't show up.

As I was sitting there mulling around what may or may not happen, I saw the sliding doors open up. In walked a girl who appeared to be searching for someone or something. She turned and looked my way, and I instantly knew it was her. She had come to pick me up!

It was a surreal moment walking up to a person I knew more about than anyone else and holding her in my arms for the first time.

We both were a little in shock and weren't sure exactly how to act or how to proceed. She helped me with one of my bags as we walked out of the airport to the parking lot. She had just gotten done driving for a couple of hours, and it was time to turn around and drive back. She drove a white Mitsubishi Outlander. I never knew that beforehand, and I honestly had never heard or seen of that vehicle. She had a South Carolina license plate and a palm tree sticker on the back glass. The rearview mirror had Hawaiian leis draped around it. It was definitely a girl's car, and I couldn't believe I was in it, and she was driving us back to her place. The drive back was an easy one. I couldn't get over how many pine trees there were everywhere.

I sensed that Lori was a little nervous. To be honest, so was I. I didn't know if we were exactly a couple at that moment, but when I put my hand on her leg, she didn't swat it away. We both kind of looked at each other with a little grin. We had done it. After almost four years of knowing each other and having a deep connection, we were together.

I wished that ride could have lasted longer, but it wasn't too long until we were getting into her part of town. She was pointing things out to me as we drove, so I knew her house was getting close.

I would be staying with Lori at her parents' house. I was confident in myself that I could make a good impression and be able to get along with them. In hindsight, though, that's a quick turnaround from meeting the girl and then her parents. I simply had to dive in headfirst.

We made it into her neighborhood, and I was wondering which house was hers. She made a turn to the left and said, "This is it." She pulled into the gravel driveway and put the Outlander into park. We sat there for a few minutes, going over what it may be like once we get inside. Our relationship had just started, and we were about to learn a whole lot about each other real fast once we got inside the house.

We shared a nice, calm moment before we got out. She said she was glad I came, and I thanked her for being there to pick me up. We looked at each other for a moment and wound up having a nice, little kiss. I started to feel like the right decision had been made. I felt ready to take on the next challenge of meeting her family.

It was a nice house, a ranch-style on a corner lot. There was a door connected to the garage, and once you were inside, you had to go up three steps to get into the kitchen. I met her dad first. He welcomed me in with a big handshake and smile. He had a strong Southern accent and seemed like a nice guy with a fun personality. Her mom was next; you could definitely tell from her voice that she was from the South, and I started to learn about Southern hospitality really quick. They both asked how the flight was, if they could get me anything, or if I needed help with my bags. They definitely tried to make a good impression on me as much as I did with them. We were off to a good start.

Any doubts or fears that this excursion would blow up in my face started to fade away. I got my stuff out of the car and into the house. I wasn't exactly sure where I would be staying. I didn't know how many rooms they had or what their rules were.

Lori had a brother, and his room was open since he was away at college. Her parents said I could stay in there. I wasn't going to make a fuss. I was happy to have a place to put my things and a bed to sleep on. After I got settled, Lori showed me around, and we eventually ended up in her room. It was the first time I was in a girl's room when the girl was actually a girlfriend. She had those glow-in-the-dark stars on the ceiling that I thought were cool and a queen-size bed. You could tell she was a college student with luggage and laundry out in the open, as she was going back and forth from school to home. Eventually, it was just Lori and me lying in her bed, looking up at the ceiling. We could finally be in the same room together and talk without needing a computer or a phone to do so. We hung out in there for a while until dinner was ready.

Lori's home life reminded me of my own to some extent. She had both of her parents at home, and they would cook a homemade meal and enjoy it around the dinner table. I helped to set the plates, and then food was served.

I don't recall what the meal was, but I do remember grits and collard greens. They all thought it was funny that I had no idea what those were. I was very much out of my element being in the South. I told them I'd never heard of this stuff where I came from. Surprisingly, they weren't half bad. The dinner went well. There were some laughs and a little teasing. I figured they at least didn't *hate* me if they were doing that. In a lot of ways, I could tell they appreciated I cared about Lori. I believe they could tell she was happy with me, which made them happy.

We chatted in the living room after dinner, and all was going well. I started to feel a lot more comfortable in my new surroundings. It was the first day of the weeklong trip, and I wasn't in any hurry to get back home.

The next morning, I awoke in my room to some nice sunshine. I sat up in my bed and found my glasses as my feet hit the floor. I stood up and saw something weird in front of me. I immediately thought it was a dog turd. Lori had a small dog, so I was really hoping it was from him versus anything that I had done. Upon further observation, after my eyes were a little more adjusted, it looked like a dead cockroach. I was a bit freaked out seeing that on the ground, but apparently they were fairly common in those parts. They call them Palmetto bugs versus cockroaches. I guess it sounds a bit nicer. The day started off a little gross, to say the least. I wasn't exactly sure what was in store for the day, but it didn't really matter. Being with Lori was what mattered.

I got a full tour of the house and the neighborhood the first day. We drove around town to see the sites until it was time for a night out at a local establishment. We were out as a little family, and Lori's parents were able to learn more about me and how I acted out in public. I could tell they were happy with me, and that's what I wanted. I didn't have a lot to offer, so I had to at least show them I was a good person with some potential. We wrapped the evening up with a little TV, and it was weird seeing the news broadcast in a different state. I looked forward to what the next day was going to bring.

Lori wasn't feeling the greatest by the next morning. It was the first time I could physically see how the Lyme was affecting her. She had a port-a-cath, or central PICC line, that allowed her to give herself intravenous antibiotics that would get pumped directly into her heart. It's important to keep everything sterile when using it; otherwise, germs can have direct access into your body. And that's what she figured had happened. She went to the hospital in the morning to get things looked at, which meant I spent an awkward day with her dad.

I'm not sure why I didn't go with her, but I think they knew they'd be gone all day, and they didn't want me being bored at the hospital. In the meantime, her dad took me out to the local golf course.

I hadn't played in a few months because of the cold up north. I didn't have my own clubs, so I had to rent a set from the clubhouse. Her dad was a very good player and had won a few local tournaments. I figured I would end up losing, but I gave it my best shot.

It was a great day to be on the course and a perfect time to show her dad a little bit of what I was made of. I was nervous as all could be on that first tee shot; however, I managed to make a decent swing to get the ball in the fairway. We talked a bit as he drove the cart around to our next shots. He was happy that I came down and said that I seemed like a "really nice Yankee boy." I got a laugh out of that. I was impressed by his consistency on the course. Shot after shot, he was right on target. I tried my best to keep up. Once we got to the back nine, I started to settle in and got used to the rental clubs I was using. I managed to outdrive him a couple of times and even bagged a birdie when I rolled in a twenty-foot putt. He was thrilled for me and gave me a spirited high five. I still lost by a fair share of strokes, but I could tell he was excited that I could play and be competitive. I thought to myself that I could really get used to being able to play golf in the wintertime.

By the time we got back, Lori still wasn't home. Her dad called to find out what was going on. I believe she had some sort of infection from the port line and was getting put on some antibiotics to help clear it up. When she did get home, I could tell she wasn't feeling the greatest, which was a little bit of rain on the parade. Lyme sucks, and the coinfections that go with it are no joke. I was getting a firsthand look at how it affected another person and not just myself. Lori and I had a lot of the same symptoms. It was definitely a big reason as to why we got along so well. I was lucky and felt fortunate that I never had to have a port-a-cath to drip drugs into my heart. In some ways, she had it worse than I did. I wished I could have given her some of the health that I was feeling. The warm weather and sunshine were recharging my batteries.

We spent the next few days at home. There wasn't a whole lot else that could be done as she simply needed to rest. It wasn't what either of us wanted to do, so we passed the time playing board games and watching whatever we could find on TV.

With only a day or two left on my trip, Lori started to feel better and wanted to take me to Myrtle Beach. We drove down there in the morning. It was a cool and windy day, so it wasn't ideal to be out there very long. While on the beach, I had the necklace I was going to give her that was burning a hole in my pocket. When we stopped to look at the waves, I reached into my pocket and pulled it out. I could tell she really liked it and was very thankful I had given it to her. I helped her put it on and the pain that I could see she had from the previous days started to go away. The joy I saw on her face made me feel like a million bucks. We started holding hands more or putting our arms around each other as we walked. I knew I would be heading home, but I wanted her to know that I was here for her. I asked her to come visit me in Wisconsin, and she said that she would love to.

It was tough saying goodbye at the airport. We knew that the next probable time we could be together was in six months once she was done with school for the year. Our relationship grew in the week that I was there, and I was looking forward to her coming to see me.

On the flight back, I knew I had to start figuring out how I could improve my situation. I thought about ways I could help people with the products that had helped me. Lori and her parents started using them with some success, so I thought I could continue finding other people who could benefit. Again, though, it was like pulling teeth. I talked to quite a few people to try and get the ball rolling, but ultimately, I would take one step forward and two steps back.

Fortunately for me, my brother Matt had just started his own construction business and was looking for some help. I figured it was something that I could handle at least part-time. I had worked with tools before and had done other projects before with him, so I gave it a shot. I started out doing what I could a few days a week, working anywhere from three- to six-hour days. I wore out absurdly fast. I had no endurance. Lugging a tool belt around my waist, carrying sheets of plywood, hauling lumber, swinging a hammer, and using power tools became a brutal test of how much I could take.

I had stretches where I would feel great for a few days, and then I'd feel like a truck ran me over. I would get dizzy and lightheaded easily. My face and hands would tingle and go numb. My body would shake, and my heart would race. I tried my best to not show how bad I was feeling. I pushed as much as I could, and a lot of times would throw up from how badly I felt. I wanted to work, but my body wasn't allowing me to do that very well. I ultimately had to take more days off than I wanted so that I could recover. In a lot of ways, I felt like how I did when I was pushing myself too hard back when I was in school. It was a terribly depressing feeling.

Pushing my body aggravated the Lyme. Lyme was daring me to work so that it could take me down. I was doing my best to not let that happen.

The cold months turned into spring and then summer. I managed to survive and make a few bucks. I was in desperate need of a break. Luckily for me, Lori was coming to town.

I was stoked she was coming to visit. I had a list of some things to do that I thought would be fun and imagined what it would be like as I drove to the airport to pick her up. I found a place to park and then headed inside to where she should be arriving. I made it to the baggage claim and waited anxiously to spot her in the crowd of people. It didn't take long until I saw her coming down the escalator. We shared a big hug and walked hand in hand to wait for her bags. I could tell she was excited and a little nervous to be in my hometown. She had never been to the Midwest, so everything would be new to her. I helped her with her luggage as we made our way back to where I parked. It was only a thirty-minute drive home, so she would be meeting my family in no time. She was concerned about everyone liking her, but I kept reassuring her that it was all going to be fine.

We arrived safely and met Mom first in the kitchen. Mom gave her a hug and welcomed her into the home. She was excited to see Lori because she knew she meant a lot to me. Dad came up from the basement and introduced himself, and after some small talk, I showed Lori the room she would be staying in for the next week.

It was interesting and unique having her in my house. It was a new experience for me, and especially for Lori being in unfamiliar territory. We kept things quiet for the first night to settle in. We played Scrabble and soaked up all the time we could being next to each other.

Over the next few days, I made some plans for us to visit the Milwaukee Art Museum and take in a Brewer game. Lori started to get more comfortable with our relationship and everyone she was meeting. It was awesome to see the smile on her face.

After a few days of walking and getting a lot of mental stimulation, she started to not feel her best. She wanted to continue doing things, but she was getting worn down. I was hanging in there just fine, but I knew when you're not feeling well with Lyme, you have to listen to your body and take a day or two to get right.

We only had ten days together, and the one day of rest turned into three. She wasn't doing well at all, and it got to the point where if she didn't improve by the next day, she was going to fly back early to get to her doctor. She was upset about the situation, and so was I. There wasn't a whole lot that either of us could do.

Lyme gets in the way of your life. I completely understood her wanting to do something, but the body just wasn't having it. I remember Lori talking on the phone with her parents and being emotional about how awful she was feeling and also not wanting to leave. We both were saddened that we were going to have to cut the trip short.

The next day, by some miracle, she felt a lot better. I was elated to see life come back into her face. She called her parents and said that she was vastly improved and would depart at her regularly scheduled time.

We went out to dinner, just the two of us. We only had one more day left. The time went by so fast. We wished we could have had more time. On the way home, my old '91 Saturn decided to lose its serpentine belt. I found a safe spot to park and called my parents to come pick us up while the car got towed away. It is a bit embarrassing when you're trying to show your lady a good time, but your old car breaks down, and you need your parents to come to your rescue. I was glad for the lift, though, and Lori didn't seem to mind. Our quick visit was coming to an end. We both knew it would be about another six months until we could possibly get together again.

I got her to the airport and waited with her until the very last minute that I could. I was about to watch her get on a plane and leave. It was tough on both of us. Aside from her not feeling well for a few days, it was a good visit that strengthened our relationship. We shared a long hug, and then she was off. She turned back and watched me as long as she could before she disappeared into the crowd. It was going to be a lonely ride back home.

Then I was back to reality in the real world.

I continued working with Matt when I could, but that was definitely taking its toll on me physically and mentally. I knew I couldn't keep up even with a part-time pace, and it sucked.

Dr. B, who I had been going to in Illinois, had left her practice earlier in the year to assist with the recovery efforts after Hurricane Katrina hit Louisiana. I was extremely bummed out by that news, as she was the first and only doctor I had any trust in. However, she did refer me to another Lyme literate medical doctor in Wisconsin, and he was only located a little over an hour away. While the drive would be shorter, I knew I would never find another doctor like Dr. B. I would gladly have driven twice as far to see her, but I didn't have a choice.

Dr. M became my new doctor. I wasn't excited for the initial consultation, but I figured I should give him a chance if Dr. B thought he was a capable doctor.

My initial impression was that he was professional. He knew a good bit about Lyme, and he had seen many different cases. He was willing to listen to my story and learn about my experiences.

It was a big relief that he didn't shoot me down and say that I was crazy.

Dr. M wanted to take some blood draws and do some lab tests to see what was all floating around inside me. He concurred with the diagnosis Dr. B had made that I indeed had Lyme, but he wanted to double-check as much as he could.

I wasn't expecting a whole lot of groundbreaking news. I knew I had Lyme. I just wanted help and guidance to figure out how to best get my life back.

The results that came back were quite interesting. It was confirmed again that I had Lyme disease. I don't recall what test I had done, but it came back positive. Then Dr. M said that I also have the coinfection Bartonella.

That was unexpected news.

Bartonella is basically just another form of Lyme that can cause varying degrees of symptoms. You can get them both together at the same time. I believe you can also just have Bartonella on its own. Either way, I had both.

Then Dr. M said that a common symptom of Bartonella is red striping on the body that can look like stretch marks or like someone scratched you.

A light bulb went off in my head.

If you recall earlier in my battle, after my last wrestling match in high school is when I looked like I had been mauled by a tiger. I had the red stripes, or red scars as I called them, all over my body. I had been dealing with the Bartonella along with the Lyme from the very beginning. I only recall seeing the striping once, but it was so prominent of an event that I could never forget how beat-up and mangled I looked. Now I knew what caused that.

It was good information to know. Having another doctor not only confirm but add to what I had been dealing with was helpful. I wasn't crazy. I wasn't making stuff up. I wasn't lazy. I was sick and dealing with not one but two terrible infectious diseases.

The Bartonella, I believe, was responsible for the swollen, burning glands in my throat that I'd experienced many times over the past few years. It can also be responsible for the brain fog or mental degradation I was experiencing. Throw in the mood swings, depression, irritability, tingling, and numbness that can also be symptoms, and it wasn't surprising why I felt like crap a lot of times.

Dr. M was impressed with how I had progressed to the point that I had. He really liked the supplements I was using and encouraged me to keep on them. He wanted to add in a few other things to try, as well as some different antibiotics. I wasn't a fan of the drugs, but I was glad to see it wasn't his first and only method of treatment. I wouldn't have gone back if he told me to stop using the products that I had because without them, I would have been in a lot worse shape.

It was off to a good start with Dr. M. I didn't need to see him nearly as often as I saw Dr. B. I wasn't in terrible health. I just wasn't in great health. It was fifty-fifty with how I felt. The more I did, the worse I felt. The easier I took it, the better I felt, but the more depressed I would become. It was very difficult finding a good balance. Knowing I had a legitimate reason for why I felt the way I did was comforting, but I still needed to push the envelope when I could if I wanted to get better.

Now that I had some more time on my hands from not being in school and only working part-time, there started to be some rumblings from Lori's parents and people in my family that I didn't have a high school education or at least a GED.

The longer I didn't do anything about my lack of education, the more annoying the gripes were about it. Lori was in college, and I wasn't. I wasn't even close. I knew I was smart, but I didn't have a piece of paper saying I was. I started to feel guilty that maybe I wasn't trying hard enough to improve my situation. Construction was hard work and not the best option at the time with me still not anywhere in the health I needed to be.

I decided that maybe if I got my GED, it would shut people up a little bit and that stress could then go away.

I went to the local technical college to see what all I would have to do to get my name on a GED diploma.

I only told Lori my intentions. I didn't want anyone else to know. For one, I wanted it to be a surprise if I was able to do it. Two, if I crashed and burned, it wouldn't be an embarrassment.

I didn't know how I would keep it a secret, as I had to leave one night a week to attend classes to prepare for the five exams and then go into the building when the time came to take the final tests.

The classes weren't that intense, and I picked up on the material quickly. A lot of it I knew, or it was common sense. I had to take practice tests before they would let me take the real ones, which I didn't like. I wished that I could have just gone in to take the tests to see how I would do.

The people who were in charge of getting students prepared to get their GED said that on average, it took one year for someone to obtain their degree. I wasn't having any of that. I wanted to get it done at least before Christmas, which was in five months. I didn't want to go back to South Carolina without something to show Lori's parents that I was trying to get my life on a good track.

I'm not sure what reasons or excuse I would use to get out of the house for a couple of hours at night, but I made up something so that my parents wouldn't know. It also helped that they were on the road with work some of the time, so I didn't have to fudge the truth as often as I thought I would need to.

I quickly made my way through the study material and was ready to tackle the practice exams. If I didn't pass those, I wouldn't be allowed to take the real one. I did the best I could and wound up passing all five practice exams on the first try. It was a relief that I got through those without too much of a problem, and after only a couple of months, I was ready to start taking the real tests.

I was well on my way to making my goal of earning my GED and maybe getting a little bit of respect from the people around me. I had a science, math, reading comprehension, English, and history exam scheduled as well as a final writing assignment.

I aced the reading comprehension and history tests. I did very well on the other three. I remember always dressing nicely before taking the tests. I felt that if I looked good, I would perform well, and I did. I ended up being in the top 1 percent in the state for GED scores.

Getting my GED was one of the first things in several years that I set out to do that I was able to accomplish. It felt great. Lori was happy for me, and her parents were, too.

I kept it a secret from my parents until Christmas when I showed them the diploma that I had framed.

They were very happy and proud that I was able to do that. They admitted they had become suspicious of what I was doing. I'm sure they were relieved that this is what it was versus me doing something I shouldn't.

It was a start to what I had hoped would be a step in the right direction. I wanted to show people that I was smart, and I did. I wanted to show that I wasn't stupid or lazy, and I accomplished that. I wanted to prove to myself that I was still capable of completing a goal.

The technical college said I should plan on a year to accomplish earning my GED, and I did it in four months. If I could have just gone in and taken the tests without having to go through courses and practice tests, I think I could have finished even sooner. I may not have been in the top 1 percent that way, but I felt I would have been able to pass.

I had gained a little bit of confidence back that I used to have. I didn't know what steps would be next for educational purposes, but I felt I had at least bought some time to try and figure that out.

My reward was another trip to see Lori. Her parents rented a vacation home on Jekyll Island in the state of Georgia. They invited me to come and stay there, too. I was really looking forward to this treat.

I flew into Atlanta first this time and then into Charlotte, where Lori picked me up. It was great to see her face again. Her parents were happy about my arrival, and it started to feel like we were becoming a family.

Speaking of family, I hadn't met any additional members of Lori's family yet. That was about to change as we were driving past her grandma's place in Savannah, Georgia, on the way to Jekyll Island. I was excited to meet and learn more about Lori's family.

The landscape was more pine trees as far as the eye could see. The weather was nice for January as we made the three-hour drive. We stayed there two nights, and there wasn't much around, so most of the entertainment was talking with people. Her grandma seemed to like me, and I felt that I left a good impression on the people there that I was a decent guy. We helped make dinner and clean up the dishes, then we played some games to pass the time. There was a little pond that we walked to later that evening. It was such different scenery down in the South compared to where I was from, but I liked it because it was peaceful.

As we prepared to depart to get to Jekyll Island the next day, we all hugged and said our goodbyes. Her grandma said she was glad that I was with Lori because she could see how happy she was. That meant a lot to me, and I said that I would try my best to keep her that way.

It was only an hour drive to arrive at our destination. I was looking forward to what the next few days would hold.

Jekyll Island is a hot spot for finding sand dollars and angel wing shells on the beach. I had never experienced finding interesting things along the ocean, but it didn't take long until I was hooked at finding these oceanic treasures. There were big ones and small ones, and some were still alive, so we sent those back into the water. It was a great time and experience that we were all able to share together.

Lori and I went out to dinner by ourselves, and I ordered an authentic crab dinner. I was very much starting to get used to fresh seafood and enjoying life in the South. We had a great first few days there, and it looked like it was going to continue, but Lori started to feel run-down again.

I could always tell when she wasn't feeling the greatest when she became quiet and stopped smiling. I guess she could have been mad at me for something, but I was pretty sure that wasn't the case. I was the same way a lot of times. When I didn't feel great, I would become quiet too. I ended up visiting the ocean by myself once or twice. I had the beach to myself. It probably wasn't the best idea to swim in the ocean with nobody else around, but I managed. I definitely wasn't as happy experiencing the ocean by myself as I would have if Lori was with me, but I had to make do. I think it did start to cross my mind at that point about our health situation. If I kept improving and she didn't, would I be able to handle that? I had a lot I wanted to experience in life. I wanted her there with me as healthy as she could be. But what if one of us got better and the other didn't? What if neither one of us got better and into a position where we could support ourselves?

It was a lot to think about as I floated alone in the ocean.

On one of the last days that we were on the island, Lori wanted to take me into town to buy me something. She was feeling better again, and I loved that it was just the two of us making our way through the beach town. She took me into a Fossil store and said that I needed a watch. I'd never worn one before, but I was excited to pick one out. I settled on one with a blue face and a silver band. She helped me get it on, and I could see the light in her eyes were bright again. I knew she cared about me and loved me, and the watch was a small symbol to show that.

We made the trek back to South Carolina as I had a plane to catch the next day. Knowing we were about to not be together for a while always seemed to spark more affection from Lori toward me. We spent the last day bleaching the sand dollars, talking, and relaxing on the swing in the backyard in the beautiful winter weather. Our connection was deepening, and I wished I could have stayed longer.

I didn't want to leave her, but I didn't have a choice. It was back to school for Lori and back to whatever life I could try and muster up.

It was cold again back home. The new antibiotics I was on were triggering some Lyme attack reactions, which made me feel awful. I continued working part- time as much as I could, but it was taking a major negative toll on my body.

I know at one job, in particular, I was fighting to stay upright. I found myself with my hands on my knees or leaning up against a wall to keep from falling over. We were doing some footing work in a hole, and some dirt needed to be cleared away. I began shoveling, but with every scoop I was getting out of the ground, I could feel my energy drop. I was getting very nauseous and shaky. It was a major struggle to keep my composure. The feeling I had wasn't a stranger to me. I had felt this badly many times before. I was just getting sick and tired of feeling that way. I had no control of when my body would decide to give out. The strain and stress of physical labor pushed me past my breaking point. I felt the uncontrollable urge to throw up again. I crawled my way out of the hole, and up came death from the pit of my stomach. It was worse than any flu visit to the toilet. I kept heaving and convulsing. I couldn't calm my body down, and everything hurt. Tears rolled down my face as I curled up into a ball on the cold, hard ground. I was done for the day, to say the least. I was able to settle down after taking some time to just sit on the ground. I made my way back to my car and drove on home. I was ashamed I was unable to help Matt out more, but I'm quite sure he saw that I wasn't in any shape to continue.

That type of occurrence would happen after I did too much for too long. I had limits on what I could do, and I hated it. It took me a long time to figure out that I need to listen to my body and take the time to recover when necessary. I paid the price multiple times when trying to do too much.

I also hated telling Lori about those kinds of episodes. Many times, I had difficulty holding back tears because I felt like I was letting her down. Even though she understood, I think she saw that maybe my health wasn't in a place where it needed to be for us to have a relationship where we could be together on more than a part-time basis.

The maddening thing about the Lyme, and now Bartonella, is that I could feel and look normal one day and then be a wreck the next. I had very little consistency. It made it very difficult to have any positive momentum. I had to take a couple of weeks off to get myself back into some sort of workable condition.

While all that was going on, Lori and I were figuring out plans for an upcoming trip for the summer.

Her parents rented a vacation house in the Florida Keys and invited me to come along. I was stoked at the opportunity. That news gave me a little bump in how I was feeling. It was going to be my longest vacation with Lori, and I was looking forward to some fun and relaxation.

I flew into Miami, and Lori was there to pick me up. It was only a two-hour drive to get to Long Key, where the house was. It was the craziest thing driving down there, especially taking the seven-mile bridge. The ocean was all around the road as we made our way past the different Keys. We arrived at our destination safely. Her dad's boat was in the water in the back of the house in a man-made channel. It was a two-story home with a covered wrap-around deck. I was excited to be there.

Lori's brother, Lane, was there too. I had never met him before. He was a bit of a rebel college student, and I know there were some rifts between him and his parents. He treated me just fine, but he wasn't as nice to everyone else, so I tried to keep my distance as much as I could, as I didn't trust him.

The first night, Lane and I slept downstairs where it wasn't air conditioned while Lori and her parents slept upstairs where it was cool. I was definitely tired and worn out from my travels, so I was looking forward to getting some rest. The plan was to get up early before it got too hot to take the boat out into the ocean for some fishing. I was excited to try out this new experience. I also hated getting up early.

I slept through my alarm and awoke to her brother shaking me to get up. I was groggy and confused. I didn't know where I was for a second or two. I got my bearings and noticed I felt like crap, but I didn't want to look like a wimp and not go. I was happy to see Lori was up and going out on the boat with us. It would have been a tad awkward if she wasn't there. For some reason, it felt like Lori was keeping her distance from me. I figured if anyone was going to wake me up, it would have been her. It would have been much nicer than her brother! Alas, we got ready to go as the sun was starting to rise.

I enjoyed watching the day come alive with Lori by my side as we slowly motored out of the channel. Once we cleared the no-wake zones, the ocean opened up, and there was nothing but water as far as the eye could see. It was quite a daunting site. The boat we were in wasn't huge, and I think I said a prayer that we would return safely. We ventured a few miles from land, and the ocean started out quite calm. I had never been fishing in the ocean. The equipment was different from what I was used to, and I struggled getting things set up on my own. I had anticipated a little help or pointers from everyone else on board, as they all had some experience, but I received none. I kind of took it as they were testing me to see if I actually was a capable outdoorsy guy. After my line was in the water well after everyone else, it was fun being out there. We caught some small groupers, mahi-mahi, and Lori's brother even caught a small shark. It was quite the experience, as you never knew what you would reel up. The waves started to pick up big time. We were floating in the water going up and down, and up and down. I was starting to get green in the face and felt awful. Lori's dad saw that I was going to lose my breakfast if we didn't start moving, so we reeled up, and he started the engine so that I could get some air on my face. My symptoms went away quickly as we started to motor off. I was exhausted when we got back. The boat needed maintenance to get the salt water washed off the deck and out of the motor, and I helped as much as I could. When we were done, I went in for a nap. I woke up many hours later. I was surprised they let me sleep as long as I did. We made a nice, fresh fish dinner with the ones we kept, and it turned into an enjoyable evening.

I was able to stay in Lori's room that night. I think they took pity on me and didn't make me sleep in my sweat from all the humidity that was in the air. It was a much more comfortable sleeping situation, even if I was in a recliner.

The next morning, we woke up to bad news. Lori's grandma had passed away.

It was a shock to everyone there. While I knew her grandma from the previous visit, it didn't impact me as much as everyone else. Lori's dad gave me a big hug and said that he was sorry. He was sorry because he knew it was throwing a wrench into my trip. I said, "It's okay. Things happen. It's out of anyone's control. I'll help however I can."

Help meant going from the Florida Keys all the way to Savannah, Georgia, the next day. Lori's brother stayed behind because he didn't like funerals, so it was just Lori, her parents, and me.

Everyone took turns driving so that we could make it there as soon as we could. The family drama ensued once we got to Georgia. Some of Lori's relatives weren't the most well-liked, and things turned quite sour when we arrived. By the time we got there, her grandma was already in the ground. Her relatives were going through items and belongings at Grandma's house. I couldn't believe the pace at which these relatives of hers tried to basically erase their grandma's memory.

The next day, we went to the cemetery where she had been buried. There was no service, and I think that really hurt Lori to not have proper closure. As we pulled up to the place of burial, Lori and her dad got out of the car, and I asked if she wanted me to come with her. She said no. I stayed by myself while she and her dad went to the grave to say goodbye. I was a little stunned that she didn't want me next to her, but she had her dad, and they knew Grandma way more than I did. I felt out of place and not part of the family. I tried not to dwell on it too much. It was a tough time, and I didn't want to make it any tougher.

We stayed in Georgia for another night or two. The rental home in the Keys was still available for a few days, so we drove all the way back.

The passing of her grandma really affected Lori, and I think it affected her affection toward me over the next few days. I started feeling like an uninvited guest in the house. I tried my best to stay out of the way but also be as helpful as I could.

On one of the evenings, a storm rolled in. I was cleaning up the kitchen to be helpful and was looking out the window, watching the downpour of rain. Suddenly, a bright flash of lightning hit a pole right by the water. The electrical arc came toward the house. My hand was on the metal stove as the lightning flashed into the electrical outlet behind it. All of this took place in a split second and was very loud! I jumped back and let out a distraught gasp. I felt my hair stand on end. I thought I had been hit hard by the lightning, but I just ended up being in the shockwave around it. It was enough to scare the living daylights out of me. Lori and her dad rushed over to see if I was okay, as they weren't that far away in the house. After I checked everything over, I was fine, just rattled. However, I didn't feel that Lori was as concerned about what had just happened as I thought she would be. My life just flashed before my eyes, but there didn't seem to be too much sympathy or compassion from her. I wasn't sure if she was still that bummed out over her grandma or if she wasn't liking me as much for some reason.

It wasn't until the last day we were at the vacation home that we went into Key West to see the sites there. I figured we would have been there earlier in the trip, as some days we didn't do much at all. Once it was just Lori and me out and about, she started to be more affectionate and loving again. We ended up having a great time on the last day there. If the whole trip had been more like that, I would have felt fantastic about our relationship and my time there.

We still had a long drive back to South Carolina. I had a few more days with Lori before I had to head back home. I was hoping we could spend a little more time together and finish out my trip on some higher notes.

Lori needed to get her items packed up so that she could move into her apartment at college. Being the nice, strong guy that I was, I was happy to help get the car and trailer loaded up. It was extremely humid that day. I was sweating profusely and getting worn out, but I kept at it because I wanted to be helpful. The college campus was almost three hours away, so the next morning, we'd get up early to drive there, unload, and come back.

Her dad drove us from Florence to Greenwood. We found where Lori's apartment was and started moving her stuff in. I remember moving furniture up a flight or two of stairs. I don't think there was an elevator big enough to fit a small couch in, so once again, I had to man up and move the heavy stuff. It didn't take long until we got Lori settled in her new place for the school year. I felt like I did most of the work by myself, and in a way, I was starting to feel like cheap labor. I got more appreciation from Lori's mom versus anyone else.

Everyone was tired, and we still had to make the trek back home. Somehow, I was pegged to drive the truck and trailer, or maybe I was half-volunteered, I'm not sure. Either way, I was tired, but it had to be done. Lori sat shotgun, and her parents took a nap in the backseat as the sun started to set as we drove. It was a strange feeling jumping into a vehicle I had never driven while also towing a trailer. I was feeling unappreciated and taken advantage of. At the same time, I wasn't paying anything to have been on some of these nice vacations to Florida and Georgia. I would have felt a lot better if I could have gotten a little bit of affection from Lori, but there wasn't much of that going around.

I got us back home safely. I was set to leave in the afternoon the next day.

That night, I had trouble falling asleep. I wanted to be home. I missed my own family. I was tired, and I wasn't feeling the greatest connection with Lori. I loved her a lot, but only getting love and affection when I was set to leave didn't feel right.

I thought of somehow quietly sneaking out, getting a cab to take me to the airport, and be gone before everyone woke up. For the first time, I didn't want to be there anymore. The distance going back and forth, the lack of appreciation and affection, and the stress of trying to get my life together quickly so that we could be together on a regular basis was starting to become overwhelming.

In a lot of ways, it felt like school, where I was getting into a hole that I couldn't get out of. I was torn between wanting to be with Lori and somehow making it work to wondering if it would be better to go our separate ways.

I eventually fell asleep. When I woke up, I was still in Florence. My mind was a little clearer after some rest, but I still wanted to skip the flight and just be home. I said goodbye to her parents, not knowing if that would be the last time I'd see them or not.

Lori was cuddlier and more affectionate again, knowing that I was going to be gone again for at least a few months. It was nice to have a little bit of the warm, fuzzy feeling again. I couldn't help but question why I only seemed to get that on the last day or two of our visits.

We had the familiar two-hour drive to Charlotte to get me to the airport. It was just Lori and me. And for whatever reason, things were just easier when it was just us. Without anyone else around, she seemed to be more relaxed. It was a great ride, and we communicated how it was tough to say goodbye again. We embraced as long as we could until we had to eventually depart. It was a different goodbye for me because I was now having mixed feelings about where things were headed. Lori had been a huge part of my life and a big reason why I was doing as well as I was. I couldn't and haven't forgotten that fact. I had a lot of thinking to do as I flew home. While I did miss Lori, I didn't miss the stress and frustration I was feeling. It felt great to be back in my own bed.

It was back to work for me, and I was dreading it. I liked the work. I liked building things and figuring out how they went together. I liked the fresh air, sunshine, and, to some extent, the exercise. However, I knew it was a nearly impossible task to consistently be able to show up and make it through the day.

I wasn't sure what else I could do. I had a little bit of freedom to work when and how much I wanted. It wasn't possible to go eight hours a day five days a week. I couldn't work full-time as part-time was difficult enough.

I looked for other jobs and even applied for some that I thought I could handle, but I was never offered a position. The lack of education and experience in anything was a big problem. I could learn fast, but no one wanted to give me a shot.

I again thought about trying to get a business off the ground by helping people with the products I used. Time and time again, nothing worked. Everyone I talked to about the supplements was extremely skeptical or thought they cost too much. I tried helping people with Lyme. I knew the products could help if people would give them an honest try. I had people purchase some supplements, but they would only use them for a few days and be done with it. It was incredibly frustrating.

The stress of trying to do something with my life, coupled with trying to maintain a long-distance relationship, while at the same time trying to be healthy was a big burden on me.

There began to be riffs and arguments in my relationship with Lori. We never used to have that problem. I wasn't necessarily unhappy with her. I was unhappy with myself. I felt that I carried all the pressure to make the relationship work instead of it being a team effort. I put a lot of time and work in showing Lori and her parents that I was a good guy. I think they saw that. They may have also seen that I didn't have a whole lot going for me.

Our relationship was starting to become a hinderance to me getting better. I knew it, but I didn't want to admit it. I didn't want to lose Lori. I loved her. She meant a lot to me. I don't know if I would even be here if she wasn't in my life when she had been. I didn't know how to let her go without hurting her, and that was the last thing I ever wanted to do. I couldn't express to Lori how I felt, but I wish I had been more honest with her at this point. I became a lot more withdrawn from her, and we weren't talking like we used to. She became frustrated with how things were going, and I couldn't blame her.

After a bit of a drawn-out process, not talking, and being disconnected emotionally, the relationship just seemed to end without either of us saying it was over.

Just like my stress level with school, once I was out and free, I felt better. However, I missed having Lori to talk to or *someone* to talk to when life seemed to go off the tracks. I was more stable mentally than I used to be, so I didn't need the daily interaction with someone to keep me from drowning in my own thoughts. Nevertheless, there were many times where I wanted to reach back out to her while we weren't together. It was difficult not having my security blanket to go to when I felt the need.

I had to get used to being uncomfortable, but I didn't like it a whole lot.

I missed the emotional connection. I missed having someone around who I could enjoy being with and who I felt at least partially appreciated the things I did.

I had hoped the girls would be lining up to be with me now that I was single, but it didn't take long to realize that wasn't going to happen.

Everyone my age was in college. They were all making new friends and forming new relationships. Life was passing me by in a hurry, and I couldn't do anything to slow it down.

I was falling behind again. I had no social life, and friends were scarce. I lived at home, and I desperately wanted something to go in my favor for a change.

Things only seemed to get worse.

Sheena, my black Lab, was unexpectedly declining in health. When she was eight, I could tell she wasn't acting like herself. She was lethargic and would hobble around, especially after being out in the woods. I started giving her the doggy supplement version of what I was taking, and in a few weeks, I could really notice a difference. She was acting much more like a puppy and had more energy to run around. It was like I had a brand-new dog again.

Fast-forward two years and whatever she had been fighting was finally catching up to her. She started to really go downhill with her health almost at the same time that Lori and I broke up. We took Sheena to the vet, and to make a long story short, an X-ray revealed cancerous growths in her spine and around her lungs. The vet gave her a grim diagnosis. My puppy, whom I thought would be around for another three or four years, would be lucky to make it another few weeks.

I was devastated.

Sheena had been fighting the cancer most likely a few years. Being on the doggy vitamins seemed to have extended her run by at least a year or two. Being that she was ten years old meant that either way, she didn't have too much longer left with or without cancer. The cancer simply sped up her limited years that I got to spend with her.

It was tough watching her struggle to get up, eat, or go to the bathroom. We picked a day to take her into the vet to let her go. I could see in Sheena's eyes that she was in pain and uncomfortable. I could also see she was grateful I was her buddy over her entire life. She had a better life than a lot of people have. I love my dogs just as I would a part of the family, and sometimes even more.

The day of her trip to doggy heaven, she was having a good day. She hadn't had any the last few weeks. It was almost like she knew her pain would be gone soon. Just for fun, I tossed her a ball, and she caught it, something she had no interest in the days and weeks before. It put a little, sad smile on my face.

I dreaded the ride to the vet. I had to carry her inside. I tried to hold it together, but I was a mess on the inside. This wasn't a routine checkup; this was the end.

Mom, Dad, and I were in the small exam room, waiting for the vet to come in. I held onto Sheena as long as I could until it was time to let her go. I took off her red collar one last time. I told her she was a good puppy and thanked her for being such a good dog. I was about to lose my best buddy at a time that wasn't good. My only regret was that I wasn't there when she eventually passed. I'm not sure if that was an option back then. If it was, though, it sucked to have her go and not be the last face she saw. It still breaks my heart to this day.

As we left the vet, we all shared a small group family hug. All three of us were fighting back tears.

When we got home, I went into my room and then into the closet, where it was really dark, and cried like I hadn't in a long time. My heart was broken in more ways than one. I missed Sheena, of course, but I also missed having someone to lean on at a time like this. I also missed Lori terribly at that moment. I felt like I was losing my sanity. I felt sick and didn't know which way was up. So, I did what I hadn't planned on doing.

I called Lori.

She picked up, and it didn't take long for her to figure out something bad happened in my life.

Any and all crap that was between us at that moment vanished. There was no pressure, no stress, and no pointing fingers on who was right or wrong. It was just us. Talking to her put some sunshine back into my life, and into hers as well. There was no doubt we cared and loved each other. The passing of my beloved dog Sheena was probably one of only a few things that would push us back together. I missed Sheena terribly in the coming days, and having Lori back in my life softened the blow that I was just dealt.

I missed having a dog. After a few months passed, I was looking forward to finding my next four-legged best friend. Mark sent me a classified ad of a guy in Iowa who had some female black Labs for sale at a very reasonable price. I called him up and was able to successfully get a spot reserved to come pick one out. Jena was born September 7, 2007. I was able to go to Iowa eight weeks later to pick one out of the litter. I stayed the night at my brother's place, and the next morning, he, his wife Lisa, and I went to pick up my new puppy, Jena. The man selling the puppies lived on a farm in the middle of nowhere. When we got there, he opened the barn door, and seven or eight little black Lab puppies came running out. Their little legs were going as fast as they could, ears were flopping, and they were falling over each other. I just sat on the ground and waited for them to come tackle me. It was a pure joy moment to have all those cute buggers around me. It was going to be hard to pick just one. I had a little red collar that would go around the chosen one. After playing with and looking at them all over, I settled on the one that liked chasing after the toys the most. I put the collar around her neck and picked Jena up in my arms. I had my new best friend.

Jena whined and cried all the way back to my brother's house. She missed her siblings, but she was going to a great home. She didn't know how good she was going to have it. Jena was a great addition to the family, and I couldn't wait to take her out in the woods and fields. I also was excited to show Lori my cute, little furball. I was looking forward to having the three of us grow together.

Lori came for Christmas and New Year's celebrations. She was filled with joy to see Jena. Lori loved dogs, which was definitely one thing I really liked about her. She even got Jena her own little paw stocking for Christmas. It was a cute, little gift and made me quite happy, too.

I was also looking forward to having her with me to show her how my family celebrated the holidays. I wanted her to see the difference in how my family got along versus how hers did. I had hoped she'd really take to my family in anticipation that maybe she'd consider being in Wisconsin versus living in South Carolina. Lori wasn't a social butterfly by any means. She was a lot quieter when there were larger groups of people. She was capable of having a good time, but meeting my family can be intimidating simply because of how many of us there are. Everyone treated her nicely, but she was a lot more subdued than I thought she would be.

My brother Matt, his wife, Jenny, and their daughters arrived early on Christmas Eve and wanted to test out how ice fishing was at the pond down the road. I immediately was excited to go as well and to also show Lori this new experience, as the lakes don't freeze in South Carolina. I was getting bundled up to go, but Lori wasn't in any hurry to come along. I asked her if she wanted to go too, but she declined. She said she didn't have the proper attire. She could have borrowed some of my clothes and boots. It wasn't like we were going to be out there for hours. I just thought it would be something easy and fun to do together to make a memory. She insisted she didn't want to go, so neither did I. They didn't end up catching anything, so we didn't really miss out. I was frustrated, though, at the missed opportunity to do something fun and different together.

I took Lori to a Milwaukee Bucks game. I wanted to show her some of the attractions around my hometown. Since it was just her and me, she was more willing to go and do things. We had a great time. I even got to go on the court after the game was done to shoot a free throw. I missed, but it was a cool opportunity that she got to see me do. I craved more adventures with her, but it was hard to get her to come out of her shell.

I don't know if the Lyme disease was holding her back or if it was just her personality. I believe it was a combination of both. I know when I didn't feel well, I simply liked being by myself, so I could understand why sometimes she was more reclusive.

The time we had together flew by, and I felt our relationship took some positive steps in the right direction, but not as much as I would have liked. I was hoping to build on that when I went down to see her next.

Lori was about to be on spring break, and it was an excellent time for us to see each other again.

I'd fly into Charlotte as usual, only this time, instead of going to a vacation home or her parents' house, we went to her apartment on campus.

We would have a week and a half together by ourselves.

There wasn't a ton to do while I was there, so we mostly stayed in, talked, cooked, and played some old school Super Mario. It wasn't exactly a blast of a time, but neither of us had a ton of money. We were limited in what we could do. I'd much rather have done more physical activities, like taking a walk, going to a driving range, playing mini golf, bowling, or something like that, but Lori never seemed to be too excited to do anything I was interested in. I wasn't sure if the reason for that was that she didn't want to or that she wasn't feeling well enough. It was more than concerning. I wanted to experience life, nature, and continually try and improve, and it felt she was more content to stay put.

It also wasn't good to learn that her parents knew I was with Lori, and when she asked if we could visit so that they could see me, they declined. They felt it was a mistake for us to be together.

It sucked not having their approval for our relationship. If I was going to fix that, I would need to really show them something. I just wasn't sure what it was.

We spent the last day going to a park. I could walk just fine, but Lori either couldn't keep up with me or didn't want to. I wasn't sure. At one point, I wanted to go explore a bridge that was a little farther up, but she stayed behind as I walked up the path to investigate further. I was starting to get the feeling that if this was a sign of what our relationship was going to be like in the future, it could be detrimental. I wanted someone to push the envelope with, to try and improve and be better versions of ourselves.

I shrugged it off. However, later on, it made me wonder if this was going to be sustainable. Was this what I really wanted? I was twenty-one years old with a whole life ahead of me. I wanted to keep pushing myself to be better in all facets of life. I wasn't sure Lori was wanting the same. She was very dedicated to school and getting through college, which I admired. She impressed me in so many ways with how she was able to handle the courses, the studying, and the stress of it all.

I didn't want to live a one-dimensional, one-speed kind of lifestyle. In my mind, I felt like I wanted to be a Lamborghini. I wasn't getting that vibe from Lori. She was stable, slow, and steady. I was adventurous, fast, spontaneous, and more of a risk-taker. We were making it work. We had one giant thing in common, which was the same dreadful Lyme disease. We understood each other and could relate to one another better than anyone else could. And I loved that. I also knew that being sick with Lyme disease didn't define me.

I had a lot of life to live, and I wanted to be with someone who wanted more of what I was looking to do. I wasn't willing to just sit on the sidelines. I wanted to get out there and do stuff and make memories. I wasn't sure if Lori was ready or willing to do that. I think deep down she did, but until school was finished, that kind of life was taking a back seat.

Again, when I was set to go back home, I got more affection, and I didn't like that pattern. She was doing just enough to keep me thinking we could make this work in the long-term. The odds were very much stacked against us now. I believed we could do it, that love would be enough to push past the barriers and limitations. I simply wished I knew how that was going to happen.

A few short months passed, and it was my turn to host. I wanted to really push to see if our relationship had what it took to survive and thrive.

This time, it was the Fourth of July, and that's a great time of the year in Wisconsin to head up north. That's where my grandpa's house was. I spent many years up there fishing and having a great time. I figured it would be a good chance to really have some fun with Lori.

Since we fished out on the ocean one time in the Florida Keys, I figured she would want to try out some fishing on the lake that I knew better than any other. I had already obtained my fishing license and thought it would be a no-brainer that Lori would get one so that she could legally reel some fish in. When I told her that we should get her a license, she didn't want to because it would be a waste of money. I was a little taken aback by her response, so I said I would pay for her to have one, but she insisted that I didn't. It wasn't the best start to the trip. I was banking on creating some memories and taking pictures of her with her best catch. Unfortunately, that wasn't going to happen. It ended up with me fishing, and Lori sitting there and watching. It wasn't the fun that I thought we would be having.

After the uneventful Fourth of July weekend, we were back at my parents' place. I was growing ever more frustrated that the only time we really could have a good time was if we were by ourselves or if we were about to be away from each other. My annoyance level turned into me shutting down and clamming up. It was how I showed that I wasn't happy with how things were going. I tried so many ways to have fun and create good times, and I didn't feel her effort was the same. I felt like I had grown out of our relationship. In a lot of ways, I thought that it might be best to really pull the plug this time.

I didn't know how to do it. I didn't know how to tell someone I loved that I couldn't be with her anymore. It's not that I didn't love her. I just knew that it would be a mistake to keep trying to make this work. I couldn't bring myself to tell her to her face.

I buried those thoughts and feelings as I took her to the airport so that she could get back home. I honestly wasn't sure if this would be the last time I would see her.

I was 90 percent sure that our relationship was going to end. I still had a small bit of hope that some magic could happen. Like clockwork, she was more loving when she knew we were going to be apart. In my head, I couldn't help but wish that part of her showed through all the time and not just when we were saying goodbye. She asked when I thought we would see each other again. I hesitated, and she noticed that hesitation. I said, "Hopefully, in the next few months." I don't know if I was being honest or just said that to come up with a neutral answer. Either way, it wasn't a good way to depart.

As I watched her go through security and head to her terminal, we waved at each other. In my heart, I felt that was probably going to be the last time I saw her.

She arrived safely back to school. We talked for a few weeks afterward, but I kept pulling away, and then she began to as well. I think she knew that I knew it was over. We never really formally broke up or had any sort of talk to have a proper closure, and that's definitely a regret that I will always have. I never wanted to hurt her, but it probably would have hurt less if I was more honest with how I felt. I wanted to still have her in my life, but only as friends. We were able to do that somewhat, but eventually, it all faded away.

I loved Lori and still do. I will always have a special place in my heart for her. In many ways, I wished we would have just remained good friends and didn't complicate it by trying to be in a romantic relationship. I look back on our time together in a positive light. She helped me grow and learn, and I think she would say the same thing. No, I didn't like how it ended, and if I could do it over, I would definitely change how it all happened. She'll forever remain an angel who was sent to me when I needed it. I believe Lori will be able to go on being an angel for someone else who needs it as much as I once did. Lyme disease brought us together, and how we responded to the Lyme and its effects shaped how it would drive us apart.

I was now free from a lot of different stresses. I definitely wanted to love again, but if I had learned anything, I knew that I needed to love myself and be happy with the person I was.

It was time to focus on myself. It was time to put the past behind me. It was time to heal. It was time to push forward.

I had a lot that I needed to work on. My health was my number-one priority. I knew that if I could get that back, then I could start to have a normal life again. At this point, I had been battling against Lyme disease for seven years. Even though I felt decent more often than not, I knew I wasn't where I needed to be.

That needed to change.

CHAPTER 10

PUSHING IT

was alone and a lot less stressed. It was still summertime. I had grand dreams of all these new women flocking to be with me. I was disappointed but also not surprised when those dreams didn't come true right away. I took a long, hard look at my situation and realized that a great relationship wasn't going to happen unless I got my life on track. Even though I could have easily leaned on many different excuses and reasons as to why I wasn't more desirable, the cold, hard truth was that I wasn't anything special.

I was twenty-one and living at home. I had no job and no way to support myself. I wasn't in school or doing anything to enhance my position in life. I was in shape, but at the same time I wasn't. I shouldn't have weighed only 110 pounds. I needed to put on muscle. I had no endurance and no stamina. I wasn't ugly, but I wasn't as attractive as I could be. I had no social life.

I didn't really want to make goals because that had blown up in my face many times before. Goals can be great in the right situations, but a lifestyle that gets you on track to what you want to achieve is a better way to reach your destination.

I still had mental health issues, and depression was the most significant one. Things weren't nearly as bad as they were before, but I had to check myself many times to try and make sure I didn't fall into a deep hole. I knew if I wanted to get over that part of the Lyme, I would have to push past a lot of limits. I knew I would be in for some bad days. On the flip side, I knew I was in store for better days. I was done with only being able to live my life at 50 percent. It was better than the 1 percent I experienced a few times before; however, I wanted more. On my good days, I sometimes felt like I was at 85 percent. I figured I could at least get to feeling like that on a regular basis. I used to have mostly bad days and rarely good days. I was determined to have a majority of good and great days and have less and less bad days.

I didn't know how I was going to do it. I didn't know how long it was going to take, but I knew I had to start somewhere, even if that starting position was at the bottom.

I wanted to set in motion a lifestyle that would eventually get me into a better place. I didn't know how my body was going to respond. I didn't know how quickly I would recover when I ultimately would fall flat on my face. I just knew I had to get up and keep going. I knew my body could take a lot. I also knew I had very low limits of what I could do. I needed to keep pushing past those limits if I ever wanted to get anywhere. I needed to be smart and listen to my body.

I started with the basics. I looked at what had been helping the most and how I could enhance that. The vitamin products I had used were great. I added in different things to see if a difference could be felt. I knew eating healthy would be a big factor. That part wasn't too hard because I usually did eat healthily. But there's always room for improvement. Exercise would be the hardest. Remembering how bad my endurance and stamina were just a few years ago, I knew getting in great shape would be a challenge.

No one else was going to do the hard stuff for me. If I could simply put in a consistent effort and slowly make progress, then I'd have a chance of getting things on track.

A lot of things needed to happen, and it was tough knowing that it wasn't all going to be accomplished in a matter of days. I figured it would take a few years to start getting some positive momentum to where I didn't feel that I would crash and burn.

I started going to the gym. I got into a habit of weighing myself when I got there to see if I was improving. There was a digital scale in a small office where I first met Dory. I mentioned Dory earlier on when I first started trying to improve my fitness. I took a liking to her from the very beginning, and for some reason, she seemed to enjoy seeing me whenever I was there.

The first workout after not doing much always seemed to feel really good when I did it, but the days after were painful. I didn't just get the regular soreness and stiffness. I would be exhausted on top of it, along with pain in my joints. It would take me a few days of doing nothing to recover.

And then I did it again.

I had to start small.

The gym was only a mile from the house. I would attempt a walk or run to get there on occasion. The only downside was that sometimes it would rain when I wanted to head home. Or I'd be exhausted from the workout and then I'd still have a mile back, which made me even more worn out.

I ended up driving more often than not just to be on the safe side.

I knew quite a few exercises and how to do them properly. I was strong but had no strength. Attempting the bench press was embarrassing at times. The maximum I could do was seventy-five pounds when I started out, and that was on a good day. On my bad days, I struggled doing the bar, which was only forty-five pounds, for more than a few repetitions.

I liked doing the incline leg press as well, but even that in the beginning wasn't easy. I could push 135 pounds with my legs when I was feeling strong. On a day I wasn't, however, just doing the forty-five-pound sled was enough to wear me out.

I struggled a lot in the early workouts of trying to get back into shape. I loved the rare days where I felt like I could go for hours, and I would do just that. I would get that "eye of the tiger" feeling. And that feeling is what kept me coming back. I didn't let the down-and-defeated feeling win very often.

Many times, I could have stopped going in those first weeks and months when it got to be difficult and overwhelming. I simply knew I had to keep doing it if I wanted to improve my health and fitness, my stamina, and how I felt on a regular basis.

After a few months of working out, I was feeling like I could take another big step toward getting my life on track. The next phase was trying to find a way to support myself a little more.

I never had a real job where I would get interviewed and hired. I didn't know what I wanted to do. I wasn't ready for a full-time job. I wanted something I could do a few hours a day.

I applied to a few different places to see if anyone would give me a chance.

I was confident in my abilities to be able to do a job, but my resume was basically empty.

I saw a local used car place was hiring, and I applied there. They liked me enough for an interview, but ultimately, they passed me up because I didn't have any experience.

I was bummed but knew I'd get another chance somewhere.

A week later, I was interviewing for a position at the local outdoor, home improvement store. I knew a little bit about quite a few different things, so I figured my well-rounded knowledge and ability to learn quickly would be to my advantage. On the plus side, I had shopped there many times, and I knew I could do the job as well as or better than some of the people they already employed. The interview went well. I answered the questions the best I could and felt confident I would receive a call for the position.

It never happened, and I was a bit irritated. I knew I could do it, but I wasn't given the chance.

I kept looking.

I saw an ad in the paper that a local sub place was hiring delivery drivers to work a few hours a day during the lunch rush. I had never heard of Jimmy Johns before. I had never eaten there. It was close to my house, and the hours interested me the most. I didn't have to wake up early, and I only had to drive for a few hours. I felt like this was something that I could do.

I wanted to put my best foot forward. I had an interview with the owner of the restaurant. My resume still sucked, so I knew I had to show that I was worth a shot. I put on a suit and drove the eight-minute trip to get there. I wasn't nervous beforehand, but I was anxious when I got in there. I was expecting to meet in an office or someplace where it was just the owner and me. The interview took place at a corner table just before the busy lunch rush. There were other employees making sandwiches and taking calls. I felt way overdressed. Everyone had their T-shirt uniforms on, and here I was dressed to the nines. I felt out of place, but after a short five-minute interview, I was asked when I could start.

It was too easy. I didn't know what to say. I thought to myself, *That's it?* I later figured out that the biggest reason why I was hired so quickly was that I took it seriously from the start. I showed up to the interview on time and dressed well (probably too well for the position), but it made an impact on the owner who was probably used to goofballs and screwups showing up and trying to get a job.

I honestly didn't know what I was getting into. I got hired as a driver for three hours a day, five days a week, and sometimes on weekends.

The only car I had was a 1997 Mercury Grand Marquis. It was a boat-style grandpa car that had some power but not very good gas mileage. It wasn't ideal for delivery, but that's all I had. I was set to start on Monday. I had a few days to prepare before I'd get thrown into the fire.

And that fire was hot.

I didn't know anybody else I was working with. I didn't know what to do. I had to learn a lot and learn it quickly.

I showed up a little early so that I could get my bearings, grab a uniform, and start learning what I needed to do to be a team player.

My main responsibility was to drive and deliver. When needed, I had to answer phones and take orders. I was terrified of taking calls. I didn't know the menu or what to do if a customer asked questions. Luckily, I didn't have to do that the first day.

I just wanted to make it through my shift.

The shop got busy quick. It wasn't long before I was up for my first run. There were four of us drivers total. We would take orders out as they would come up and keep rotating. Whoever got back to the shop first would take the next deliveries in line.

For some reason, I remember my first order. It was to a company I had never heard of, and I didn't know where it was. We didn't have GPS. I was given a map printout and was shown where it was. I had to figure out how to get there, find it, and come back. It seemed simple enough. I only knew the main roads in the area, so anytime I was off the main path, everything was new to me.

I successfully found the location, walked in, and said I had an order from Jimmy Johns. I gave the food to the lady at the front desk, she gave me cash and said, "Keep it," so I did.

I walked out and counted what she gave me. There was an extra five dollars for me. It was a good yet strange feeling that someone gave me a tip for delivering their food. As I drove back, I thought to myself that this could be fun getting tips. I could make some decent money doing this!

When I got back, the other owner working said, "Congrats on making it back." He then proceeded to give me another delivery. I did that a few more times during my shift. I wasn't the fastest driver, but I was learning and getting it done.

Unfortunately, that five-dollar tip was the best one of the day. The rest were one or two dollars. I made about thirty bucks in tips to go along with my small hourly rate. For three hours of work, I was at fifteen bucks an hour. At that time, that was a decent wage, especially if that was done for a full eight-hour shift. I wasn't ready for that, though.

I was exhausted when I got back home. I had planned on going to the gym afterward, but I had no energy left for that. Mom and Dad were excited for me that I got through the day and that I was able to finally start doing something with my life.

I went to bed early that night. I was hurting. Three hours was more than enough work for me in the beginning. It wasn't a hard job in general, but it was for me. I had to be physically active, except while driving. Driving required a lot of mental stimulation, and then adding in the stress of trying to figure out everything and not making mistakes was draining.

The next day was a little easier. I knew what to expect. I just had to keep learning and try and be more efficient. My biggest fear was forgetting a sandwich, a bag of chips, or a drink. I didn't want to get to a customer and tell them, "I forgot an item." I really didn't want a customer to call the store and say that I messed up. I tried extra hard to make sure I wasn't missing anything.

I was bummed that the second day, I only made fifteen dollars in tips. I heard from the other drivers that it was simply a slow day and that sometimes you get a bad day out delivering. When I heard one of the drivers say that he averages fifty bucks for tips on a lunch shift, I was seeing dollar signs in my head. I couldn't wait to get some of that.

I started to get to know a few of my fellow coworkers. One in particular was Chrissy, who was a manager at the time. She was younger than me and in charge of running the store. I was surprised how well she handled everything for being only eighteen. She was the one to go to if I had questions. Chrissy was super sweet and nice to me. I liked her instantly and wanted to do a good job for her. She made coming to work a whole lot easier.

Before I knew it, I had made it through my first week of work. I didn't miss a day. I didn't make it a goal to not miss a day of work, but I wanted to show up every day no matter what. The shop needed me, I liked the money that I could earn, and I wanted Chrissy to know she could count on me to be there.

No one knew that I was sick. No one knew that I had Lyme disease. I did not want that to be known, at least in the beginning. I didn't want sympathy; I didn't want to be treated differently. I wanted to be judged, good or bad, based upon what type of work I was doing.

I needed the weekend. It was only fifteen hours of work for the week, but it felt like eighty to me. All I could do was rest and recover and hope that my body would be ready by Monday.

Work became my workouts for a while. I couldn't work and workout at the same time. I had no stamina for it. It was one or the other. Since work was technically a workout, and I could make money, that won out.

After the second week of work, I was in bad shape. Not only was I exhausted, but I got the dreaded sickness that started in my lymph nodes, swelling up in my neck. The Lyme disease was aggravated and angry. I couldn't talk, and my voice was gone. It felt like a flu and cold hit me all at once.

It was the same type of symptoms I experienced when I first was getting sick with the Lyme.

I knew it wasn't good. I knew my body was pushing itself over its limits.

I couldn't call in sick. I wasn't going to call in sick, but I *wanted* to call in sick.

I went to work.

I wasn't going to miss work after two weeks on the job. I didn't want people to think I wasn't committed or that I couldn't handle it.

I knew that my body needed rest. I also knew I had to push back. It was a hard thing to balance. I risked permanently taking myself down a hole I wasn't going to get back out of. I also didn't want to go down without a fight.

I fought back. That week of work was one of the hardest things I have put myself through. I had massive headaches, I was hot, I was cold, I was in pain, my throat felt like it had sharp sword in it, my eyes were blurry and burning, I couldn't stop coughing and sneezing, I had to constantly blow my nose, and I was exhausted. I had to deal with that and still deliver with a smile on my face and a nice attitude.

The weekend came, and all I wanted to do was to rest until I realized I was on the schedule for a closing shift on Saturday night.

I was so out of it that I was only focused on the week that I didn't even think about the schedule. I knew I would periodically be called upon to work a weekend, and it just had to be this one. I couldn't get out of it. I didn't ask to get out of it. I sucked it up and did it.

I kept telling myself to just survive, that I could get through it. It was a six-hour shift, the longest I had ever worked there. It wouldn't have been a big deal if I wasn't fighting off death, but it felt like I was, and then some.

Thankfully, it was a slow night. I had to help with cleaning and to get things prepared for the next day. I couldn't go home until everything was done. It sucked. I felt terrible, and I needed to rest. I was only going to have Sunday to recover just so that I could start another workweek.

I was starting to doubt that I could hold up. I had seen and experienced this movie before, and I knew how it ended. I had to push it, but if I went too far, that could be the end of me like it almost was seven years before.

I wasn't on the schedule for the coming weekend, so I had to just get through the five days. I was half-recovered, but working made me feel worse. I didn't want to quit; however, it was seriously crossing my mind. I thought that maybe it would be better to continue to exercise, get in shape, and *then* go back to work.

I liked having the money, and I didn't want to lose that. I was starting to get to know people at work, and I didn't want to miss out on some friendships. Work was now my school. I wanted people to like me, and the only way that was going to happen was if I was there on a regular basis. Chrissy was always there. She quickly became someone I gravitated toward. She had started working there a few months before I did. She handled so much, and I was impressed by how she stayed on top of everything. She kept people in line too. I don't know how she had the confidence to manage a whole shop of people from all different backgrounds at such a young age. I felt small in comparison. I was the quiet, little mouse just trying to do a good job and not ruffle feathers, and here Chrissy was running an entire team of people.

I learned quickly that as long as you tried your best and helped out, you were on Chrissy's good side.

I wanted to do just that. I needed Chrissy to trust me. I needed her to know that I was there to go through the battles of the lunch shift with her. I needed her to know that because, eventually, I was going to fall apart. She was my manager, but I also felt that I could trust her with my life.

The weekend shifts were too much for me on top of my regular five-day schedule. After a couple of months, I worked up the courage to talk to Chrissy about it. I told her that I wasn't looking for special treatment or that I was wimping out on her. I simply needed every weekend off. I told her about my situation with the Lyme. I told her that just getting through the week could be torture on my body. I told her if she wanted me to continue to be available during the weekdays, that I needed all future weekends off.

I was pleasantly surprised with her reaction. She was *glad* I told her what I was dealing with. I held back tears because the trust I had earned paid off. The two months I put in and pushing through all that I did was worth it. Chrissy listened to me and was willing to work with me. I thanked her over and over for understanding. It was a huge weight off my shoulders. I knew what my schedule was now, and I knew I could handle the work before me.

Chrissy quickly became another angel to me. I enjoyed working with her. She helped me tremendously, and even though I had more of a legitimate excuse to skip out on work when I wasn't feeling the greatest, I never took advantage of that situation unless I was in dire need of a day off.

The cold, snowy winter months were again in full swing, and 2008 turned into 2009. When it snowed, deliveries became extremely hectic. Nobody wanted to drive in the snow, so more people than normal would order delivery. Orders would be backed up for up to an hour. It was crazy trying to keep track of all the bags of food and making sure they were delivered in the right order.

One particularly snowy day, the wind was blowing the snow sideways out of the north. It was tough to see, and the white stuff was sticking to the signs and traffic lights. I always had terrible traction in my Mercury. The weight was in the front end, and fishtailing was quite easy to do. It was also hard to stop that boat of a car on slippery roads.

I had just finished up my run of deliveries and was headed back to the shop. I was coming down a decent hill with four cars ahead of me that had just started turning left through a green light. I had my foot on the brake, but once I saw the other cars turning left, I knew I could easily coast through the intersection and follow the tracks in front of me. As I approached the intersection, the light was still green, so it felt safe to proceed. I took a quick glance to my right and then to my left and saw a giant semi pulling a trailer barreling straight at me. I reacted as fast as I could by hitting the brakes and then braced for impact. I knew my car wasn't going to stop in the snow on time, and I was about to get T-boned hard by the semi. I quickly said, "Lord, help me!" as the impending collision was about to take place. All of it happened so quickly.

And then my car stopped on a dime.

I didn't slide a single inch. It was like I was on completely dry pavement. The semi blew past me and missed hitting my front end by a few feet. Several other cars followed in behind the semi.

I was dead meat, or I should have been. There was no way possible that my car could have stopped as fast as it did. I collected myself and made sure all my body parts were intact. I couldn't believe what had happened. I was flabbergasted why the semi and other cars didn't stop. I looked up at their traffic light, and it was covered with snow. They couldn't tell if it was red or green. My traffic light was on the east side, so it was shielded from getting covered and was still green, as I sat there in the intersection. I was 100 percent in the right. I couldn't believe a semi wouldn't have slowed down and been more cautious. The people behind it were probably just following the leader, so to speak.

The only reason I wasn't in an accident was because of a small miracle. I didn't stop my car. God did. I said a thank-you prayer as I made my way back to the shop. I easily could have been killed or badly injured that day, yet I was spared. Even though I had been through a lot in my life up to that point, it could always be worse. I was very grateful that on this day, it wasn't made worse.

Not many people know that story. I think about it time to time as a reminder that even when it may feel like I'm alone on this earth, God is watching over me.

My health was okay, but *okay* wasn't what I wanted. I felt like I could only do the minimum. I could work part-time, and I could occasionally work out. I wanted more good and great days.

Mom had been going through her own health issues and had recently begun acupuncture treatment. I had heard about the practice but never thought there could be a benefit for me. After a few months, Mom was definitely having some improvement. She asked if I wanted to try it out, so I said, "Sure, it can't hurt."

My initial consultation went very well. The acupuncturist and the staff there were warm and welcoming. They explained how the treatments could be beneficial and were confident that if I stuck with the treatment, I should notice some improvement.

The biggest takeaway I had from the consultation was that a disease or sickness can fester in the body for a long time before symptoms emerge, and by then, it could be too late. A heart attack is a good example. You may not know you have an issue with your heart until it stops, or cancer could fester in your body for a long time, but you may not know you have it until you're in the late stages, which are very difficult to treat.

Acupuncture is about helping the body get in a good state so that your organs can function at the highest level. It's done by placing needles in certain areas so that the energy in your body can move more efficiently and freely. It didn't make a ton of sense in the beginning, but I pictured the needles being conductors for the electrical system of your body. The different points the needles would go helped everything flow better. Therefore, your body doesn't have to work as hard fighting through bad traffic jams in your system. The less your body has to fight against the bad stuff, the better it is able to heal and rejuvenate itself.

I was optimistic and eager to see what treatments could do for me. There was a scoring system of how well my body was working. I'm not exactly sure how it was calculated but on a scale of one to one hundred, I was operating around a ten. I wasn't surprised they could figure out I wasn't in the best of health. I knew I needed to improve, and I was willing to try different things to help me do that.

We started on an aggressive treatment plan. I was set to go twice a week for a couple of months to kick-start my system. I believe I would go Tuesday and Thursday after I got done with work. It was about a half-hour drive from work, and a lot of times, it was through the lovely Milwaukee traffic. I didn't like going into

Milwaukee because it added a lot of unneeded stress, but I wanted to feel better.

The treatments were more relaxing than I thought they would be. I started out with only a few needles being inserted in my body as I lay on the table. There was nothing I could do but endure it and wait. I would either think about stuff or take a quick nap. The needles didn't ever hurt too badly, but if I moved my body, I could feel where they were, so I remained as motionless as possible.

I felt the treatments were beneficial, but it was difficult to tell in the beginning. With me working and then traveling to the facility twice a week, I was adding more stress and exhaustion to my body. I was just starting to get used to working fifteen hours a week, and adding in an extra few hours to get to my appointments was pushing me way past my limits. I felt like I was falling apart.

A month or two later, I was at my breaking point. I couldn't keep up this schedule. I had a re-exam coming up in which the acupuncturist would evaluate how I was doing and make adjustments. My graph, which was at ten, went down to a five. I felt a lot worse, and the chart reflected that. The acupuncturist was surprised at my step backward.

I wasn't.

I told them that I either needed to reduce my treatments or spread them out, or I was done.

They agreed that spreading out the number of times I would come in could be a good thing. I immediately felt a relief come over me. I wanted to give this type of treatment an honest try, and I was glad they were willing to work with what I felt would be correct.

I started going once every two weeks, and it was so much easier on me. To the average person, it wouldn't be a big change, but I was fighting to get my health back. Every little thing that I could do to help my situation was needed. Even something as small as adjusting a schedule to reduce the amount of stress I was putting on myself made a huge difference.

I had another re-exam a couple months later and knew this one would be better. I felt it. I bounced back from a five (my lowest point) and improved to a twenty. I was starting to head in the right direction and was excited to see how I could progress with this ancient Chinese healing modality.

I had made it through the winter months, and spring was approaching. I had finally started to make some consistent, positive momentum.

I was looking for that to continue.

I had been going to the gym on occasion and would mostly play basketball by myself. I got pretty good at shooting, and it helped with getting my coordination back. My endurance was improving, but I now needed to start adding muscle to my frame.

As I mentioned before, if I felt strong, I could get through some weightlifting. I knew the only way I could put and keep muscle on was to hit the weights consistently. It wasn't going to be easy, but I had to start somewhere.

I would get there as often as I felt I could. Some weeks, I'd be there five days. Other times, I'd be there for maybe one or two days. Even when I knew I'd fall off the proverbial horse and I'd be out a week or two with how I felt, I kept coming back to fight again.

Getting through the first few weeks was the toughest. My body needed to get used to the change. I started off slowly because I had to. There was no point in pushing past what I could do and then quit. I listened to my body the best I could. I would always try and get three sets of whatever exercise I was doing, but sometimes it was only two. It didn't matter as long as I was sticking with it. I knew that if I could do that, results would show up.

Dory was a huge factor in helping me stick with my plan of getting into better shape. Knowing she would be there when I was became a giant mental boost. I wasn't going to be there alone. Dory was always happy to see me. We would hug and chat about anything and everything. She was a role model, friend, and confidant. She didn't have to give me the time of day. She did a lot of personal training, but I wasn't her client. I'm not sure why she took a liking to me, but it was easy to like her.

I had opened up to Dory about the Lyme and what I had been through. I wanted her to know my story. Main reason being, I would sometimes push way too hard when I was working out. I wanted someone at the gym to know about my condition in case something was to happen to me while I was there. I didn't know if there would come a time when I would collapse and need CPR or if I would just end up dying there.

More than a few times, I would black out, collapse, need a shoulder to lean on, or assistance to get up off the floor. Dory watched out for me and would keep an eye out if she hadn't seen me for a while to make sure I was okay.

Over time, Dory could see it in my behavior if I was having a great day, good day, or a day where she might want to keep an extra-close watch on me. A lot of times, I would tell her how I was functioning so that she would have a heads-up in case something was to happen.

Fortunately, she only had to pick me up off the floor a few instances. I leaned on her many times so that I would stay upright and not collapse. She would bring me water if she saw me gassed and sitting down. She really became my best friend. I never would have expected us to have the kind of relationship we did. She helped me so much, and I was grateful for that.

On days when I wanted to work out but felt terrible, or on just a random day, I would still go to the gym to see her. Sometimes all it took was a quick embrace and a minute to chat, and I'd feel better about things. Going to the gym and having Dory there was one of the best forms of therapy I could have had. I was just a kid trying to get my life back. It wasn't going to happen overnight. It was going to take a consistent effort, and Dory was an integral part in helping me with that effort. I honestly don't know what she got out of our relationship. I had nothing to offer. I think she did it out of the goodness of her heart. Whatever the reason may be, I was happy to have her in my life.

I had been working for a solid nine months as the summer of 2009 was fast approaching. I had been wanting to get my own car with my own money since the Mercury was terrible on gas. I figured I could increase my bottom line if I used a vehicle that could double the mileage I would normally get. I had been looking at Honda Civics for a few months and came across one I thought would be a good fit. It was a 1999 EX with a factory spoiler in the back and a five-speed manual transmission. I knew how to drive stick, and even though I knew it was going to be a lot of shifting when I drove for work, it was much more fun to drive versus an automatic.

Mom took me to pick it up. I paid for it in cash from the tips I had made. As I drove it home, I had a nice feeling of accomplishment come over me. I may have started in last place, but the race was far from over. In a lot of ways, I used to view life as a sprint, and I thought I had to hit certain life goals by a certain age. That was all thrown out the window with me having to battle back from a sickness that I had no control over happening. Life was now a marathon. It didn't matter if I finished first; all that mattered was I felt like I was now competing and had a chance to run a good race.

That Civic purred nicely as I cruised home on the highway. I made sure to take good care of it. I wanted it to last as long as it could. I was excited to see everyone's reaction at work when I pulled up in a sporty coupe versus an old, gas-guzzling boat of a car.

I felt a little confidence again for the first time in a long time.

Delivering was fun for the most part that summer. I could roll the windows down, have the sunroof open, blast some music, and make money all at the same time.

After a few weeks of driving manual, my left knee was hurting and aching terribly. Every day at work, my left leg would have to push the clutch anywhere from a few hundred times to some days probably close to one thousand times. I would hobble in and out of the car as I made my deliveries. In hindsight, it wasn't a smart decision to get a manual car, but I liked it too much to sell it.

I worked on healing and strengthening my legs at the gym and asked Dory for some pointers of what I could do. I essentially put myself into physical therapy so that I could get my legs strong enough to take the daily pounding I was undoubtedly going to put on them.

It took a few weeks for the legs to strengthen, but putting in the work fixed the problem. I didn't want to just pop some pain pills and deal with it. I wanted to get stronger and more flexible. The more I did that, the better my quality of life would be.

Work was going well. I had good days, bad days, and an occasional great day. I liked most of the people I worked with and tried to stay away from the ones I didn't care for as much. Working there opened me up to many different kinds of people and new things. I heard swear words I'd never heard before. Some people smoked cigarettes or weed. I'm quite certain some people were doing some hard drugs too. We had people from all backgrounds. Some people had good families, and some didn't. I had a clean background while others were on work release from a juvenile detention center. We were a mixed bag of all races and cultures.

Peer pressure can develop in any work environment. Sometimes where you work, you can start to adopt different practices of things that people do. This can be positive or negative.

My health was extremely important to me, and so the smoking, drinking, and any drug use I stayed away from. I had worked extremely hard to get to where I was, and I wasn't going to be influenced by other people's bad habits just to fit in or have anyone like me.

I could get along and have a good time with just about everyone at work, but that's typically where it stayed. I had people I could be friendly with at work, but very few of them became friends outside of work.

My objective was to grow and improve, so I didn't see the benefit of late-night parties where drinking, smoking, or other crazy things might be taking place. I had to walk a very straight line if I wanted to continue to ascend.

After a while of working there, more and more people knew about my Lyme health condition. Most didn't know what it was, so I educated them about it the best I could. No one gave me any grief over it, and I never tried to use it as an excuse for anything. I was part of the team, and as long as I was doing what I should, I was accepted.

I didn't like making mistakes at work, so I tried to operate perfectly, even though it was impossible with everything that I did.

I would occasionally mess up an order on the phone or forget to take an item with me, but I didn't make a habit of it.

On one extremely busy day, I was getting set to take a bunch of orders out the door. Two of them were in similar boxes with the same price on them. I grabbed those, along with a handful of other orders, and went out the door. I knew where the first two similar orders were going. I quickly got to the first destination, got the money for it, and took off to deliver the second one. I had four or five smaller orders to get to before I headed back to the shop. When I got back, one of the managers working that day told me I messed up big time. I had switched the two similar orders around so neither customer had the right order. I had no idea I did that; it was an honest mistake. The manager was quite upset with me and said that it may be grounds for firing me. All I could do was apologize that it happened. I was paranoid the rest of the day that I was taking the correct order to where it needed to be. I wasn't sure if I would have a job when my shift was over.

Thankfully, it all blew over and was forgotten about by the end of the day. People said a lot of things in the heat of the moment. It would get extremely stressful at times. I was glad I was a driver so I could escape the craziness that would take place. I honestly don't think I could have handled the amount of multitasking that a lot of the employees had to handle. My Lyme brain wasn't fully back to operating at a high capacity. Looking back just a few short years ago, simple math and remembering how to write my name was a challenge. It was a miracle I could handle what I was doing and not messing up more.

I was finally starting to keep and maintain a consistent schedule. Granted, there were a lot of ups and downs along the way, but the bottom line was I was moving forward.

With acupuncture, I made slow and steady improvements. Most days, I'd feel rested and relaxed after treatments, and other times, not so much. On more than a few occasions, I'd be done with a session and get set to leave. Out of the blue, I would get hit with an intense wave of old symptoms. It felt a lot like a Herxheimer reaction. The first time it happened was just like how I felt back when I was wrestling. My heart would race, I'd feel sick to my stomach, and then I'd shake, and my hands and face would go numb. I'd simply feel terrible. It was a major onslaught that was short-lived, especially if I was able to throw up. It wasn't a pretty scene a few times. I'd be back in a public restroom, clinging to a toilet, praying for the reaction to pass.

I mentioned it to the acupuncturist, and he said even though I might feel a little bit worse once in a while, it shouldn't be like what I was experiencing. The Lyme didn't like the treatment. The Lyme didn't like any of the healthy habits I was trying to adopt. I kept pushing back. Acupuncture was helping, even though, at times, it put me through a short-lived hell.

I added a few more supplements to my regimen as well. With me doing more and more, I needed whatever help I could get. If that meant putting high-quality supplements in me, that's what I was going to do. When I was working out, I used pre- and post-workout products to help me get through and recover. I started taking more digestive and liver support products to help get rid of bad stuff that could be living in there. And then I always took my regular regimen of antioxidants, vitamins, and minerals. The more ways I could help my body, the better.

I was trying to do the best that I could, and it was slowly starting to work.

My workouts were getting longer. I was lifting more weight and doing more repetitions. I had a goal of being able to bench press my own weight at least one time. I felt that if I could do that, then anything after would be icing on the cake. I wasn't looking to become the next world's strongest man or a bodybuilder, but I did want to become the strongest version of myself that I could be.

After a couple of years of dedication, I not only benched my weight, but I was also doing more than my own weight. I had doubts I would ever be able to do the bar plus a forty-five-pound weight on each side for a total of 135 pounds. I enlisted a spotter to help me in case I needed it, but I successfully pushed that weight up to my amazement. A few short months ago, there were times when it was a struggle to simply get the forty-five-pound bar off my chest for more than a few repetitions.

I had come a long way. Instead of having mostly bad days and a few good ones, I was starting to have more good days than bad days. The bad days were still bad and a humble reminder that I wasn't where I wanted to be yet.

The only thing I could do was keep pushing forward. I had to be smart about it. The recipe I was finding for success was to simply do the things that worked and keep on doing them.

I didn't stop.

I would still get lonely and down on myself from time to time. I didn't have a ton of friends, and dates were nonexistent.

Rich was at the University of Wisconsin, and he invited me out there to hang out. It was an hour drive from home. I was able to stay the night at his apartment so we could do some fun stuff and catch up. His then-girlfriend was there too, and I was looking forward to meeting her. Maybe she had friends?

There was a documentary showing at a local theater that we went to see called *Under Our Skin*. It was a movie about Lyme and the effects it had on different people as they went about their daily lives.

It was difficult seeing other people struggle as much as or worse than me with their battle against Lyme disease. My fight wasn't ever caught on camera like the people in the film. I suppose if it was, it could look perilous if I was captured at some of the moments I've endured. In a lot of ways, I felt blessed that I was doing better. I knew I could be in a much more challenging situation.

It was impossible to not be emotional after sitting through and watching the whole thing. I wasn't surprised by any of it, but it just sucked knowing what this disease can do to people. No one chooses Lyme. There's nothing we did to our bodies to cause it. For most of us, we were in the wrong place at the wrong time. Some of us didn't know for years what the cause was of all the terrible carnage. Doctors didn't know what to do with it and would call us crazy. Friends and family couldn't understand it. The mental, emotional, spiritual, and physical toll it can take on a person is almost indescribable. It can leave you isolated and bankrupt; health insurance has denied many people coverage.

I was glad Rich believed me and cared about how I was doing. I thanked him and his girlfriend on the ride back for coming with me to the movie and showing their support. It meant a lot. As I mentioned before, I didn't have that many friends, but with Rich, I had a great friend. He believed what I had was real. He believed it so much that he went on to write his final dissertation paper on Lyme. It was called the "Epidemiology of Post-Treatment Lyme Disease Syndrome in Wisconsin." I was the inspiration behind that, which made me feel like maybe going through this whole ordeal may benefit others somehow or in some way.

I started reaching out to the Lyme community more and seeing if I could be of service to someone. A lot of people I talked to were glad I was doing better, and they always asked me how I had improved so much. I would tell them about the supplements I used, acupuncture, chiropractic care, exercise, and doing the little things that help consistently.

It seemed like more often than not, people were looking for a quick fix. They would ask what supplements I used, but then I would get accused of trying to sell them something. If, by chance, they did try them, they would only use them for a week and be done. That's not how it works. You don't get better after a week. I always said that supplements can help if you take them consistently and then add in whatever else you feel may be helping. There was no magic pill. There wasn't an all-knowing doctor who was curing 100 percent of their patients. Lyme and the coinfections are extremely difficult to figure out, and everyone reacts differently. How I got a lot of my health back may not work for everyone, but it will at least give a person some ideas on what they can try.

When I was talking with people with Lyme, I had always wondered if I could find another girl to talk to just like I had with Lori and Kelsey previously.

It didn't take long before I had my answer. I started talking with a girl named Erin who lived in Alabama. She was six years older than me, but we got along great. We would chat online quite often and, on occasion, text each other on the phone. She definitely was having more bad days than good days when we were conversing, but she always had a good spirit about her. She didn't want me to worry too much about her either. She'd always wanted to know how I was doing. She was really happy for me that I was through the worst of it, and she was determined to get through it just the same.

We started talking in the summer of 2010. It was nice to have someone to chat with again on a regular basis. I wished we lived closer, but that was the case for me a lot of times. I'd find someone fun to talk to, but they were always a good distance away from me.

By the end of 2010 and into 2011, I would hear from her more sporadically as her health wasn't very good at all. I always kept her in my prayers that she could get some relief. She was such a sweet person who really cared about people, and you could always tell she was trying to smile through the pain she was going through.

I completely stopped hearing from her in April 2011. A few weeks passed, and I thought it was strange that she wasn't coming around at all. I had no way of contacting anyone else in her family to see if she was okay or not. I began to think that maybe she got tired of talking to me and just blocked me from communicating with her. I didn't really believe that would be the case, but it had happened before with other people. As one month and then two rolled by, I figured something bad happened. I thought that she may be in the hospital and just wasn't able to communicate.

I still had to live my life. There was nothing I could do. If she was ignoring me, I wouldn't know. If she was in the hospital or worse, I had no way of knowing. It was a crappy position to be in. I cared about her and just wanted to know how she was doing.

Fall was creeping in, and the colder weather was knocking on the door. I was scrolling through a Lyme page and saw an obituary posted.

I froze when I saw it was Erin's obituary.

She passed away due to complications of Lyme on April 28, 2011.

I was shocked and saddened. I couldn't and didn't want to believe it. She was only thirty years old.

I doubt anyone else besides us knew we had a connection and friendship, so I was never able to be informed of what happened. I wish it would have been a case where she just slowly drifted away from me versus her passing away. Her number is still in my phone and always will be. I scroll past it from time to time to remember her.

It didn't seem fair. It didn't seem right. Why did this sweet girl pass away while I was still standing?

Lyme is not an easy thing to diagnose, treat, or get better from. It can slowly torture you for years and years. Erin was not the first person to die from Lyme, and she won't be the last. She was the first person I personally knew who died from it, and since then, there have been others. Erin's memory is something I want to remember, and adding a little bit of her story into mine is one way I can do that. Even though our little friendship together was short, she made a big impact on me. It made me even more determined to try and do something good with my life.

The gym became the place where I began to set purposeful action to start the process of that good.

There would be no story if I didn't push it. There would be no reason to write this story if I didn't go through the hell and live to tell the tale.

I was healthier than I had been in a long time. Yet, I still wasn't healthy.

I wasn't satisfied with my fitness level. I wasn't content to be just good enough to get by.

I wanted to be able to power through the day and not pay for it the next.

I wanted to have a good week. I wanted to have a good month. I wanted to have a good year.

It was now a physical and mental battle. I had started my climb up the mountain, and I didn't want to go back down. I wanted to keep ascending.

Up until the start of 2012, my workouts were light and didn't require too much exertion. I started small on purpose. There was no reason to try and sculpt Mount Rushmore in a week, so to speak. I could handle the minimum, but I wanted to handle the maximum. The only way to do that was to chisel away over a long period of time. Three weeks was not going to do much. Three months would be a great start. I needed to push for a few years. The time was now to start ramping things up. I knew it wasn't going to become any easier the older I got.

My plan was to gradually push past what I thought I could do, just to see how my body responded. Sometimes, I fell apart, but other times, I could push the pedal down more.

Walking up a flight of stairs used to cripple me to the ground. Now, being able to get up and down the basketball court with no pain was joyous. Being able to run a mile and not collapse was exhilarating. Lifting more and more weights than I had ever been able to before made me feel like a tank.

I was finally able to start pushing back without falling apart.

I started to feel a little bit like I used to, and I wanted more.

I drank my pre-workout supplement to get me revved up to hit the weights. I was pushing and moving heavier and heavier loads. Curling twenty to twenty-five pounds was good, but not what I wanted. I could do that for ten and fifteen rep sets. I gradually was able to increase that to thirty pounds. After a while, I upped it to thirty-five. I wanted to get up to forty pounds for a single arm curl. It took a while, but I eventually was able to take a forty-pound dumbbell and curl each one individually. I then proceeded to max it out at eight reps.

I did all sorts of leg exercises as well. The incline leg press was the one that I wanted to really move some weight on. Starting out only being able to do a measly 135 pounds and sometimes only forty-five pounds when I felt really weak was something I was determined to improve upon. I thought when I crossed the three- hundred-pound weight line that I was getting quite strong, but I knew I had a lot more in me. I started to enlist some spotters when I did this exercise, as I didn't want all that weight coming back down on me in case my legs gave out. I passed four hundred and five hundred pounds and was at the point where I could do five hundred at ten-rep increments. I knew I could get to the six hundred mark. On the day that I attempted it, I made sure to have two spotters. The two guys who were there looked a little dumbfounded when I kept telling them I needed more forty-five-pound plates added. We kept taking them from wherever we could. I used almost all of the ones that were available. There was some serious doubt on their faces that I could even come close to pushing up that much weight. I needed twelve forty-five-pound plates plus the sled, two five-pound weights, and two two-and-half-pound weights to make an even six hundred pounds. I sat myself down and lifted my feet up to get them in a comfortable position on the sled. The two spotters were a little anxious, but I assured them I would be able to do it. I took a few deep breaths and focused my mind on what I was about to do. I knew it was a little risky, but I needed to prove to myself that I could accomplish this task. As I exhaled, I exerted all my strength into my legs. I could feel the weight pushing down on me. I extended my legs up and then slowly brought my legs back toward my chest. I stopped when I was in the proper position, then started to slowly push the sled back up higher and higher. That was one repetition. I kept going. The second one was easier than the first, then the third and fourth. I could feel my legs start to shake when I pushed up the fifth one and thought it was a good place to stop. I didn't need to go anymore. I did what I wanted to do. The spotters couldn't believe it. They said there was no way I could have done that and that there was no way *they* could have done that. I felt very good about myself. It didn't happen overnight. It took me nearly three years to get there.

In the same time period I was able to do that, I was also closing in on my bench press goals. I used to struggle sometimes with being able to do the forty-five-pound bar a few times, but now I was getting closer to where I wanted to be. It was mind-blowing.

My first goal was to be able to do my own body weight, which, at the time, was around 115 pounds. I needed the bar plus two twenty-five-pound plates and two ten-pound plates. It took me about a year to be able to do that one time. I increased that to five and then ten reps. I thought it would be the coolest thing ever if I could push up the full-size forty-five-pound plates on each side plus the bar for a whomping 135 pounds. That doesn't sound like a lot of weight, but there is only a small percentage of people who can bench press their own body weight. Luckily, I didn't weigh that much!

I wanted to go way above my body weight to prove to myself that I could be the 1 percent of people who could push up more than what they weigh.

It took another few months before I could do 135 comfortably. The first time pushing that up was extremely difficult for me to do. I kept at it, and it wasn't long until I was doing that same 135 pounds ten times in a row. I kept going. The strain I was putting on my body was intense. The odd thing was that there were days that doing the 135 pounds ten times felt easy. A few days later, mustering ninety-five pounds was incredibly hard. The bench was the most difficult thing to be consistent with. I needed to feel great to even attempt lifting a lot of weight. I learned the hard way a few times when I tried to push through the weakness I would feel. It was a little embarrassing and a little dangerous when I tried to do more than I should. Getting to the point where I couldn't get the weight off of me, I either had to call for help or somehow roll it off of me. After a few close calls, I always made sure I had someone spot me when I got to the heavier sets. One hundred fifty pounds was on my radar. I wanted to do that ten times. I had to start with one. One turned into three, and three turned into five. I kept rolling. Sometimes I'd fall back and have to start back at one. Eventually, I did make it to the tenth rep, and man, did I feel good.

I started wondering how high I could or should go. I had already pushed past so many limits, but I also knew there was no point in getting stupid in seeing how much I could do. It didn't matter to me or prove to me anything if I could bench 150 or 250. What mattered was that I was strong and fit. My odds of injury would definitely go up if I tried to go crazy, and I didn't need that.

So, I decided to push just a little more. I was around 120 to 125 pounds, so I thought if I could do fifty pounds more than I weighed, then that would be something worth writing home about. I mean, just seven years ago, I couldn't get up off the wrestling mat after pinning my opponent in thirty seconds. It started to seem inconceivable how rough of a shape I used to be in.

I made sure I was feeling good and strong on the day I attempted 170 pounds on the bench press. I found a capable spotter and told him what I wanted to do. I made sure I could do 135 and 150 a few times to warm up. I did those with no problem. I knew I could add twenty more pounds and knock this out of the park.

As I lay back on the bench, I put on my angry, upset-at-the-world, punch-you-in-the-mouth, get-back-at-you revenge attitude and gripped the bar. I exhaled and pushed up, then steadied myself as I slowly let the weight come back toward my chest. I put all my strength into pushing that weight up, and it slowly got higher and higher. I got one. I went back for another and struggled to get two. I told myself that one was a fluke, two was luck, but three would be validation. I went in for number three. When it came down, I could feel myself wearing out, but I dug deep and pushed up as hard as I could. My spotter saw my struggle and brought his hands under the bar. I didn't want help. Knowing I did have help just in case gave me another gear to push upward. I squeezed up as hard as I could, and it felt like I was a large locomotive slowly charging up a hill with two hundred cars attached to me. Every inch I went up, I felt I would get to the top. With my arms fully extended up, I was able to drop the bar back to its starting place.

I did it: 170 pounds, three times.

Not bad, not bad at all for the chronically ill kid who used to be skin and bones and only ninety pounds.

Hitting those milestones was not easy. It took a lot of time, dedication, pain, setbacks, and patience.

I would get close to hitting a goal and then have to take a few days or weeks off because I would be exhausted. I still needed to work, and sometimes that's all I could do for the day.

There were many times I'd work out and be really upset with myself that for whatever reason, I just simply could not muster the strength or energy to even come close to what my baseline workout had become.

I had to stop my workouts when I was only halfway done or before I could even start it multiple times.

I fought through exhaustion, depression, weakness, and low self-esteem. I had days where I didn't want to work out, but when I was able to get through even a small one, it was a victory.

A lot of people feel great after a workout. That was the case for me multiple times; however, other times, I thought I might die.

I would get super nauseous, and I threw up on many occasions. I'd have extreme dizziness where I thought the room wouldn't ever stop spinning. I'd get major headaches, black out, see stars, or I'd be so exhausted that I'd pass out on a workout mat and even once or twice on the bench. I stared up at the ceiling hundreds of times, wishing it would crash down on top of me and take me out of my misery.

Dory saw my struggles, as did a lot of the other trainers who worked there. I didn't want them to see it, but I had no choice. I was a limp noodle, dead to the world, beaten down like a smashed carton of eggs in front of quite a few people more times than I'd like to admit. Dory and the others saw me at my worst and at my best. I didn't know, and they didn't know what was in store when I walked through the doors to the workout area. I would have bet that at some point, I would have needed the ambulance called for me because of how awful I felt. Thankfully, that never happened.

I worked hard, pushed through a lot, and never gave up.

I could have stopped. But I knew that if I wanted to live a healthy life, I needed to keep going. No one was going to do it for me. I had way too much life ahead of me to not try and put my best effort into being able to live it at a high level.

I will always be in good shape. That was the path I wanted to be on. I knew it was going to be the easiest to do it now versus what it would be like when I got older.

In my mind, I knew what it was like to be unhealthy, sick, and weak. I didn't like that feeling. I never felt that way before Lyme. Lyme took a lot away from me. What I had to push through to get some normalcy back I will never forget, and it's the main reason why I want to be fit and strong for as long as I can.

I may never get back to the point of lifting as much weight as I did. That took an extraordinary amount of effort, time, and dedication. As long as I'm staying in shape, eating well, exercising, and fitting into the clothes I want to and looking the way that makes me feel good, I'm winning, and the Lyme is losing.

I will always be pushing it, but in a smart way. I could run myself into the ground, but then I may not get back up. That's not worth it. I'd rather put in a consistent effort to maintain a high-level fitness and not burn out.

There's no way I'd want to go back to how I used to have to live. Being sick as bad as I was sucked.

I felt lazy, and it sucked.

I could barely do anything that I wanted, and it sucked.

Life for me was a lot better being fit and healthy. I had more energy, drive, ambition, self-esteem, and confidence.

I felt like I was on the right track. I was excited and looking forward to the future a lot more than I was looking back at the failures and disappointments of the past.

CHAPTER 11

KEEP IMPROVING

was the strongest I had ever been. I was having more good days than bad days. I was starting to sprinkle on more great days and having less and less horrendous ones.

Unfortunately, the horrendous ones would still happen occasionally.

I could be flying high and feel like I could take on the world, and the next day, it would be a struggle to do anything.

I was still on a roller coaster of emotional and mental ups and downs.

I could be happy and optimistic, but if I didn't feel like I could dominate the day, I'd get pretty down on myself.

I was still learning and adjusting. Trying to find a good balance in everything was difficult.

Work was going well. I hardly missed any time at work. I pushed through a lot of sickness, exhaustion, and pain.

Sometimes, I probably should have taken the day off, but I didn't.

One day, I should have called in sick because I was struggling mightily at work. I was insanely exhausted. All I wanted to do was get through my shift, go home, and take a nap. I probably had overdone a workout the day before and was paying for it at work. I felt like I couldn't catch my breath. I was weak, and my legs felt like rubber. I knew it wasn't a good day, and it just wouldn't get any better. I was making my deliveries at a snail's pace. I was taking the elevators instead of the stairs. I would walk at a drastically reduced pace versus my typical running around like crazy. I just did not have it, and I couldn't break out of the tiredness.

I was dizzy and lightheaded and kept struggling through the hours. I would glance at the clock in my car, and I couldn't believe how slowly time was passing. I told Chrissy that I was struggling. She could see it in how I was not acting like my normal self. There wasn't anything she could do, but she did say if things slowed down that she would send me home early. I loved it when she did things like that for me.

I could feel myself slowly spiraling down. I felt that if I stopped for any period of time, I would fall over. If I had been working out or attempting to, I would have stopped a long time ago. It wasn't that the work was hard. It was simply my body not allowing me to do what I was normally capable of.

I hated those kinds of days. At the same time, I was grateful because I knew it could be worse. I'd been through much worse. However, I still very much disliked it.

The hours ticked by, and the deliveries slowed down. Chrissy asked if I wanted to go home. I tiredly nodded yes. She started cashing me out as I was leaning on her shoulder so I wouldn't fall over. A few seconds later, I felt my eyes close, and everything went black.

I collapsed to the ground like I had done many times before. I was only out for a few seconds; thankfully, the hard ground broke my fall.

I came to with a bunch of my fellow employees around me, making sure I was okay. I was helped to my feet, and someone got me some water. I wanted to get home, but I wasn't in much shape to do so. One of the girls I worked with volunteered to drive me because she knew how to drive a stick shift. It was extremely kind of her to do that.

I didn't plan on collapsing. My body decided it had had enough and just gave out.

There were limits to what I could do safely. Sometimes pushing those limits would get me in trouble, so I had to be smart with what I did and what I allowed myself to go through. Otherwise, I could end up on the floor.

Thankfully, with an evening of rest, I was okay by the next day. If this same kind of thing had happened eight years ago, I'd probably be out for months. I had been in this rodeo before, and the biggest difference now was that I could get back on the bull a lot faster than before and go another round.

I also continued battling through back and neck issues. I went through a lot of it when I first was sick with the Lyme, and they still lingered. Sometimes all I had to do was move my head, and something in my neck would catch. Other times, I could just be sitting at the table and having dinner, and my back would twinge, and I'd be in a world of pain.

Add in the occasional searing, stabbing, shooting pains that I would get in my chest, and I didn't know when or where something would pop up and bring me to my knees. It was a terrible surprise.

I don't know if my back and neck going out had anything to do with those piercing shots to the heart or not, but it was a major inconvenience to deal with when it would randomly appear.

As an example of how it would just happen, I was in the kitchen one time talking with Mom, and out of nowhere, it felt like someone stabbed me in the chest. The pain was instant and intense and would make me collapse to the floor. It never lasted for more than a few seconds, but it was enough to bring tears to my eyes. Those episodes would happen at the most random times. They happened at work, when I worked out, or when I was sitting down relaxing. There was nothing I could pinpoint that would trigger it.

The pain in my neck and back would come on in the same way and, unfortunately, would leave me in terrible pain and limited movement for days on end.

Sometimes my neck and back would both go out at the same time, which made it almost impossible to do anything.

A few times, I attempted to go to work; it wasn't the safest thing to be doing when I couldn't turn my head to see if any traffic was coming my way. Shifting would hurt, and getting in and out of the car would hurt. I tried to work through it as much as possible. In a lot of instances, I'd recover faster if I kept active and moving. It would be terribly painful, and it might not have been smart, but it showed me I could work through a lot more than I thought.

More than once, however, I just needed to stay home and let my body heal. It had to be exceptionally bad for me to at least not give work a try. Sometimes I'd test it out and just go right back home; other times, I could manage.

The back, neck, and pain in the heart issues persisted for quite some time. The chiropractor would help, but I was only going in for adjustments after I started hurting. It wasn't until quite a few years later that I committed to going on a regular basis. Once I did, the frequency and severity of those events went down dramatically.

If there was a way I could improve my body, I was open to it. If I had an issue, I wanted to treat it as naturally as possible. I didn't want to be prescribed a drug or have to do any sort of surgery unless it was a last resort. For me, I found the idea of taking care of myself and doing what I could naturally was a better route than having to be prescribed something or needing some sort of hospital or doctor care.

I had been working at Jimmy Johns for a few years. I liked it on most days. I was starting to have a normal life after ten-plus years of pain, sickness, sadness, and despair.

I started thinking, *What else can I do?*

I didn't want to be a delivery driver forever.

I didn't know what I wanted to do next. In some ways, I was hesitant to change anything. I was functioning and fitting into society. I wasn't doing that in the years past.

I was scared.

I was worried that this was all I could do or be capable of.

I felt like a loser at times.

All the people I knew and the friends I had were doing bigger and better things with their lives. Some were starting families. Some were getting nice jobs, and some were continuing with higher education.

And there I was, a part-time delivery driver.

Even though I had overcome a seemingly insurmountable mountain to get to where I was, I felt inadequate.

I was grateful and happy to be out of the crap I was in, but I wasn't content feeling mediocre. I couldn't help but feel like I was falling behind in the race of life.

I battled through depression again. I felt like I was trapped in quicksand as other people passed me by. I had worked so hard, and I still felt like I was in last place.

I was stuck. I felt immature and not socially developed. I had friends but nobody that I'd hang out with on a regular basis. I was alone. I kept seeing people at work and their significant others. I started wondering, *Am I ever going to find someone to share my life with?*

I couldn't think of anything that I wanted to do.

I tried some online dating, but aside from a few dates, nothing materialized after a few years of being on them.

I had nothing to live for. I got down on myself. It wasn't the same kind of depression that I experienced in my teenage years, but the end result was the same. *Why don't I just take myself out?*

I wrestled with those thoughts again. I hated it. I kept telling myself I've put in too much effort to just give up now.

Ending it seemed like a valid idea for a while.

I had the house to myself for a few days, and in isolation, my mind was allowed to run wild. I kept thinking about what would happen if I didn't exist. I know people would miss me. But I didn't know if I would miss anything.

I made myself a little deal with God.

I would physically put myself in a position to hang myself.

If I was caused to slip or fall by an outside force outside of my own doing, then I'd die, and it wouldn't entirely have been my decision.

I found some rope, tied it up in the garage, and made a loop that I put around my neck. I went to the top of the garage and sat there.

In a way, I wanted to feel what it was like, but I knew I couldn't undo the feeling after it was done. I don't think I had any real intention of dropping down and letting gravity and inertia take its course.

However, the deal was on the table. If, for some reason, I'd be caused to black out and fall, or if the house shook and I fell, then I felt like I wouldn't have been responsible for what happened to me. It would just be a tragic accident.

I sat there for a few hours thinking about life, what I was doing, and my situation.

Nothing ever happened.

I wasn't meant to die. I didn't make it this far to have to end it now. More importantly, God didn't carry me this far for it to end like this.

I removed the rope and climbed down.

I needed to keep improving. I didn't know how, but I wasn't going to stop trying to improve my situation, which became my mindset. That kept me focused on positive ideas and away from the depressing ones.

Four years at Jimmy Johns, in a lot of ways, felt like my high school. I didn't know anybody going into it. Along the way, I had a lot of laughs, made a few friends, and learned a lot about myself. I proved to myself that I could commit to something for a long period of time and be successful.

I was at the point where I needed to graduate and move on.

I didn't know what I wanted to do or what I could do.

I had a few ideas that I entertained. I loved golfing, so I looked into what it would take to be a PGA professional. I didn't know if my body would hold up to that.

I was also good at tinkering and fixing things. I loved cars, so I thought about going to school to learn how to work on those. I believe the schooling would have been a two-year commitment and a little on the expensive side. I didn't really want to get into something for too long or invest too much money in case I couldn't get through it.

While driving around for work, I kept hearing about this computer school. I heard the ad on the radio many times a day for weeks on end. I started taking it as some sort of sign to look into it. It turned out to be a year-long education in computers and Microsoft technologies. There wasn't any degree that I would get out of it, but I would be Microsoft-certified on various systems, and I thought that was interesting. I also figured that if I was in IT, I wouldn't have to physically wear myself out. I decided to check it out.

When I got to the building, I realized I had delivered to the school a few times in the past. The school wasn't a regular customer, but I had no problem finding where I needed to go. I met with a guy who was in charge of qualifying and onboarding new students. He was friendly and helped me to see that it could be a good opportunity to pursue.

I went back home and told Mom and Dad what I was thinking of doing, and they agreed to go with me to see what it was all about.

Long story short, it was going to cost me a little less than $20,000. I qualified for a small grant from the government, but it didn't make much of a dent in the price. I would be on the hook for that full amount. I didn't have that much saved up, but I knew I could pay it back in time as long as I was able to work.

I started betting on myself to win. I was nervous about taking the education and the loan all on my own. That's the way I wanted to do it, though, so I had no one else to blame but myself if I didn't make it. I had a lot of skin in the game. I felt that because of that, I was more likely to see it through to completion.

My schedule was going to get intense. There would be a lot of studying in the evenings. A lot of the course was online, and I could work at my own pace. As long as I was getting the assignments done, I figured I would be good to go. I had to go into the building every Monday night. The class went from five o'clock in the evening until ten o'clock at night.

There were multiple Microsoft certifications I could achieve, and one of the bigger ones was Windows 7. I know that's a bit of an ancient technology now, but it was a big deal at the time. There were also Windows certifications in networking, server, and a few others. I believe there were seven of them total spread out through the year. My plan was to be prepared enough to pass them all on the first attempt. I didn't want to screw around and have to take them multiple times.

There were roughly seventeen of us in the class to start with. We were a mixed bag of people. I didn't know if I was one of the smarter ones in the room or if I was on the bottom of the totem pole. I only knew the basics of computers. I didn't know how to take one apart and put it back together, but I was going to learn.

That was one of the first in-person classes. We got to play around with an old computer. I had very little idea of what I was doing. Some people already seemed to have done this kind of thing before, so I felt I was behind right out of the gate. I took notes, paid attention, and tried staying on top of things as best as I could. I didn't want to let myself down.

I was still working at Jimmy Johns and working out while studying and going to class. It was the fullest schedule I had taken on in a long time. I was concerned about how I would hold up.

It didn't take long before I got hit hard with a Lyme attack. So many times, when I added more stress to my life, it made me feel a lot worse for a while. I was prepared for it to happen, though, and with me being healthier, I got through it quicker than I ever had in the past. It sucked to deal with, but I was happy to see I was able to recover from it a lot quicker than I used to.

A few weeks in, my class of seventeen was down to twelve. Another month after that, we were down to seven.

It was wild to see people drop like flies out of the program. There was a clause in the loan where if you dropped out before a certain point, you could get a percentage of your loan back. I think a lot of people wanted to see if it was for them, and if they didn't like it, they bailed.

I wasn't bailing.

I passed the opening exam on the first attempt. It wasn't one of the harder ones, but it showed that I understood the basics of computers. I could check one off the list. I was off to a good start, and I felt confident moving forward.

After having been though the live class a few times, I started to get to know some of the people there. I gravitated and connected with one guy there named Joel. He was older than me, but we became buddies. He had the same kind of drive I had and wanted to pass all the exams straight away. We even started having a little competition about who was getting the higher grades on the coursework throughout the week. It was extremely important that Joel was there with me; it made the experience a lot more enjoyable.

After class on Monday night, I got into a routine of going out to eat. There weren't many places open at that time of night, but Hooters always had their lights on. So that's where I would go. It was a little weird going there by myself that late at night, but I didn't mind the atmosphere, and it was a fun place to unwind after a long day of work and studying.

A few more weeks passed, and we were down to five people remaining in the class. We weren't even halfway through the course. At the rate we were going, there would be none of us left who finished, but I wasn't going to let that happen. I was going to complete what I began.

I was starting to wonder to myself if the people who dropped out knew something that I didn't. Perhaps this education was going to be a waste of time? Or could it possibly be that they weren't cut out for this, but I was? Only time would tell.

The school said they would help me land a job after I successfully graduated, and I thought a lot about what type of position I could get into. I was getting good scores and passing the exams, but I still didn't think I knew much about anything.

I kept knocking the exams out of the park, but I could feel the toll everything was taking on my body. I was tired, and I went through another Lyme-related sickness. With the finish line in sight, though, I wasn't going to give up.

The class was down to me and Joel in the final two months. Our friendship and competition together kept us motivated to keep on trucking. We were in the home stretch, and the in-person sessions were starting to become a real drag. I just wanted to be done.

My body was wearing down.

During one class, while the professor was on the video screen, I was just sitting in my chair, listening and paying attention as best I could. I didn't feel well at all and needed to adjust my position in my seat.

In an instant, pain shot up and down my back, and my whole body tensed up. I tried to contain my yelp of pain as I fell out of my chair and down to the floor.

Luckily, we were going on break. I couldn't get up off the floor without being in tremendous pain. Any movement would hurt, so I just stayed on the floor. When break was over, the professor asked where I was because he couldn't see me on the floor. Joel spoke up and said that my back went out, and the only spot to be comfortable in was on the ground. Thankfully, I had some pain relievers with me, and by the end of class, I was at least able to move enough to drive home.

I didn't go into work for a few days. My body simply needed to rest and recover. Studying was difficult because it was hard to stay focused. My health had been slowly going downhill since I started this educational journey, but I wasn't about to quit now.

I only had the Windows 7 exam left. Up until this point, I had done what I set out to do, and that was to pass every exam on the first attempt. I wasn't able to prepare how I had for the other tests. My energy and ambition levels were so much lower than they were at the beginning. I wasn't nearly as confident with how I would do on this one as I was with the others.

I used all the time allotted to me to finish the exam. I sweated through the whole three hours that I had. I remember marking down how many answers I thought I had wrong or that were a complete guess. I did the math and concluded that as long as I wasn't a terrible test-taker, I should be able to pass.

And that's exactly what I was able to do.

It was over, and I felt a major weight off my shoulders. I don't think I could have handled another year of schooling; it would have been tough. I was relieved to be done.

I accomplished what I wanted to do, albeit in a crash-landing style, but I showed myself that I could take on a project and win.

Seventeen students down to two. I only had one person to compete with for the highest GPA in the class, and I narrowly achieved that. I also had the highest score on the Windows 7 exam between the two of us. The competition was in good fun. All that mattered was that we both successfully got through the course.

I was hoping for a little break after I finished, but that wasn't going to happen. I had been asked to interview with the school for an internship. In my class, there was always a teacher who would physically do some teaching in the last hour of the in-person session. The school was looking for me to do that same thing.

They offered me a position, and I took it. It wasn't the glamorous IT job that I thought I might be able to get, but I figured I had to start somewhere.

On the one hand, I wanted to be done with the school. After my experience of going through it, I wasn't very impressed with how it was all run. On the other hand, if I wanted to get out of delivery driving, I needed to get into the IT field as quickly as possible.

I didn't feel like an IT expert, but now I had to try and share my knowledge with students who were in the position I was in just a short year ago.

My first night on the job, I was expected to instruct a class full of people on something related to IT. I had no idea what I was doing. I wasn't a teacher. I barely knew the stuff I had just learned. I had thought that the school would have given me some sort of syllabus I could use to go over with the class. No such thing existed. Apparently, I just had to wing it.

Since I had nothing prepared, I let the students work on whatever assignments they had, and if they needed help, I'd try and do that. It was terribly awkward. I was supposed to be the smartest person in the room, but I definitely did not feel like it.

The next few weeks, I got zero help from the school with what I could maybe cover with the class. There were a few areas I knew quite well and felt comfortable with attempting to teach, but it was difficult.

I hadn't felt like the school adequately prepared me for the IT world, and I didn't feel like they put me in a good position to succeed as an employee.

I was exhausted and didn't like what I was doing. I was done.

I thanked the school for the education and the opportunity with the job, but I had to leave. My health needed to be put first again. If I didn't reduce my workload, I might set myself back ten steps. I wasn't going to continue to push myself through something I didn't believe was a good situation.

Leaving turned out to be great for my health. Even though I was back to just delivery driving, I had confidence that I could find a better job.

As a side note, the school permanently closed its doors about six months after I left. I wasn't surprised. It wasn't the greatest education or the best institution. Nor was it a great place to work. I definitely would not do it again, but I'm glad I did.

It gave me confidence.

I knew I was capable of bigger and better things. I just had to figure out what that was.

Finding another job wasn't as easy as I had hoped. Any serious IT jobs required at least two years of experience and sometimes five or more.

With IT, it appeared that the only way you get experience was to bounce around from one temp job to another.

I was frustrated.

On top of that, my hands became a major problem.

I spent a lot of time typing on a keyboard and working with a mouse over the last year. My hands were on fire as soon as I hovered over either one of them.

It was a symptom that just came out of nowhere. Nothing was helping. I thought the only way the problem could be fixed was through surgery.

I was starting to get bummed out. I felt my education was a letdown. The process of getting a good job was years down the road, and now I couldn't even use a computer because of the pain.

It was depressing.

In the midst of all this happening, something special was brewing.

CHAPTER 12

KEEP GOING

I had been single for the last five years. I couldn't ever seem to find anyone who was worth it. I had been on different match-making sites and went out on a few dates here and there; however, no girl impressed me that much. I ran into my fair share of crazy girls and ones who would seem to be a good fit, but then I wouldn't hear from them ever again. I even had some who faked being in the hospital or in an accident as a reason why they went missing in action. I couldn't believe a person would do that, and it was more unreal as it happened three times with three different girls. I started thinking there was a secret club where girls had to devise ways to mess with a guy's head.

I was rather sick of the games. I just wanted something real and fun. I knew I was a good guy, yet I couldn't believe how difficult it was to find a good girl.

It was Fourth of July weekend 2013. I made the three-hour trek to my grandpa's place for a nice holiday weekend with my family.

The lake, campfires, fish fries, and the scenery were all things I enjoyed. I just wanted someone to enjoy those things with.

I slept in the basement alone. It was cooler down there, so I didn't mind that, and neither did my dog Jena. The house didn't have air conditioning, so it would be twenty to thirty degrees cooler in the basement.

I slept on an old, squeaky trundle bed. My dog Jena was on her pillow on the floor next to me. The house was quiet, and I just lay there looking up at the ceiling. I had just turned twenty-seven years old, and I kept thinking that I hated doing everything by myself. I wanted to share my life with someone great.

That night, I prayed and talked with God for a few hours. It was a different type of conversation I was having with the only One who I felt could truly bring someone to me. I didn't beg or plead, but I stated my case. I felt I had gotten through the worst of the Lyme. I was working, I had more of an education, and I was looking to continue to grow and move forward. I asked God, "If it wouldn't be too much trouble, and if it's the right time, please, can You help me find a good girl I can enjoy life with?"

I ended up having a great night of sleep, and I felt a calmness come over me about the whole being-lonely situation. I put my concerns on God and had the comfort and confidence that my request would be taken into consideration.

It didn't take long to get an answer.

By the afternoon of the next day, I saw that I had a message from a girl on one of the dating apps I was on. That, in and of itself, was rare. I didn't have the greatest access to the internet, so all I could respond was, "Hey, I got your message. I'm in a dead zone for internet, so I'll reply back to you once I'm back home."

The next few weeks, we spent emailing and texting back and forth. It was an awesome feeling communicating with a girl who actually had the intelligence to be able to carry on long conversations. We then started talking on the phone, and it was like we had known each other our whole lives. It was easy, it was fun, and she never disappeared or faked a hospital visit.

The relationship started off great. I had someone I could celebrate my successes with and someone to help the not-so-great times be better. It was truly a blessing to have her in my life, and I was excited to see where life would take us.

I wanted to keep the good times going. I was riding a big wave of momentum and didn't just want to do better for myself but for this new girl in my life.

I wanted to see if I could handle a full-time job. I knew I had to keep pushing forward. I was still working at Jimmy Johns; however, I knew I couldn't keep working there forever.

I applied at a few different places. There was one IT job at a place I had delivered to many times. It sounded like a nice position. I knew the building and the people there already. I interviewed well, and they asked me to come back for a second interview and then a third. I knew I was close to landing the job. They said there would be some training down in Texas, and I was already thinking about what the job was going to be like.

It was between me and another person. But in the end, the other person won out. They said this other guy had more experience, which was probably true because I had zero.

I was bummed but also encouraged that I almost had this job based purely on what they liked about me. I knew the lack of work experience would hurt me, so I had to impress people with how I acted and presented myself.

A few weeks later, I was back interviewing for another position. They didn't exactly tell me where it was located or who it was for. All they said was that it was a contract job at a large, well-known company.

The first interview went well, and it was off to the second one, where I would meet with the guy who was in charge of whether I'd get hired or not.

I learned a little bit from my previous failed attempts at landing a job. This time, I emphasized a lot more on my willingness to learn and that I could pick up on things very quickly.

This guy liked my ambition and offered me the job.

I wanted to know where it was and who it was for.

The job was going to be located about twenty minutes from my house for a small company called GE Healthcare.

Of course, GE wasn't a little mom-and-pop shop. I wasn't actually hired by GE but for a copier and printer company called Xerox. Xerox had a contract with GE to provide machines and support to their locations. I was going to be in charge of the largest contract they had in the area.

I didn't know much about Xerox or GE. I had no experience with copiers, printers, and the networks they were involved in.

I was willing to learn.

The pay wasn't great, but the experience would be worth it.

I left Jimmy Johns. I left my comfort zone. I left a part-time life to see if I could start living a full-time one.

I had to keep trying to improve my situation. The best way to do that was to get uncomfortable. That was the only way I was ever going to feel good about myself and the only way I was going to get my health as close to normal as I could.

I had on-the-job training for a week in Milwaukee with a lady who managed that location by herself.

It was my responsibility to keep track of all the printers and copiers, making sure the ink or toner was kept supplied, fixing them if I could, and calling in technicians when I couldn't.

After following my colleague around for a week, we then went to the location that I would be overseeing. My contract covered twice as many machines spread out over seven different buildings. I was a little surprised that they gave me the largest contract, but I felt I could handle it.

I understood what needed to be done on a daily basis. I was the most comfortable with the network portion of the job. I knew about IP addresses, how to update software, check things remotely, and enough about troubleshooting to feel confident in what I was doing. I had the support of my colleague if I had questions. She was only a call away and could always come on site if I needed help.

I started out enjoying what I was doing. Most days, the job wasn't too stressful, which was huge for me.

To the surprise of no one, I got quite sick a few weeks into the new job. Even though the job wasn't overly taxing, any new amount of stress took ten times the effect on me as I think it would normally have.

I didn't work out as much as getting my eight hours in was more than enough exercise for the day. Some days were filled with a lot of walking, as the copiers were spread out all over the place. I hated it when one machine needed help and the next one was in a completely different building a half mile away.

I didn't miss a day of work, though. I fought through any sickness and fatigue. Occasionally, it was slow enough where I could sit at my desk and close my eyes for thirty minutes on my lunch break. Being able to recharge when I needed it helped out big time. It really was the perfect type of job for me to start working full time. I could figure things out on my own, and no one looked over my shoulder as long as I was getting things done.

I could work at my own pace, especially after I figured out how to best manage my day. I could start predicting what was going to happen, and I got really good at prioritizing what was the most important thing to be doing.

A few months passed, and the lady who was the area manager overseeing the contracts stopped in. She was a little surprised and worried as to why she wasn't hearing of any issues or complaints from my site. After she talked with me, she figured out why that was. I took care of a lot of things on my own. I tried to figure things out so that I could resolve an issue before involving someone else. She said this site had never run this smoothly before, and she was impressed with what I was doing.

I wanted to make a good impression and show that I could handle the job. I figured that if I could show I was capable of providing great service, I could be in line for a raise or maybe even a better position down the road.

Thirteen years after I initially got sick, I was starting to live a more normal life. I, in no way, felt like I was twenty-seven years old. In my mind, I felt like I was still a teenager with a lot to prove. I believe that helped me in a lot of ways to keep my head down and drive forward. I still had the Lyme, but I was slowly putting the worst of it behind me. Every day that I was able to go to work, not fall apart, and come back again the next day was a victory for me. Oh, you bet there were days where I felt like absolute garbage, and I probably should have taken the day off, but I didn't. I didn't want to stop. I think I felt that if I took one day off, then I might be tempted to take two and then three. I was scared to fall back. That fear of falling back into the hell that I was in kept me focused on completing the task at hand and winning the day.

CHAPTER 13

LIVE HUMBLED

wanted to get to a point where I had more good and great days than bad days.

I was able to do that.

I've kept that consistency and have gotten even healthier in the years since.

Writing this book has been a challenge. It took me multiple years to do it. I started and stopped many times because life sometimes got busy, or it was difficult to figure out how I wanted to word different parts. It wasn't until I found myself in a position where I had some extra time and less responsibilities to be able to finish it.

I didn't want to write a simple book with little to no effort put into it. I told myself that if I was going to put my story out there, I had to make it count. I had to dig deep and sort through a lot of paperwork and memories. When I didn't have the memories, I had to ask for help.

Reliving a lot of the pain and anguish that I went through was uncomfortable, but that's life.

I always found I was most inspired by other people's stories when they laid it all out on the line. When a movie, book, or a song gets great feedback and ratings, it's typically because there was a lot of emotion, energy, and effort into making it.

It's not easy to be vulnerable, to open up, and to let the world in. There is trepidation in thinking that someone isn't going to like it or that someone will say bad things about me or my experiences. I'm learning on a regular basis that I'm not going to please everyone. As long as I'm being true to myself and feel good about what I'm writing, then that's good enough for me to sleep easy at night.

I never would have thought that after the small amount of years I have lived, I would have enough material or words to fill a book.

In some ways, I don't feel worthy to have my own story put to print. I mean, what do I know? What do I have to offer? Could someone really benefit from the experiences that I have gone through?

Even if my story, as told in this book, only inspires, motivates, or helps one person live a better life or have a relationship with God, then I will consider it a success.

I do hope and pray there is more than one, though.

There are so many inspiring stories that have been told and many more to come that will blow mine out of the water. I'm not a professional writer, and I know I can't hold a candle to some of the great writers out there. All I can do is be real and authentic.

I hope that's been enough.

While I ended the book on a good note, that wasn't the end of my story.

I wish I could tell you that everything was sunshine and smooth sailing for the rest of my life. Unfortunately, that's not how it works. As much as I may have wanted to or tried, it's darn near impossible to have everything go according to plan. Life will always throw you curveballs, and you may not end up where you thought you would be. While I may have dreamed off the following, it just didn't happen.

I didn't become a great athlete and make millions of dollars. That would have been fun, though.

I didn't go on to start the next billion-dollar company, at least not yet.

I didn't reinvent the wheel and change the world. Though, hopefully, I can make a positive impact.

I didn't suddenly have perfect health and achieve remarkable athletic feats like climb a mountain, swim across the ocean, run across the US, or anything like that. While that would be cool and add a lot to the story, it wouldn't be true.

I did, however, finish a 5K run after twenty years since my last near-fatal race in high school. I finished with a time that was close to what I used to be able to do. I still have goals of being able to be faster now than I was then. I'm not sure if I will accomplish it, but trying to do so keeps me in a healthy mindset.

A healthy mindset is probably the best thing I've learned from my illness. I didn't have that for many years while I struggled to get better. While I had every reason to be sad, depressed, and angry, it didn't make my situation any better.

Sometimes, I was my own worst enemy.

It's impossible to always be 100 percent focused and positive. And it's even harder to be that way while going through a major disease or sickness. Friends, family, teachers, and doctors didn't believe what I was going through, either, which only added to my difficulties in getting myself on the correct path.

It took me a long time to realize that I had every right to feel all the emotions I did. Even though I was ashamed and embarrassed to feel the bad and negative feelings, I couldn't help it.

To this day, I can still feel the pull from the past whenever life gets tough. It's frightening to think how easy it could be to slip back to a depressed state. I'll let myself feel the sad emotions for a while when they are warranted. I try my best to not let them linger any more than they need to. I'll let it hurt, I'll feel the pain, and then I'll move forward and put it all behind me as much as I can.

Holding onto the hurt and sadness only prevents you from feeling the good things that are all around you.

I've learned that there will always be challenges, ups and downs, and obstacles to maneuver around. Bad stuff will happen, and unexpected twists will take place. Good will also happen, and you have to enjoy it when it does. Going through what I did armed me to be able to handle life better. Live humbled means that you appreciate what you have but use your talents to strive for more.

All the crap I went through has helped me appreciate all the blessings I have around me. I find myself thanking God for the big things and sometimes even little random stuff. It's easy to be thankful for family, friends, a car, or a house, but sometimes being thankful for a pair of socks can be just as important and impactful.

One of the biggest things I'm thankful for now is the health that I enjoy now. Even though it's not perfect, I could be in a lot worse shape. Even when I don't feel the greatest, I'm still thankful because I know how bad things could be. I've lived with chronic Lyme disease for a long, long time. If I have to live with it forever, I believe I'll be okay. God willing, I'm going to live a healthier life than maybe I otherwise wouldn't have.

How I've been able to improve my health and my situation may not work for everybody. We're all different, and our circumstances won't be the same.

However, I have found one thing that will work for everyone.

Find something that works and keep doing it.

I knew nothing about supplements or vitamins before I was sick. I found some great nutritional products that helped me improve, and I stuck with them. I owe Kathy a great deal of thanks for getting me started on them. I can count on both hands the number of days I have missed taking my daily regimen. Yes, it costs money, but it's been money well spent. I'd rather spend two thousand dollars on healthy habits every year and try and avoid the tens, if not hundreds, of thousands of dollars in medical bills that could be easily racked up in this day and age. I pray that my plan continues to work. I haven't been under a doctor's care or on any medication since my early twenties. I would love to keep it that way.

I knew about chiropractic care since I had received treatments off and on since I was a kid. The Lyme ravaged my body, and I had more than my fair share amount of back and neck pain. I finally got the majority of my issues to disappear once I made regular adjustments a priority. Up until that point, I would only go in when I had a problem. Once I realized my body needed continuous work to keep everything aligned, my spasms went down drastically. Over the years, the chiropractor has saved me multiple trips to the doctor's office as well as from having to have potential surgeries. I always joked with him, saying, "I need a good crack to keep me in line." The craziest story was when my hip would scream in agony when I'd either bump into something or move in an awkward way. The pain would send me to the floor, but after a minute, I would be fine. After experiencing that a few too many times, I asked my chiropractor about it. He gave me my regular treatment and said to come back in a week if it wasn't any better. I came back a few days later to try and figure it out. I thought I would need to go to a hip specialist or, worse yet, get a hip replacement. Luckily and painfully, I let the doctor do his thing. He performed a psoas release. I didn't know it was a thing. Apparently, there's a muscle that connects to your lower back and goes down to your hip. When he did the release, I had to hold back tears; I was in so much pain. After a few minutes, the pain subsided, and a few weeks later, I was pain-free.

I do my best to make sure I'm getting straightened out on a regular basis to hopefully prevent future issues from popping up. Dr. Kurt was a lifesaver. I am 100 percent certain I would not be where I am if I didn't have his help in fixing me up. The treatments and consistent care have helped, so I will keep doing them.

Acupuncture is something I never thought I would do. Mom first benefited from it, and then I did. My little graph to indicate how I was doing started at ten, dropped to five and then up to twenty before slowly climbing up to near eighty. One or two sessions won't do a whole lot for you. A continual approach worked the best for me.

The hand problem I was having at the end of my computer schooling was drastically improved because of my acupuncture treatments. I typed every single word of this story with minimal to no discomfort in my hands. At one point, I thought I would need surgery to fix the issue, but acupuncture freed my hands of the agony they were in. I owe that to my acupuncturist, Curry, and his team that kept adjusting the needle points until I would get relief.

I also want to include and thank my favorite acupuncturist, Mindy. She was the best at getting the needles to go in so I wouldn't feel a thing. There were times I wanted to be done going, but once she started working there, I always looked forward to my treatments. Her kindness, friendship, and genuine care for me would put a big smile on my face. She was always happy to see me, which went a long way to helping me stick with another healthy alternative habit. In a lot of ways, she was another angel who helped me to be healthier and happier.

I continue to exercise, stay active, and eat mostly healthy food. I want to be fit and mobile as long as I can. Dory was and still is an inspiration to me. I have seen the results of what a healthy lifestyle looks like, and I want the same. I've seen way too many people struggle with poor health choices, bad eating habits, lack of exercise, and being overweight. I want to try my very best to stay away from all that. I had to work extremely hard to get my health back and into the best shape of my life. It's one habit I hope I never take for granted.

One thing I didn't expect, though, was now that I am healthier, I'm not just fighting against the Lyme, I'm fighting against Father Time. There's no way around it. The body breaks down as we get older. It doesn't get any easier to get or stay in shape, and I'm sure a lot of people have already figured that out.

The key is to not stop. I've seen too many times someone who wants to get in shape does something for a few weeks, then doesn't get immediate results, so they quit. It has to be a lifelong journey to stay active and fit. You may have to work a little harder for a year or two to get into the form you want, but it's a lot easier to stay in shape than it is to get in shape. In addition to exercise, eating healthy is another thing I have stuck with and will continue to do.

I've only made it this far because I've had faith and trust in the Lord above. I know not everyone believes God exists, but I'll argue that you're crazy if you think like that. I had faith, questioned it, almost lost it, and regained it so that it is now stronger than ever.

I think a lot of reasons why some people question if God exists is because bad things have happened to them or to people they know. I was in that boat. I couldn't figure out why all this bad stuff happened to me and why bad stuff continues to happen. The easiest answer is because there is sin in the world. And since there is sin in the world, bad things will happen. It's really that simple.

Sometimes bad things might happen to get your attention to make you go on a different path or change your thinking.

I could have been going the wrong way and didn't even know it. Maybe I needed this bad stuff to happen so that I would find a different way in life.

Maybe the unfortunate turn of events that happened to me and the ensuing story that has followed will help someone else find their way.

Sometimes bad things can happen to us our whole lives until we realize God is trying to get our attention so that we follow Him.

People can be stubborn, and that includes me, too. We can be stubborn our whole lives and not realize we need to change until it's too late. We think we know best, but it's actually God who does.

We have free will to do what we want.

I know I don't always do the right things or make the best choices. I'm still a sinner and always will be, and everyone else is in the same boat as I am. Bad things will continue to happen because of sin. Good things will happen because of God's grace, love, and forgiveness through Jesus.

It's the greatest gift of all. I know that my sins are forgiven, and I'm washed clean in God's eyes. You can be, too, by simply accepting that gift, acknowledging your sin, asking for forgiveness, and accepting Jesus as your Savior.

I had to go through hell and sometimes back through it again to get to where I am.

Without God putting the right people in my life when He did, I may not be here. Without God's mercy, my situation and story could have been much worse than it was. Without salvation through Christ, I wouldn't have a place prepared for me in heaven.

I had a glimpse of what heaven was like for a very brief moment. I know this life isn't all there is. If I didn't have salvation, I would be terrified of day-to-day living, not knowing what happens after I die. I have peace knowing where I'm going when I do eventually die. I have peace knowing that all my earthly struggles, problems, and worries will be forgotten and replaced with eternal joy and happiness. That's unfathomable now and impossible to wrap my mind around, but it's fun to try to think about.

As I wrap this up and put a bow on it, I want to reference what I started off with in the beginning.

I'm just a regular guy writing a story about what I went through. It won't be the greatest, most inspirational story ever written. Other people have gone through much worse than I have. Better stories have been written and will continue to be written. The cool thing is that this story is mine.

I was inspired to write this because of different books I have read. I loved the idea that my story could go on and impact anywhere from one to millions of people.

If this book gives you hope, healing, or faith, then I'd love to hear about it one day.

In a lot of ways, I wrote this for myself as a reminder that God is in control no matter how bad things get.

I pray that I have gone through the majority of my earthly struggles, but I have no doubt there will be more. I know I'm better equipped now than before to be able to handle what life throws my way. Hopefully, after reading this, you will be, too.

We're all in this together.

We're all going to struggle in one way or another.

I leave with this scripture: "For by grace are ye saved through faith; and that not of yourselves: it is the gift of God: Not of works, lest any man should boast" (Eph. 2:8–9, KJV).

There is nothing I can do to earn forgiveness, be 100 percent healthy, live free of any pain or hardship, survive any situation on my own, live forever, or please everybody.

Despite all of that, I will still try and improve and become a better version of myself as long as I can. Knowing that I will never reach perfection or know it all keeps me *humbled*.

ACKNOWLEDGMENTS

The only reason why I am here is because God has allowed it.

I first thank God for the blessings that I have and for putting the right people in my life to help me to get to this point.

Thank you to my mom and dad for your continued love, support, meals, rides, hospitality, and allowing me time to heal and improve at my own pace. I am very fortunate to have the parents that I do.

To my late Grandpa Art. One hundred two years you had on this earth, and the best thing you taught me was to not take life too seriously. Laugh at yourself and carry a tune in your heart; we will meet again.

Thank you to all the members of my family. There really are too many to list. In some way, shape or form, you have all helped or inspired me to be where I am today. We may not have always gotten along or seen eye to eye, but I'm very thankful and blessed to have such a great family. Maybe one day we can all stop having to work so hard and enjoy the fruits of our labor just a little bit more.

Thank you to my fellow friends and warriors in the Lyme community who have fought just as hard or harder than I have. We may not talk as much as we used to as life takes us down different roads, but I'll never forget your support when I needed it the most. To Lori, Kelsey, and later down the road, Jessica, Kayla, Nikki, and Kelsey, respectively, what we have gone through together shouldn't have had to happen, but I'm eternally grateful that I had you there with me. We kept each other alive and moving forward.

I wouldn't be as far along in life without Sheena being a friend and sounding board about anything and everything. How in the world we've kept a friendship going for this long is sometimes mind-boggling, considering the distance between us. The chats we've had, the insight you've given me, and the prayers you have sent my way have all been a blessing. I truly hope we can continue the unique relationship we have for as long as God keeps us on this earth.

High school was not the experience I envisioned. It was downright terrible and depressing. Having Rich emerge as a lifelong friend out of the mess that was, is truly unfathomable. The rounds of golf and fun that Rich and I have had over the years have been awesome. I always look forward to those times we can get together. Hopefully, we're only on the sixth hole of life, and we can make it a full eighteen.

Abbie, you are a bigger part of my life than I'm sure you ever considered. You kept me alive and gave me kindness in high school, and especially throughout the majority of the book-writing process when my life yet again was flipped upside down. You always seem to be there when I've needed someone to lean on. You could have easily ignored me and looked the other way, but God gave you a big, beautiful heart and soul that you could spare some to give to me. May God always bless you and your family.

Dory, words can't express the impact you've had on me, having you as a positive role model, friend, and mentor. I never would have gotten myself into the fitness level I did if I didn't have your care and support. Though our time of seeing each other on a regular basis is over, the memories of pushing my limits knowing you had my back when I faltered I will always carry with me.

Chrissy, you have one of the biggest hearts of anyone I know. Thank you for working with me and allowing me to start the process of getting my life back on track. Your kindness, patience, and friendship you showed to me while I faltered and stumbled to work the few hours a day I did will forever be appreciated.

Mindy, you came in later in my journey, but you are a big part of keeping me healthy. At times, I thought maybe I could do without acupuncture; I was burnt out from going. When you started working there, your kindness, friendship, and ability to perfectly place the needles where they needed to go furthered my ability to heal. You were the only one who could get the needles into my sensitive hands without making them jump, and I always appreciated that. You have a great heart, and it's an honor to have you as a friend.

Lizzy, thank you for your friendship, especially in the year prior to completing this book. You're truly one of the best people I know. You have a beautiful and kind heart; I wish there were more people in this world like you.

Amber, God entered you into my life when I least expected it. You're the continuation of the angels who have been sent to help and guide me. Your struggle with Lyme pushed me to get this book done. Having someone who understood everything I had to relive and supporting and encouraging my progress was immeasurably important. Knowing your story and situation helped me realize that people need to be aware of the devastation Lyme and other tick-borne diseases can cause. What you have had to deal with is incomprehensible, and to still have the heart and kindness that you have shown me, I will never forget.

Curry, without your in-depth knowledge of acupuncture, I wouldn't be as healthy as I am now. The time you put in tweaking my treatments for my various symptoms paid off. The graph of my progression is proof that the treatments work. Thank you to you and your staff for improving my quality of life.

Dr. Kurt, you fixed me up numerous times with your chiropractic adjustments. There were times I thought I would have back and neck pain forever, but with your dedication and expertise, you've saved me from multiple doctor and hospital visits and even possible surgeries. I have a much more mobile and pain-free life because of your service, and for that, I'm forever thankful.

Dr. B, Thank you for being the first doctor to really listen to me. Your kind heart and knowledge about Lyme helped me and many others in leading healthier lives. I am forever grateful that you were my doctor. I wish there were more like you.

To the people who have helped get this story turned into a book. I had no idea what I was doing in the beginning. To find my initial editors, Jenna and Blair, was a huge first step; thank you so much for getting the process going. Your skills contributed into turning my story into something worth reading. Lastly, thank you to Publify Press for taking on my project and getting it across the finish line. You have helped polish and perfect my story to be the best that it can be. Thank you.

CONNECT

Enjoyed the story? David would love to hear from you! Please consider giving a positive online review or five-star rating wherever you made your purchase. That is one of the best ways to help this book reach and impact others who may need it. One small act can truly change someone's life. Be that positive force.

To contact David about potential engagements or if you would like to share a message about how this book has helped you, please use the contact information below.

Email: support@livehumbled.com

Facebook: Live Humbled or David Bugenhagen

Instagram: Live_Humbled

Website: LiveHumbled.com

www.ingramcontent.com/pod-product-compliance
Lightning Source LLC
Chambersburg PA
CBHW070847160726

48004CB00003B/965